Contents

First published in 2003 by Philip's
a division of Octopus Publishing Group Limited
2–4 Heron Quays, London E14 4JP

First edition 2003
First impression 2003

Cartography by Philip's

Printed and bound in Slovenia

Road map symbols

bbreviated local authority areas

Area	Page	Grid
Bridgend	9	U16
Bracknell Forest	6	V22
Blaenau Gwent	9	U17
Brighton and Hove	6	W23
Blackpool	15	Q17
Bournemouth	5	W20
Blackburn with Darwen	15	Q19
City of Bristol	4	V18
City of Edinburgh	25	L17
Cardiff	4	U17
Clackmannanshire	24	K16
City of Nottingham	11	S21
Caerphilly	4	U17
Dundee City	25	K18
Derby City	11	S21
Darlington	16	N20
East Dunbartonshire	19	L15
East Renfrewshire	19	L15
Falkirk	24	L16
Glasgow City	19	L15
Hartlepool	21	N21
Halton	15	R18
Inverclyde	19	L14
Kingston upon Hull	17	Q23
Leicester City	11	S21
Luton	12	U23
Middlesbrough	16	N21
Merthyr Tydfil	9	U17
North East Lincolnshire	17	Q23
North Lanarkshire	19	L16
Newport	4	U18
Neath Port Talbot	9	U16
Plymouth	3	X15
Portsmouth	5	W21
Poole	5	W20
Redcar and Cleveland	17	N22
Reading	6	V22
Renfrewshire	19	L14
Rhondda Cynon Taff	9	U17
Southend-on-Sea	7	U25
Slough	6	U22
Stockton-on-Tees	21	N21
Southampton	5	W21
Stoke-on-Trent	10	R19
Swindon	5	U20
Torbay	3	X16
Torfaen	4	U17
Thurrock	7	U24
Telford and Wrekin	10	S19
Warrington	15	R18
West Dunbartonshire	24	L15
Wokingham	6	V22
West Lothian	24	L16
Windsor & Maidenhead	6	V22

Motorway
junction – full / restricted access
service area – full / restricted access
under construction

Primary route – dual / single carriageway
under construction
primary destination

A road / national secondary road
under construction

B road / regional road
under construction

Other road

Major Distance (in miles)

Minor Distance (in miles)

Tunnel

Railway

International boundary
National boundary
County / local authority boundary

River
Canal
Lake / reservoir
Car ferry
Hovercraft
Major airport

Built-up area

National park, forest park, area of outstanding natural beauty

Spot height in metres

Scale

0 5 10 15 20 25 miles

0 5 10 15 20 25 30 35 40 km

12 miles to 1 inch, 1:760320

Route Planner

0 20 40 Miles
0 20 40 60 Km

North Channel

NORTHERN IRELAND

Dunfanaghy
Coleraine
Ballymoney
Limavady
Londonderry
Dunglow
Letterkenny
Stranorlar
Strabane
Ballymena
Larne
Newtownstewart
Antrim
Carrickfergus
Killybegs
Donegal
Cookstown
Newtownabbey
Bangor
Ballintra
Belfast
Newtownards
Ballyshannon
Irvinestown
Lisburn
Ballygawley
Lurgan
Saintfield
Grange
Aughnacloy
Portadown
Enniskillen
Armagh
Sligo
Manorhamilton
Monaghan
Ardglass
Ballysadare
Newry
Newcastle
Belturbet
Warrenpoint
Castleblaney
Charlestown
Carrick-on-Shannon
Boyle
Cavan
Castlebar
Carrickmacross
Ballaghaderreen
Dundalk
Westport
Virginia
Ardee
Ballindine
Longford
Drogheda

REPUBLIC OF IRELAND

Clifden
Tuam
Navan
Balbriggan
Mullingar
Swords
Oughterard
Athlone
Dunshaughlin
Aughrim
Lucan
Dublin
Galway
Loughrea
Dun Laoghaire
Newbridge
Bray
Naas
Gort
Portlaoise
Roscrea
Wicklow
Nenagh
Ennis
Johnstone
Carlow
Arklow
Limerick
Kilkenny
Gorey
Cashel
Abbeyfeale
Rockhill
Tipperary
Carrick-on-Suir
Enniscorthy
Tralee
Caher
New Ross
Castleisland
Clonmel
Wexford
Mallow
Fermoy
Mitchelstown
Waterford
Rosslare
Killarney
Rathcormack
Youghal
Macroom
Cork
Bantry

N56, N13, N14, N15, N17, N5, N59, N4, N16, N3, N2, N1, N6, N18, N7, N8, N9, N10, N11, N21, N20, N24, N30, N25, N23, N22, N71, M1, M2, M4, M7, M9, M11, A2, A5, A6, A8, A26, A29, A36, A37, A32, A4, A28, A3, A505, A509, A20, A7, A24, A1, A21

IRISH SEA

St. George's Channel

CELTIC SEA

Girvan
Cairnryan
Newton Stewart
Stranraer
Anglesey
Holyhead
Cardigan Bay
Fishguard
Haverfordwest
Carmarthen
Milford Haven
Pembroke
Tenby
Bude
Launceston
Wadebridge
Bodmin
Newquay
Redruth
Truro
St. Austell
Penzance
Falmouth
Isles of Scilly

A77, A75, A40, A39, A30, A390, A394

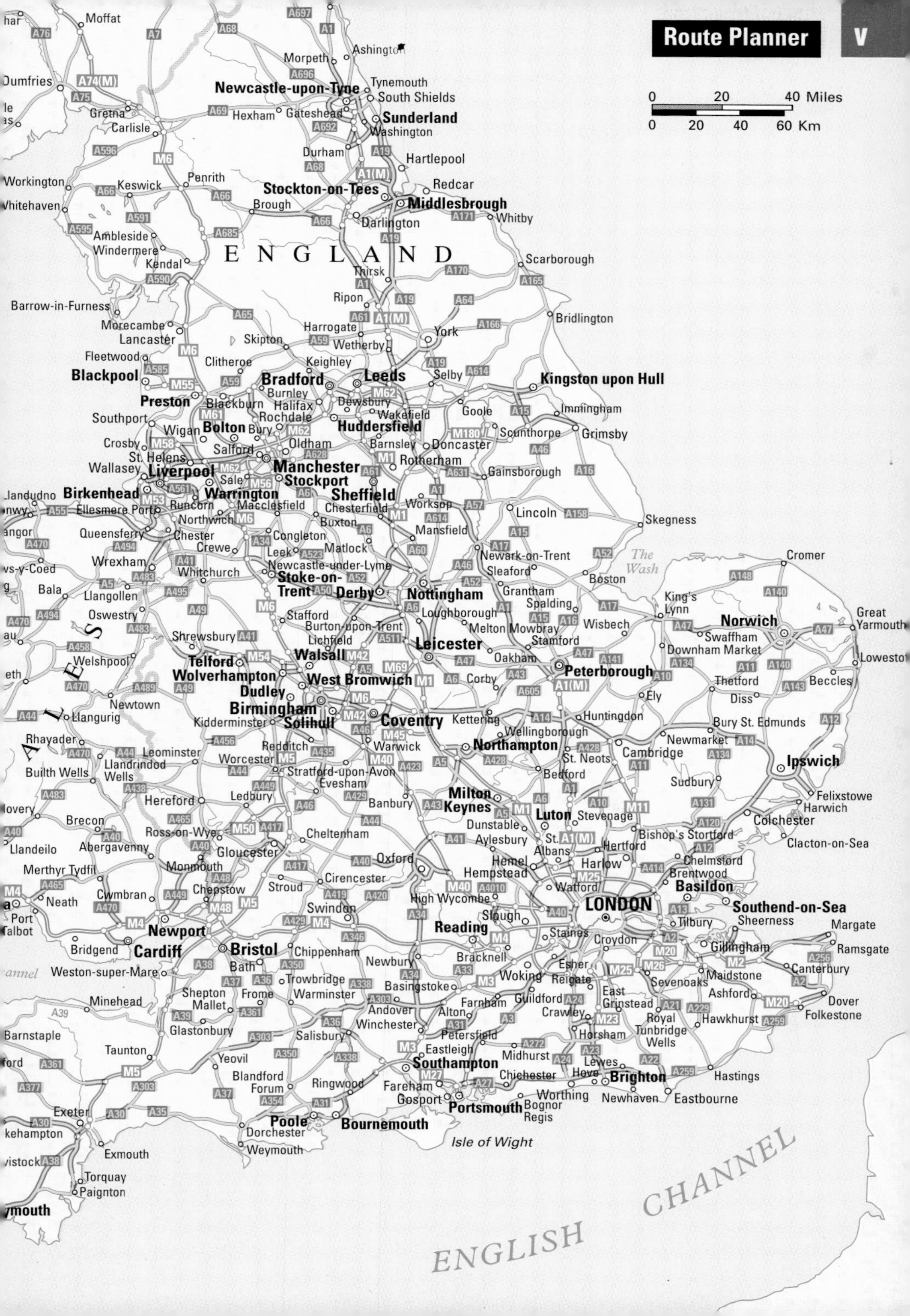

0 20 40 Miles
0 20 40 60 Km

Moffat
Ashington
Morpeth
Dumfries
Newcastle-upon-Tyne
Tynemouth
South Shields
Gretna
Hexham
Gateshead
Sunderland
Carlisle
Washington
Durham
Hartlepool
Workington
Keswick
Penrith
Stockton-on-Tees
Redcar
Whitehaven
Brough
Middlesbrough
Darlington
Whitby
Ambleside
Windermere
ENGLAND
Kendal
Thirsk
Scarborough
Barrow-in-Furness
Ripon
Bridlington
Morecambe
Harrogate
York
Lancaster
Skipton
Wetherby
Fleetwood
Clitheroe
Keighley
Blackpool
Bradford
Leeds
Selby
Kingston upon Hull
Preston
Burnley
Blackburn
Halifax
Dewsbury
Goole
Immingham
Southport
Rochdale
Wakefield
Wigan
Bolton
Bury
Huddersfield
Scunthorpe
Grimsby
Crosby
Oldham
Barnsley
Doncaster
St. Helens
Salford
Wallasey
Liverpool
Manchester
Rotherham
Gainsborough
Sale
Stockport
Llandudno
Birkenhead
Warrington
Sheffield
Ellesmere Port
Runcorn
Macclesfield
Chesterfield
Worksop
Northwich
Buxton
Lincoln
Skegness
Queensferry
Chester
Congleton
Mansfield
Crewe
Matlock
Leek
Newark-on-Trent
The Wash
Cromer
Wrexham
Newcastle-under-Lyme
Sleaford
Whitchurch
Stoke-on-Trent
Boston
Bala
Llangollen
Derby
Nottingham
Grantham
King's Lynn
Spalding
Oswestry
Stafford
Loughborough
Norwich
Great Yarmouth
Burton-upon-Trent
Melton Mowbray
Wisbech
Swaffham
Shrewsbury
Lichfield
Stamford
Downham Market
Leicester
Lowestoft
Welshpool
Telford
Walsall
Oakham
Peterborough
Wolverhampton
West Bromwich
Corby
Thetford
Beccles
Dudley
Ely
Newtown
Diss
Birmingham
Llangurig
Kidderminster
Solihull
Coventry
Kettering
Huntingdon
Bury St. Edmunds
Rhayader
Wellingborough
Newmarket
Redditch
Warwick
Northampton
Leominster
Cambridge
Ipswich
Worcester
St. Neots
Llandrindod Wells
Stratford-upon-Avon
Builth Wells
Evesham
Bedford
Sudbury
Hereford
Ledbury
Milton Keynes
Felixstowe
Banbury
Harwich
Luton
Stevenage
Brecon
Colchester
Dunstable
Ross-on-Wye
Cheltenham
Bishop's Stortford
Llandeilo
Abergavenny
Aylesbury
St. Albans
Hertford
Gloucester
Clacton-on-Sea
Oxford
Hemel Hempstead
Harlow
Chelmsford
Merthyr Tydfil
Monmouth
Cirencester
Brentwood
Stroud
Watford
Basildon
Neath
Cwmbran
Chepstow
High Wycombe
LONDON
Southend-on-Sea
Swindon
Port Talbot
Slough
Tilbury
Sheerness
Newport
Reading
Margate
Staines
Croydon
Gillingham
Bridgend
Cardiff
Bristol
Chippenham
Ramsgate
Newbury
Bracknell
Esher
Maidstone
Canterbury
Bath
Weston-super-Mare
Woking
Trowbridge
Reigate
Sevenoaks
Basingstoke
Shepton Mallet
Frome
Warminster
East Grinstead
Ashford
Dover
Minehead
Farnham
Guildford
Andover
Crawley
Alton
Folkestone
Winchester
Royal Tunbridge Wells
Hawkhurst
Barnstaple
Glastonbury
Petersfield
Horsham
Salisbury
Taunton
Eastleigh
Midhurst
Yeovil
Southampton
Lewes
Blandford Forum
Hove
Brighton
Hastings
Ringwood
Fareham
Chichester
Gosport
Worthing
Newhaven
Eastbourne
Portsmouth
Bognor Regis
Exeter
Poole
Bournemouth
Okehampton
Dorchester
Isle of Wight
Exmouth
Weymouth
Tavistock
Torquay
Paignton
Plymouth
ENGLISH CHANNEL
WALES

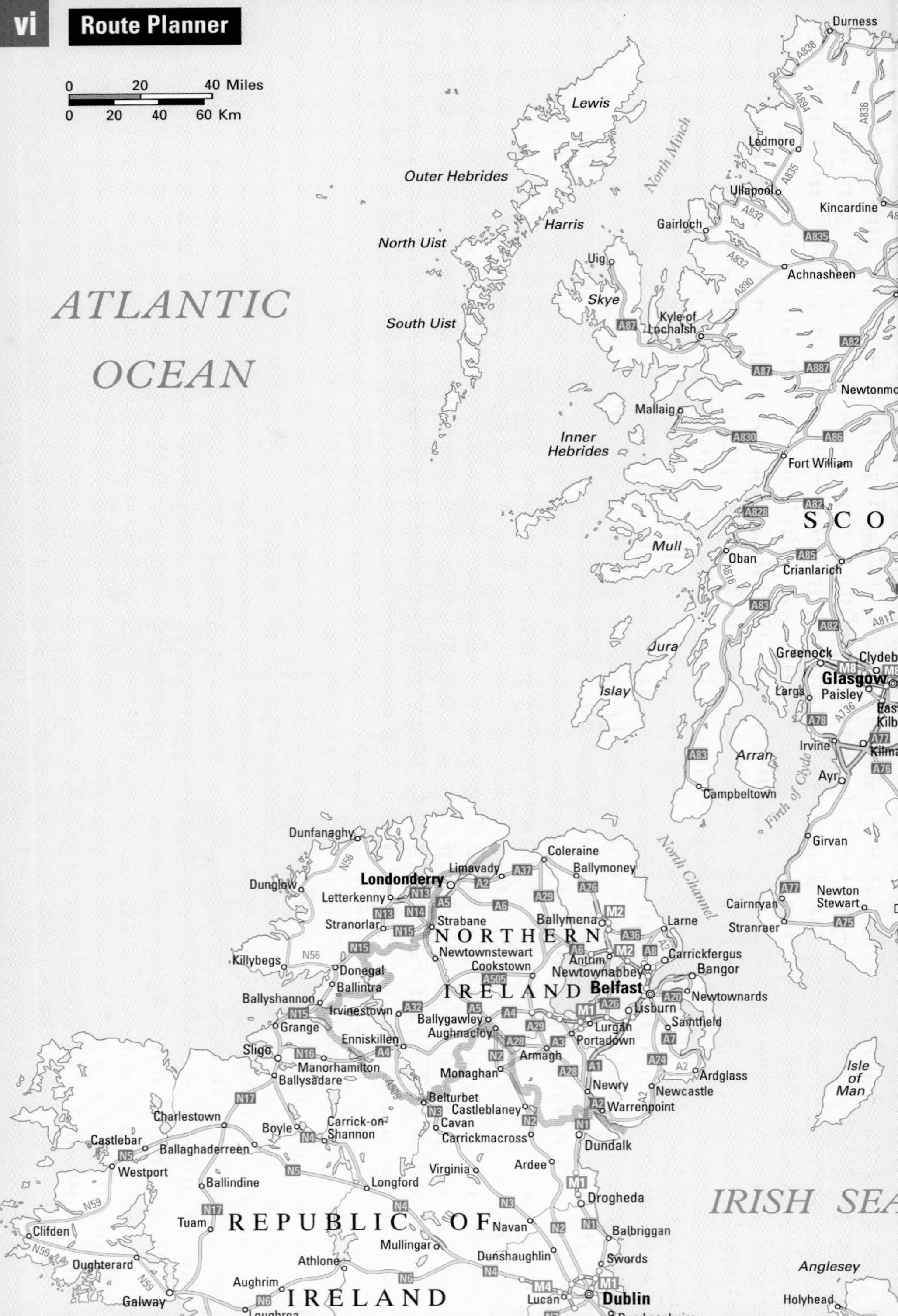
0 20 40 Miles
0 20 40 60 Km
ATLANTIC OCEAN
IRISH SEA
North Minch
North Channel
Firth of Clyde
Lewis
Outer Hebrides
Harris
North Uist
South Uist
Skye
Inner Hebrides
Mull
Jura
Islay
Arran
Isle of Man
Anglesey
SCOT
NORTHERN IRELAND
REPUBLIC OF IRELAND
Durness
Ledmore
Ullapool
Kincardine
Gairloch
Achnasheen
Uig
Kyle of Lochalsh
Newtonmore
Mallaig
Fort William
Oban
Crianlarich
Greenock
Clydebank
Glasgow
Largs
Paisley
East Kilbride
Irvine
Kilmarnock
Ayr
Campbeltown
Girvan
Cairnryan
Newton Stewart
Stranraer
Dunfanaghy
Coleraine
Limavady
Ballymoney
Londonderry
Dunglow
Letterkenny
Strabane
Ballymena
Stranorlar
Larne
Newtownstewart
Carrickfergus
Killybegs
Donegal
Cookstown
Antrim
Bangor
Newtownabbey
Ballintra
Belfast
Newtownards
Ballyshannon
Irvinestown
Lisburn
Ballygawley
Saintfield
Grange
Aughnacloy
Lurgan
Portadown
Enniskillen
Armagh
Sligo
Manorhamilton
Monaghan
Ardglass
Ballysadare
Newry
Newcastle
Belturbet
Castleblaney
Warrenpoint
Charlestown
Carrick-on-Shannon
Boyle
Cavan
Castlebar
Carrickmacross
Ballaghaderreen
Dundalk
Westport
Ardee
Virginia
Ballindine
Longford
Drogheda
Tuam
Navan
Balbriggan
Clifden
Mullingar
Oughterard
Athlone
Dunshaughlin
Swords
Aughrim
Galway
Lucan
Dublin
Loughrea
Dun Laoghaire
Holyhead
A838
A894
A836
A835
A832
A890
A87
A82
A887
A830
A86
A828
A85
A816
A83
A81
M8
M80
A78
A736
A77
A76
A75
N56
A37
A2
A26
A29
M2
N13
N14
A5
A6
N15
A36
A8
A505
A20
A32
M1
A4
A28
A3
A24
N16
N2
A1
A509
N3
N1
N17
N4
N5
N59
N6
M4
M50
A7

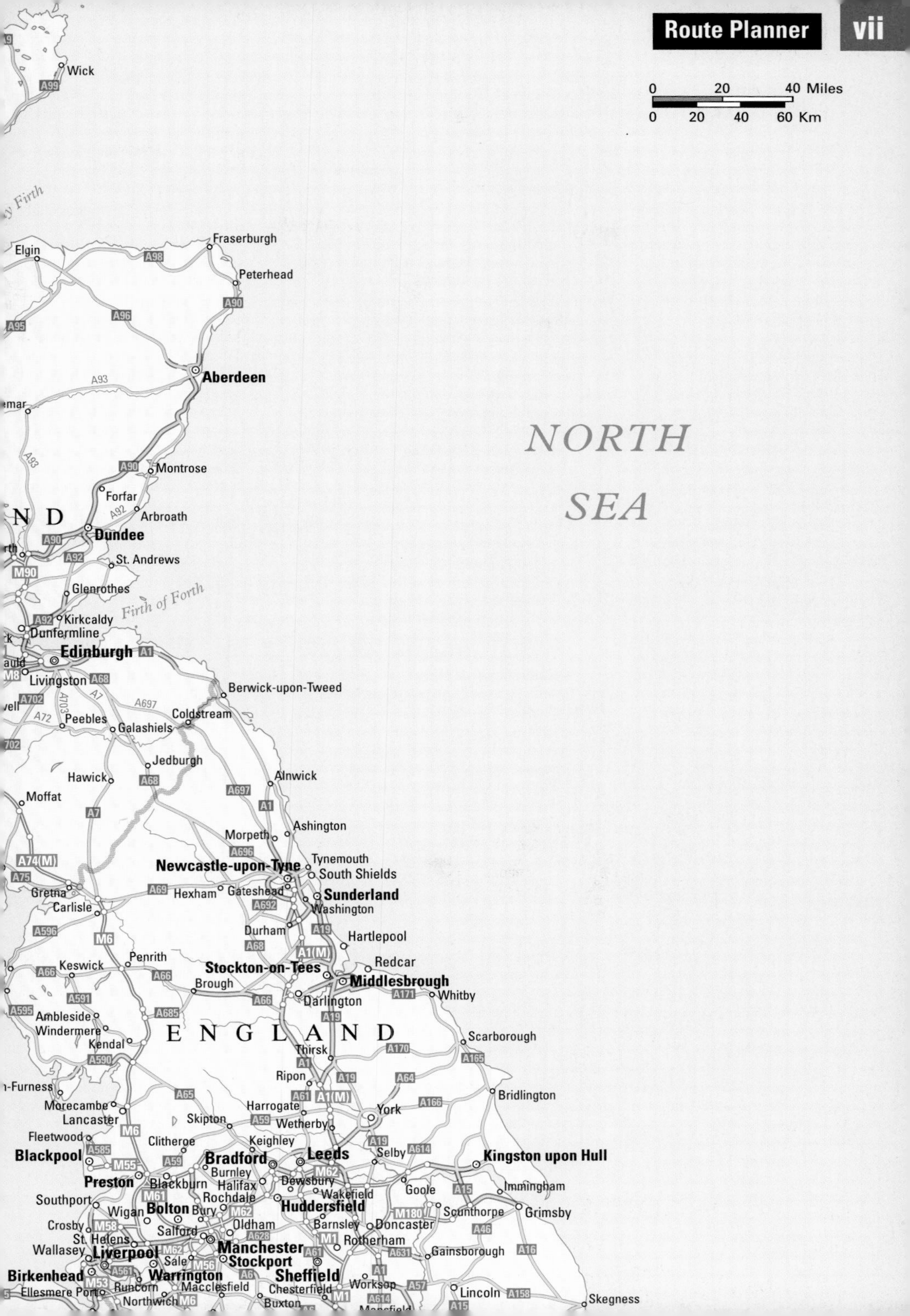

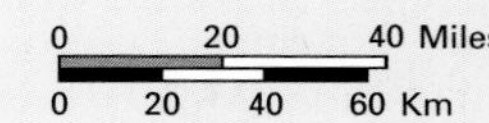

NORTH SEA

Wick
A99
Firth
Fraserburgh
Elgin
A98
Peterhead
A90
A96
A95
Aberdeen
A93
Braemar
A93
A90
Montrose
Forfar
A92
Arbroath
N D
Dundee
A90
A92
St. Andrews
M90
Glenrothes
Firth of Forth
A92 Kirkcaldy
Dunfermline
Edinburgh A1
Livingston A68
M8
A702
A7
A703
A697
Berwick-upon-Tweed
A72 Peebles
Galashiels
Coldstream
A702
Jedburgh
Hawick
A68
Alnwick
Moffat
A697
A1
A7
Morpeth
Ashington
A696
A74(M)
Newcastle-upon-Tyne
Tynemouth
South Shields
A75
Gretna
A69
Hexham
Gateshead
Sunderland
Carlisle
A692
Washington
A596
M6
Durham
A19
Hartlepool
A68
A1(M)
Penrith
Redcar
Keswick
A66
Stockton-on-Tees
A66
Brough
Middlesbrough
A591
A66
Darlington
A171
Whitby
A595
Ambleside
A685
A19
Windermere
ENGLAND
Scarborough
Kendal
Thirsk
A170
A590
A1
A165
Ripon
A19
A64
Barrow-in-Furness
A65
A61
A1(M)
Bridlington
Morecambe
Harrogate
York
A166
Lancaster
Skipton
M6
A59
Wetherby
Fleetwood
Clitheroe
Keighley
A19
Blackpool
A585
M55
A59
Bradford
Leeds
Selby
A614
Kingston upon Hull
Burnley
M62
Preston
Blackburn
Halifax
Dewsbury
Goole
A15
Immingham
M61
Rochdale
Wakefield
Southport
Wigan
Bolton
Bury
M62
Huddersfield
M180
Scunthorpe
Grimsby
Crosby
M58
Oldham
Barnsley
Doncaster
St. Helens
Salford
A628
M1
Rotherham
A46
Wallasey
Liverpool
M62
Manchester
A61
A631
Gainsborough
A16
Sale
M56
Stockport
Birkenhead
A561
Warrington
A6
Sheffield
A1
M53
Runcorn
Macclesfield
Worksop
A57
Ellesmere Port
Chesterfield
A614
Lincoln
A158
Northwich
M6
Buxton
M1
A15
Skegness

HOW TO USE THIS TABLE

Distances are shown in miles

Example: the distance from Cambridge to Dover is 125 miles

Cambridge				169
Cardiff			190	45
Carlisle		289	264	277
Dover	389	238	125	202
Dundee	523	152	441	406	430

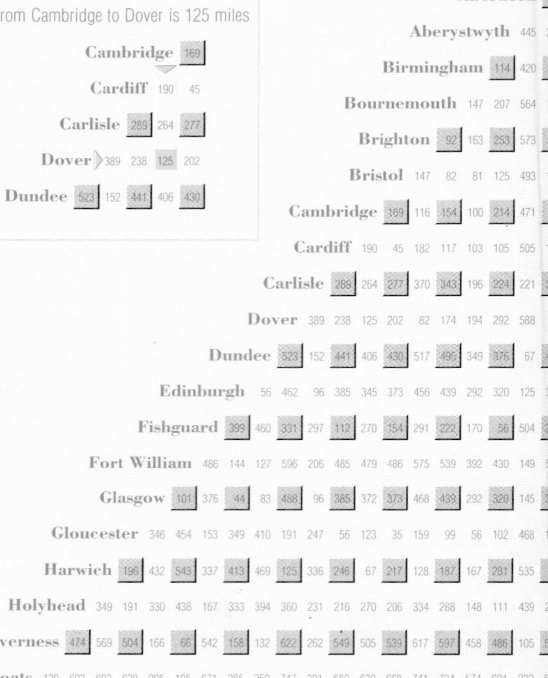
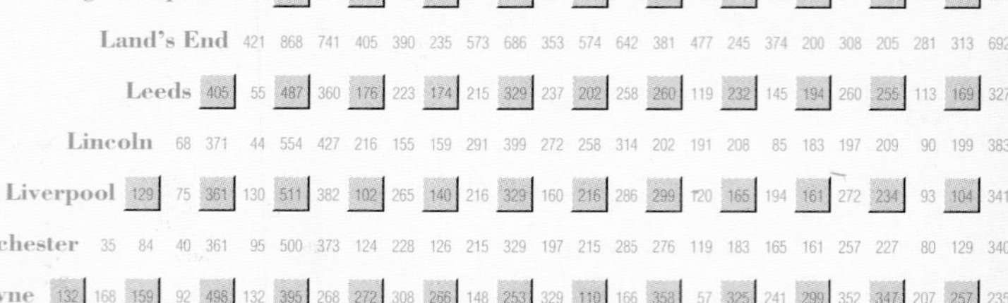
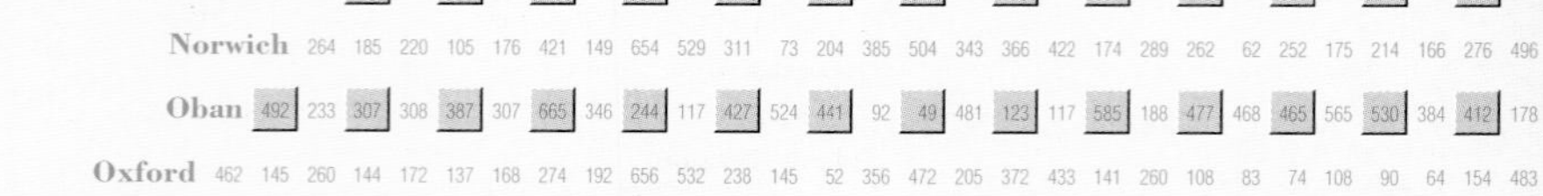
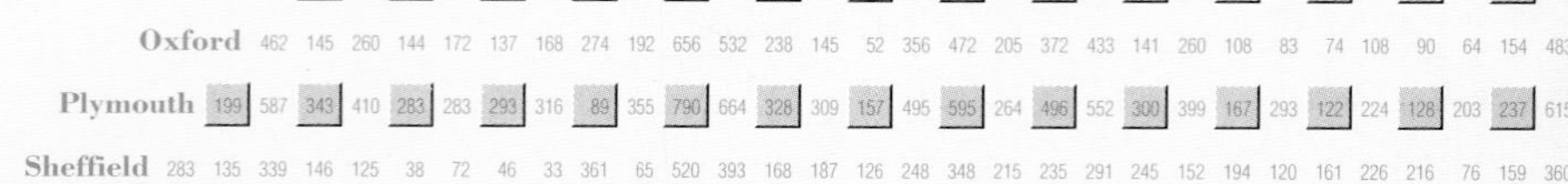

London																																					
Aberdeen																																					[illegible]
Aberystwyth																																				445	[illegible]
Birmingham																																			114	420	[illegible]
Bournemouth																																		147	207	564	[illegible]
Brighton																																	92	163	253	573	[illegible]
Bristol																																147	82	81	125	493	[illegible]
Cambridge																															169	116	154	100	214	471	[illegible]
Cardiff																														190	45	182	117	103	105	505	[illegible]
Carlisle																													289	264	277	370	343	196	224	221	[illegible]
Dover																												389	238	125	202	82	174	194	292	588	
Dundee																											523	152	441	406	430	517	495	349	376	67	[illegible]
Edinburgh																										56	462	96	385	345	373	456	439	292	320	125	[illegible]
Fishguard																									399	460	331	297	112	270	154	291	222	170	56	504	[illegible]
Fort William																								486	144	127	596	206	485	479	486	575	539	392	430	149	[illegible]
Glasgow																							101	376	44	83	488	96	385	372	373	468	439	292	320	145	[illegible]
Gloucester																						346	454	153	349	410	191	247	56	123	35	159	99	56	102	468	[illegible]
Harwich																					196	432	543	337	413	469	125	336	246	67	217	128	187	167	281	535	[illegible]
Holyhead																				349	191	330	438	167	333	394	360	231	216	270	206	334	288	148	111	439	[illegible]
Inverness																			474	569	504	166	66	542	158	132	622	262	549	505	539	617	597	458	486	105	[illegible]
John o' Groats																		129	603	693	628	295	195	671	285	259	747	391	680	630	668	741	724	574	601	232	[illegible]
Kingston upon Hull																	518	394	231	196	198	254	369	280	234	295	256	158	244	139	233	245	264	134	223	364	[illegible]
Land's End																421	868	741	405	390	235	573	686	353	574	642	381	477	245	374	200	308	205	281	313	692	[illegible]
Leeds															405	55	487	360	176	223	174	215	329	237	202	258	260	119	232	145	194	260	255	113	169	327	[illegible]
Lincoln														68	371	44	554	427	216	155	159	291	399	272	258	314	202	191	208	85	183	197	209	90	199	383	[illegible]
Liverpool													129	75	361	130	511	382	102	265	140	216	329	160	216	286	299	120	165	194	161	272	234	93	104	341	[illegible]
Manchester												35	84	40	361	95	500	373	124	228	126	215	329	197	215	285	276	119	183	165	161	257	227	80	129	340	[illegible]
Newcastle upon Tyne											132	168	159	92	498	132	395	268	272	308	266	148	253	329	110	166	358	57	325	241	299	352	347	207	257	235	[illegible]
Norwich										264	185	220	105	176	421	149	654	529	311	73	204	385	504	343	366	422	174	289	262	62	252	175	214	166	276	496	[illegible]
Oban									492	233	307	308	387	307	665	346	244	117	427	524	441	92	49	481	123	117	585	188	477	468	465	565	530	384	412	178	[illegible]
Oxford								462	145	260	144	172	137	168	274	192	656	532	238	145	52	356	472	205	372	433	141	260	108	83	74	108	90	64	154	483	[illegible]
Plymouth							199	587	343	410	283	283	293	316	89	355	790	664	328	309	157	495	595	264	496	552	300	399	167	293	122	224	128	203	237	615	[illegible]
Sheffield						283	135	339	146	125	38	72	46	33	361	65	520	393	168	187	126	248	348	215	235	291	245	152	194	120	161	226	216	76	159	360	[illegible]
Shrewsbury					82	225	106	364	205	201	69	58	133	109	303	169	567	438	113	240	77	272	382	145	274	330	251	176	111	159	103	226	185	45	77	399	[illegible]
Southampton				185	199	151	64	530	206	324	221	239	204	232	228	256	723	598	293	164	105	433	541	233	438	500	143	324	121	148	76	61	31	128	201	547	[illegible]
Stranraer			445	277	263	500	379	148	403	158	220	221	298	220	585	259	379	262	338	435	343	84	195	392	124	167	496	101	390	379	378	475	444	297	325	228	[illegible]
Swansea		417	161	118	217	206	141	506	301	347	187	195	233	248	285	264	696	572	184	267	89	409	496	67	412	473	274	309	41	227	85	222	167	119	73	507	[illegible]
York	272	222	258	133	52	333	181	309	181	84	64	99	75	24	411	37	479	352	204	228	189	217	330	261	194	250	282	121	244	165	222	275	269	130	195	319	[illegible]

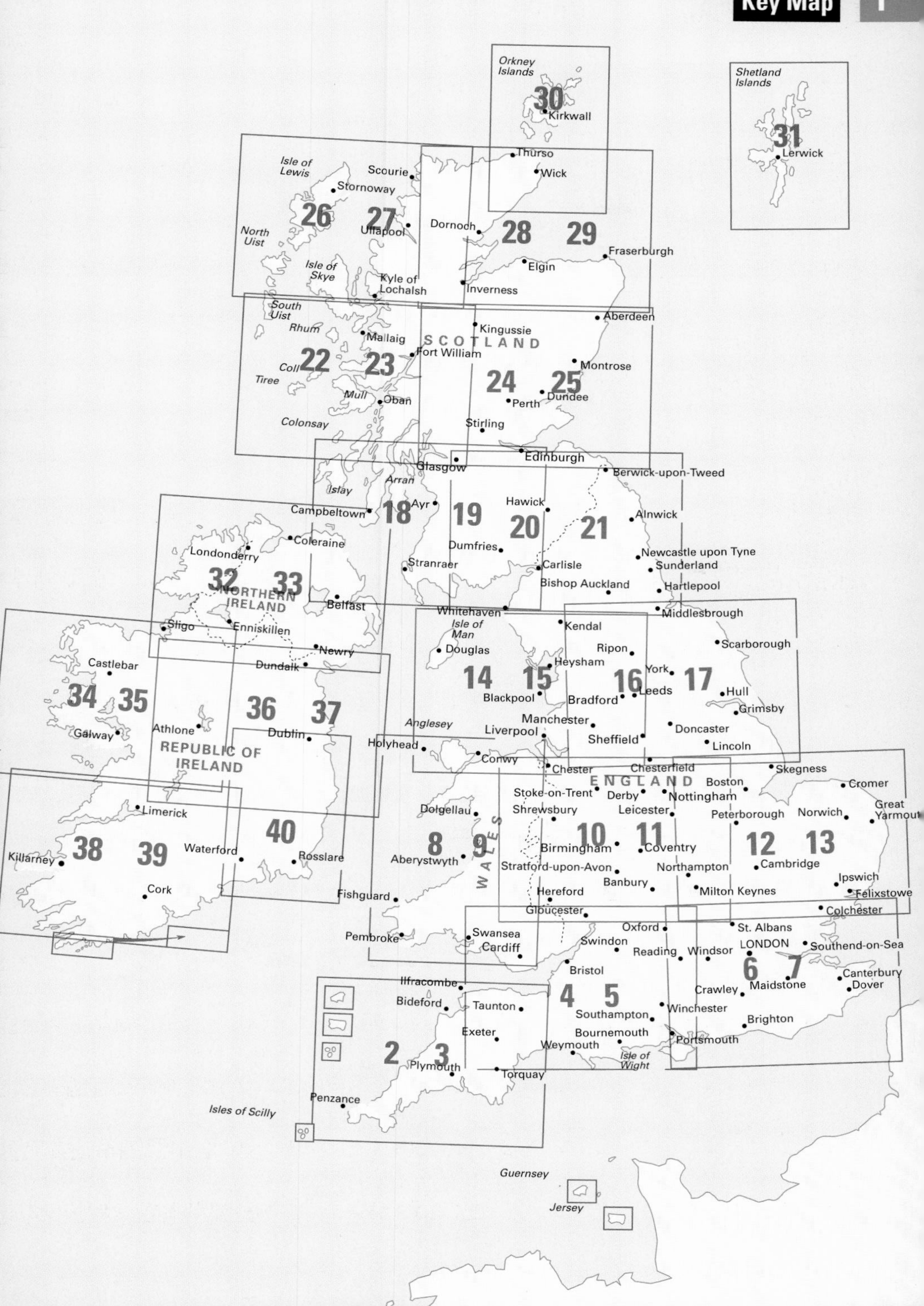
Orkney Islands
30
Kirkwall
Shetland Islands
31
Lerwick
Thurso
Wick
Isle of Lewis
Scourie
Stornoway
26
27
Ullapool
Dornoch
28
29
North Uist
Fraserburgh
Elgin
Isle of Skye
Kyle of Lochalsh
Inverness
South Uist
Aberdeen
Rhum
Kingussie
Mallaig
SCOTLAND
Fort William
Coll
22
23
Montrose
Tiree
24
25
Mull
Oban
Perth
Dundee
Colonsay
Stirling
Edinburgh
Glasgow
Berwick-upon-Tweed
Arran
Islay
Hawick
Campbeltown
18
Ayr
19
20
21
Alnwick
Coleraine
Dumfries
Londonderry
Newcastle upon Tyne
Stranraer
Carlisle
Sunderland
32
33
NORTHERN IRELAND
Bishop Auckland
Hartlepool
Belfast
Whitehaven
Middlesbrough
Sligo
Enniskillen
Isle of Man
Kendal
Ripon
Scarborough
Newry
Castlebar
Dundalk
Douglas
Heysham
York
34
35
14
15
16
17
Hull
Blackpool
Leeds
Bradford
36
37
Grimsby
Manchester
Anglesey
Doncaster
Athlone
Galway
Liverpool
Dublin
Sheffield
Lincoln
Holyhead
REPUBLIC OF IRELAND
Conwy
Chester
Chesterfield
Skegness
ENGLAND
Boston
Cromer
Stoke-on-Trent
Derby
Nottingham
Great
Yarmout
Dolgellau
Shrewsbury
Leicester
Peterborough
Norwich
Limerick
WALES
40
8
9
10
11
12
13
38
39
Waterford
Birmingham
Coventry
Killarney
Rosslare
Aberystwyth
Cambridge
Stratford-upon-Avon
Northampton
Ipswich
Cork
Banbury
Fishguard
Hereford
Milton Keynes
Felixstowe
Gloucester
Colchester
Oxford
St. Albans
Pembroke
Swansea
Swindon
LONDON
Cardiff
Reading
Windsor
Southend-on-Sea
6
7
Bristol
Canterbury
Ilfracombe
Maidstone
Crawley
Dover
Bideford
Taunton
4
5
Southampton
Winchester
Brighton
Exeter
Bournemouth
Weymouth
Portsmouth
2
3
Isle of Wight
Plymouth
Torquay
Penzance
Isles of Scilly
Guernsey
Jersey

12
13
14
V
W
X
Y
GUERNSEY
St. Sampson
St. Peter Port
Herm
Sark
Rocquaire Bay
St. Martin
Torteval
POOLE WEYMOUTH
JERSEY ST. MALO
18
19
JERSEY
Grosnez Pt.
Rozel
Trinity
St. Martin
St. Ouens Bay
St. Peter
St. Helier
Gorey
St. Brelade
St. Aubin
la Rocque Pt.
GUERNSEY WEYMOUTH POOLE
ST. MALO
ISLES OF SCILLY
Tresco
St. Martin's
Bryher
Hugh Town
Crow Sound
St. Mary's
Broad Sd.
St. Agnes
St. Mary's Sd.
11
Lundy
Hartland
Morwenstow
Bude Bay
Bude
Widemouth
Dizzard Pt.
Poundstock
CORNWALL
Boscastle
Tintagel Hd.
Tintagel
Delabole
Camelford
Port Isaac Bay
Pentire Pt.
Port Isaac
BROWN WILLY
St. Breward
Padstow Bay
Polzeath
St. Teath
Trevose Hd.
Padstow
St. Minver
St. Tudy
St. Merryn
Wadebridge
St. Mabyn
Washaway
St. Issey
Camel
Colliford Lake Res.
Trenance
BODMIN
Watergate Bay
St. Columb Major
Lanivet
NEWQUAY
St. Columb Minor
Roche
Bugle
Lostwithiel
St. Enoder
St. Dennis
St. Blazey
Tywardreath
Fraddon
Newlyn East
St. Stephen
Perranporth
Bodinnick
St. Agnes Hd.
Goonhavern
Ladock
Fowey
Polruan
St. Agnes
Perranzabuloe
Grampound
ST. AUSTELL
Mevagissey Bay
Portreath
Probus
Mevagissey
Illogan
Tresilian
REDRUTH
Chacewater
TRURO
Tregony
Kea
St. Ives
St. Ives Bay
St. day
Gorran Haven
Carbis Bay
Pool
Gwennap
Gurnard's Hd.
Hayle
Camborne
Dodman Pt.
Zennor
Lelant
Feock
Veryan
Veryan B.
Leedstown
Gerrans B.
Pendeen
Penryn
Ludgvan
St. Erth
St. Mawes
C. Cornwall
PENZANCE HELIPORT
St. Just
Marazion
HELSTON
FALMOUTH
Kelynack
LAND'S END
Newlyn
PENZANCE
Breage
Helford
Falmouth Bay
Praa Sands
Sennen
Gweek
Mawgan
Mousehole
St. Buryan
Land's End
Mount's Bay
Porthleven
St. Keverne
The Manacles
St. Levan
Mullion
Ruan Minor
Coverack
Black Hd.
Lizard
Wolf Rock
Lizard Pt.

3
15
16
17
Bridgwater
Bay
Foreland Pt.
Burnham- on-Sea
Highbridge
Hinkley Pt.
Lynmouth
Lynton
Porlock
Minehead
Ilfracombe
Combe Martin
Morte Pt.
Mortehoe
Parracombe
EXMOOR
EXMOOR
Timberscombe
Dunster
Carhampton
Watchet
Combwich
Nether Stowey
Cannington
Holford
Morte Bay
Woolacombe
Challacombe
DUNKERY BEACON 520
Washford
Williton
QUANTOCK HILLS
Bridgwater
VON
Baggy Pt.
Georgeham
Simonsbath
Exford
BRENDON HILLS
Croyde
Bratton Fleming
Braunton
NATIONAL PARK
SOMERSET
384
North Petherton
Middlez
Barnstaple or
Bideford
Bay
Fremington
BARNSTAPLE
Brompton Regis
Wimbleball L.
Bishops Lydeard
Instow
Landkey
Appledore
Westward Ho!
Northam
Bishop's Tawton
South Molton
North Molton
Dulverton
Wiveliscombe
TAUNTON
Curr
Milverton
Norton Fitzwarren
Langford Budville
BIDEFORD
Buck's Cross
Bampton
Trull
Hatch Beauchamp
Buckland Brewer
Bishop's Nympton
Wellington
STAPLE HILL 315
High Bickington
Meshaw
Rackenford
BLACKDOWN HILLS
Horton
Great Torrington
Stibb Cross
Langtree
Chulmleigh
Witheridge
Culmstock
Hemyock
Uffculme
BLACKDOWN
Chard
Bradworthy
Dolton
Chawleigh
Tiverton
Halberton
Willand
Shebbear
Lapford
Cheriton Fitzpaine
Cullompton
Kentisbeare
HILLS
Yarcombe
Winkleigh
Morchard Bishop
Broadhembury
Torridge
Hatherleigh
Monkokehampton
DEVON
Silverton
Holsworthy
Exbourne
North Tawton
Copplestone
Thorverton
Crediton
Honiton
Hawkchurch
Whimple
Halwill Junction
Sampford Courtenay
Bow
Colebrooke
Newton St. Cyres
Wilmington
Axminster
Clawton
Broadclyst
Ottery St. Mary
EAST
Colyton
Pinhoe
Musbury
DEVON
Okehampton
South Tawton
Spreyton
Tedburn St Mary
EXETER
Ashwater
South Zeal
Newton Poppleford
Sidbury
Axmouth
Roadford Res.
Teign
Dunsford
Alphington
Topsham
Beer
Seaton
Sidford
Bridestowe
621 HIGH WILLHAYS
Chagford
Woodbury
Sidmouth
Moretonhampstead
Christow
Exminster
Kennford
Lympstone
Otterton
Lydford
DARTMOOR
Lifton
DARTMOOR
Starcross
Budleigh Salterton
Bovey Tracey
Chudleigh
EXMOUTH
Milton Abbot
Marytavy
Postbridge
South Petherwin
Widecombe
Dawlish
Bishopsteignton
Kingsteignton
Teignmouth
Tavistock
Princetown
NATIONAL
Bickington
Shaldon
Whitchurch
Newton Abbot
Linkinhorne
Gunnislake
Ashburton
Kingskerswell
Callington
Calstock
Horrabridge
Buckfast
TORQUAY
Pensilva
St. Dominick
TAMAR
Yelverton
Buckfastleigh
Torbay
Bere Alston
PARK
Dartington
VALLEY
Plym
Liskeard
Landrake
Tamerton Foliot
South Brent
PAIGNTON
TOLL
Totnes
Stoke Gabriel
Tor Bay
Saltash
PLYMOUTH
Ivybridge
Galmpton
Berry Hd.
St. Germans
Dittisham
Brixham
Torpoint
Plympton
Ugborough
Dartmouth
Devonport
Plymstock
Modbury
Kingswear
East Looe
Looe
Millbrook
Brixton
Yealmpton
Loddiswell
Whitesand Bay
Stoke Fleming
Rame Head
The Sound
Wembury
Newton Ferrers
SOUTH
Kingston
Bigbury
Aveton Gifford
Churchstow
Kingsbridge
Start Bay
Chillington
Bigbury Bay
Thurlestone
DEVON
Torcross
X
Marlborough
Salcombe
Bolt Tail
Start Pt.
ROSCOFF
SANTANDER (Mar-Nov)
ST. MALO (Nov-Mar)
Bolt Head
Prawle Pt.
Y
15
16
17

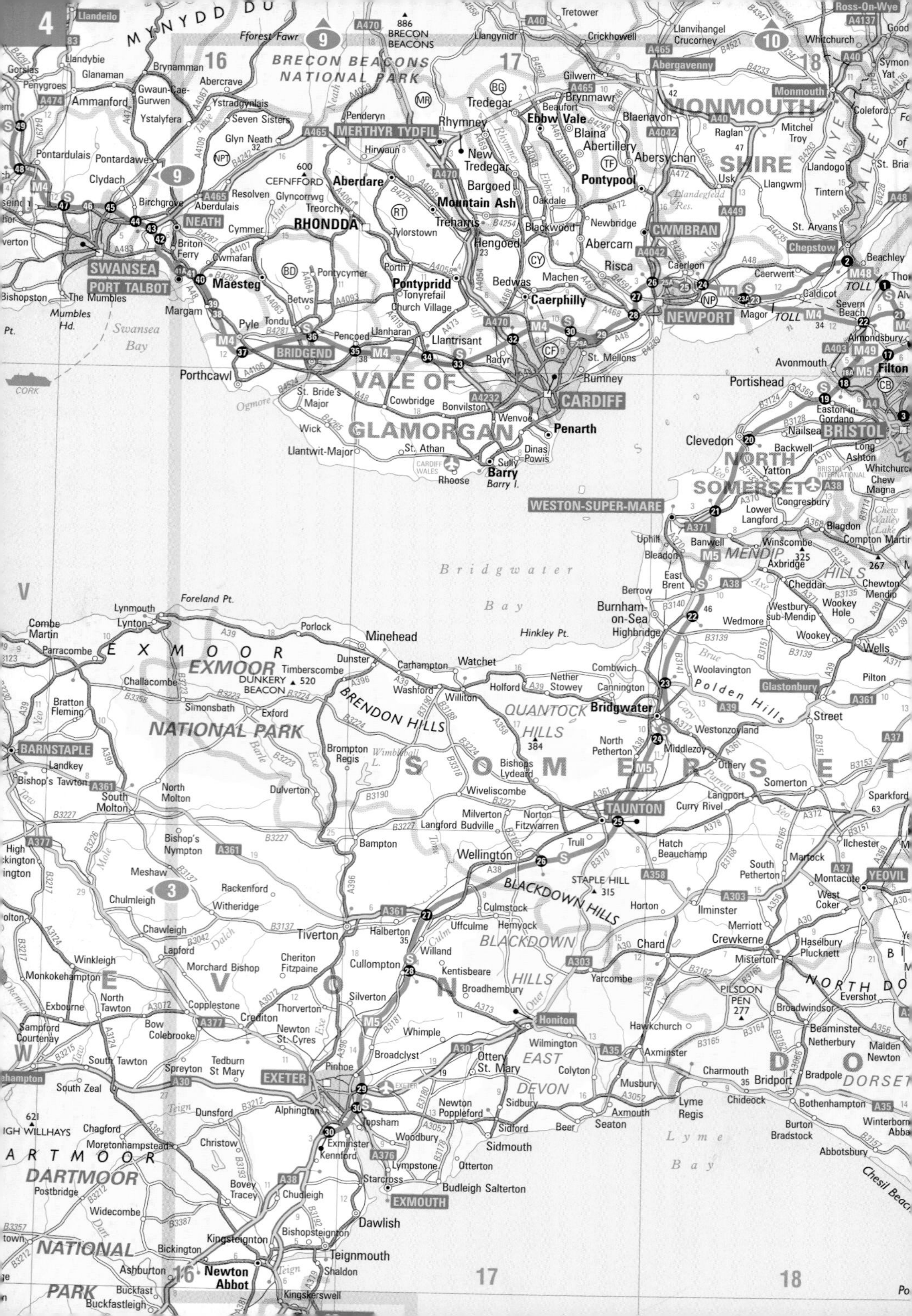
MYNYDD DU
BRECON BEACONS NATIONAL PARK
886 BRECON BEACONS
Fforest Fawr
Llandeilo
Ammanford
Swansea
Neath
Port Talbot
Bridgend
Merthyr Tydfil
Rhondda
Pontypridd
Caerphilly
Cardiff
Penarth
Barry
Newport
Cwmbran
Pontypool
Abergavenny
Monmouth
MONMOUTHSHIRE
Chepstow
Ross-On-Wye
Bristol
Weston-Super-Mare
Clevedon
Portishead
NORTH SOMERSET
VALE OF GLAMORGAN
Bridgwater Bay
MENDIP HILLS
Cheddar
Wells
Glastonbury
Street
Bridgwater
QUANTOCK HILLS
Taunton
SOMERSET
Yeovil
Minehead
Lynton
Lynmouth
EXMOOR
EXMOOR NATIONAL PARK
DUNKERY BEACON 520
BRENDON HILLS
Barnstaple
South Molton
Tiverton
Wellington
BLACKDOWN HILLS
Chard
Crewkerne
Honiton
Exeter
Exmouth
Sidmouth
EAST DEVON
DEVON
DARTMOOR NATIONAL PARK
Newton Abbot
Teignmouth
Dawlish
Axminster
Lyme Regis
Lyme Bay
Bridport
DORSET
NORTH DORSET
Chesil Beach
16
17
18
9
10
3

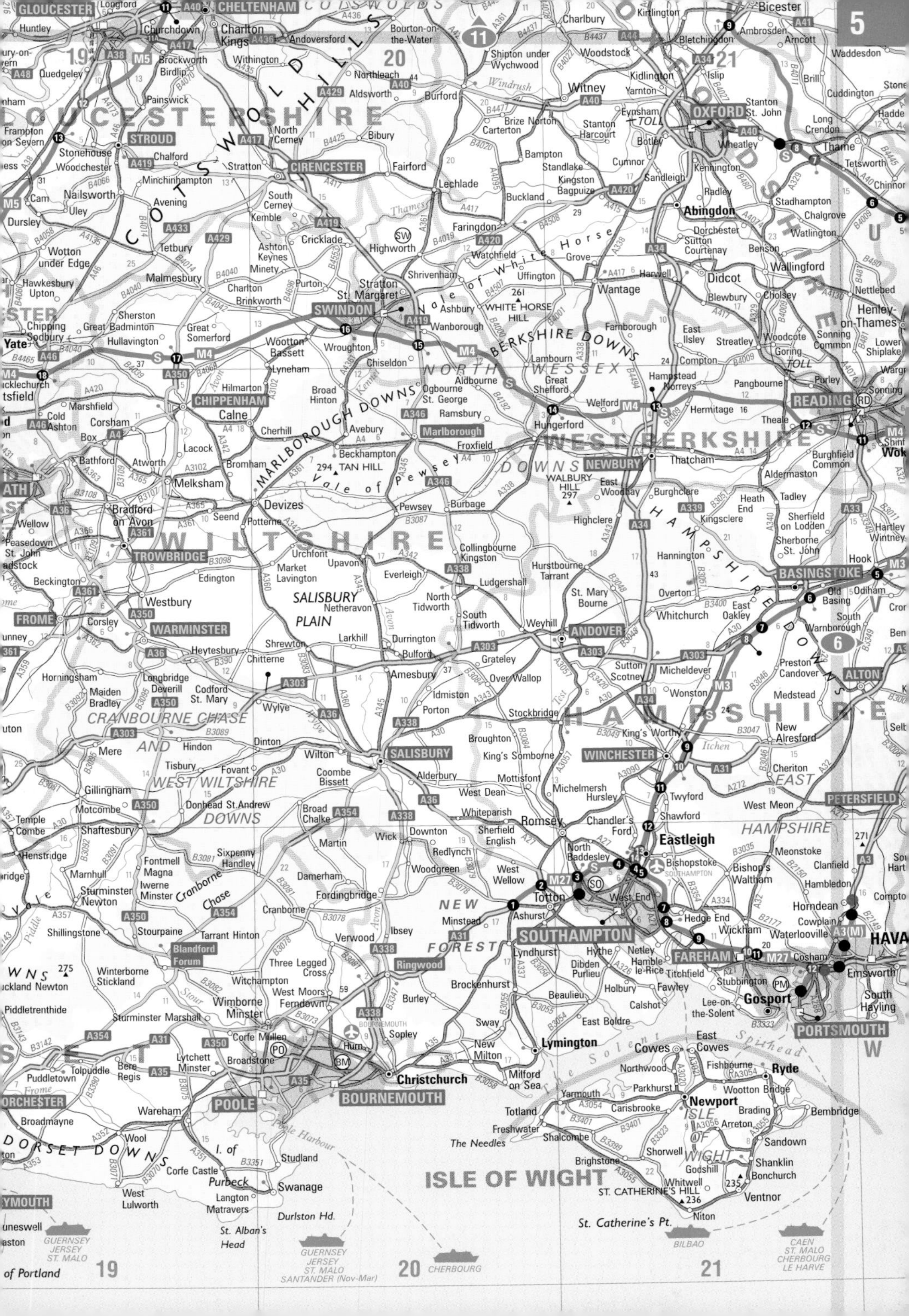
GLOUCESTER
CHELTENHAM
COTSWOLDS
GLOUCESTERSHIRE
COTSWOLD HILLS
Charlton Kings
Andoversford
Bourton-on-the-Water
Churchdown
Brockworth
Birdlip
Huntley
Quedgeley
Withington
Northleach
Aldsworth
Burford
Charlbury
Shipton under Wychwood
Woodstock
Kirtlington
Bicester
Ambrosden
Arncott
Bletchingdon
Islip
Kidlington
Yarnton
Witney
Eynsham
Brize Norton
Carterton
Stanton Harcourt
OXFORD
Botley
Wheatley
Stanton St. John
Thame
Long Crendon
Waddesdon
Brill
Cuddington
Painswick
North Cerney
Bibury
Frampton on Severn
STROUD
Stonehouse
Woodchester
Chalford
Stratton
CIRENCESTER
Fairford
Lechlade
Bampton
Standlake
Kingston Bagpuize
Cumnor
Sandleigh
Kennington
Radley
Abingdon
Tetsworth
Chinnor
Stadhampton
Chalgrove
Watlington
Minchinhampton
Nailsworth
Avening
Cam
Uley
Dursley
South Cerney
Kemble
Buckland
Faringdon
Cricklade
Highworth
Tetbury
Ashton Keynes
Minety
Dorchester
Sutton Courtenay
Benson
Wallingford
Wotton under Edge
Malmesbury
Charlton
Purton
Brinkworth
Stratton St. Margaret
Shrivenham
Watchfield
Vale of White Horse
Uffington
Grove
Wantage
Harwell
Didcot
Blewbury
Cholsey
Nettlebed
Henley-on-Thames
Hawkesbury Upton
Sherston
Great Badminton
Chipping Sodbury
Yate
Hullavington
Great Somerford
SWINDON
Ashbury
WHITE HORSE HILL
Wanborough
Wootton Bassett
Wroughton
Chiseldon
Lyneham
NORTH WESSEX
BERKSHIRE DOWNS
Lambourn
Farnborough
East Ilsley
Streatley
Woodcote
Sonning Common
Compton
Goring
Great Shefford
Hampstead Norreys
Pangbourne
Purley
READING
Hermitage
Chipping
Tormarton
Marshfield
Cold Ashton
CHIPPENHAM
Hilmarton
Calne
Broad Hinton
Ogbourne St. George
Aldbourne
Ramsbury
Hungerford
Welford
Theale
MARLBOROUGH DOWNS
Marlborough
Avebury
Beckhampton
TAN HILL
Vale of Pewsey
Froxfield
Cherhill
Corsham
Box
Lacock
Bathford
Atworth
Melksham
Bromham
WEST BERKSHIRE
NEWBURY
Thatcham
Burghfield Common
Aldermaston
DOWNS
WALBURY HILL
East Woodhay
Burghclere
Heath End
Tadley
Kingsclere
BATH
Bradford on Avon
Devizes
Seend
Potterne
Pewsey
Burbage
Highclere
Sherfield on Lodden
Sherborne St. John
Hartley Wintney
Wellow
Peasedown St. John
Radstock
TROWBRIDGE
WILTSHIRE
Urchfont
Market Lavington
Upavon
Everleigh
Collingbourne Kingston
Ludgershall
Hurstbourne Tarrant
Hannington
Overton
HAMPSHIRE
BASINGSTOKE
Old Basing
Odiham
Hook
Beckington
Edington
Westbury
SALISBURY PLAIN
Netheravon
North Tidworth
South Tidworth
St. Mary Bourne
Whitchurch
Oakley
East Oakley
Warnborough
South Warnborough
FROME
Corsley
WARMINSTER
Heytesbury
Shrewton
Chitterne
Larkhill
Durrington
Bulford
Weyhill
ANDOVER
Grateley
Over Wallop
Sutton Scotney
Micheldever
Preston Candover
ALTON
Horningsham
Longbridge Deverill
Maiden Bradley
Codford St. Mary
Wylye
Amesbury
Idmiston
Porton
Wonston
Medstead
CRANBOURNE CHASE
AND
WEST WILTSHIRE
DOWNS
Mere
Hindon
Dinton
Wilton
SALISBURY
Stockbridge
King's Worthy
New Alresford
Broughton
King's Somborne
WINCHESTER
Itchen
Cheriton
EAST HAMPSHIRE
Tisbury
Fovant
Coombe Bissett
Alderbury
Mottisfont
Michelmersh
Hursley
Twyford
West Dean
Gillingham
Motcombe
Donhead St. Andrew
Broad Chalke
Whiteparish
West Meon
PETERSFIELD
Temple Combe
Shaftesbury
Sherfield English
Romsey
Chandler's Ford
Shawford
Eastleigh
Wick
Downton
Martin
Redlynch
North Baddesley
Bishopstoke
Bishop's Waltham
Meonstoke
Clanfield
Hambledon
Henstridge
Fontmell Magna
Sixpenny Handley
Woodgreen
West Wellow
Marnhull
Iwerne Minster
Cranborne Chase
Damerham
Fordingbridge
Totton
West End
Hedge End
Horndean
Cowplain
Waterlooville
Sturminster Newton
Cranborne
NEW FOREST
Minstead
Ashurst
Wickham
HAVANT
Shillingstone
Stourpaine
Tarrant Hinton
Verwood
Ibsey
SOUTHAMPTON
Lyndhurst
Hythe
Netley
Hamble-le-Rice
FAREHAM
Cosham
Emsworth
Blandford Forum
Three Legged Cross
Ringwood
Dibden Purlieu
Titchfield
Stubbington
Winterborne Stickland
Witchampton
West Moors
Ferndown
Burley
Brockenhurst
Beaulieu
Holbury
Fawley
Calshot
Gosport
Lee-on-the-Solent
PORTSMOUTH
South Hayling
Piddletrenthide
Sturminster Marshall
Wimborne Minster
Sway
East Boldre
Corfe Mullen
Sopley
BOURNEMOUTH
Lymington
New Milton
Milford on Sea
Christchurch
The Solent
Spithead
Cowes
East Cowes
Ryde
Hurn
Broadstone
Lytchett Minster
Bere Regis
Tolpuddle
Puddletown
DORCHESTER
POOLE
Wareham
Broadmayne
Wool
DORSET DOWNS
Poole Harbour
I. of Purbeck
Corfe Castle
Studland
Swanage
West Lulworth
Langton Matravers
Durlston Hd.
St. Alban's Head
Northwood
Parkhurst
Fishbourne
Wootton Bridge
Yarmouth
Newport
Carisbrooke
Brading
Bembridge
Totland
Freshwater
ISLE OF WIGHT
Arreton
Sandown
The Needles
Shalcombe
Brighstone
Shorwell
Godshill
Shanklin
Bonchurch
Whitwell
ST. CATHERINE'S HILL
Ventnor
Niton
St. Catherine's Pt.
WEYMOUTH
Fortuneswell
Easton
of Portland
GUERNSEY JERSEY ST. MALO
GUERNSEY JERSEY ST. MALO SANTANDER (Nov-Mar)
CHERBOURG
BILBAO
CAEN ST. MALO CHERBOURG LE HARVE
19
20
21
6
11

Steeple Claydon
Upper Heyford
Bicester
Hockliffe
Leighton Buzzard
Houghton Regis
Linslade
Whitchurch
Wing
DUNSTABLE
LUTON
STEVENAGE
Knebworth
Stansted Mountfitchet
Bishop's Stortford
BUCKS
Kirtlington
Ambrosden
Arncott
Quainton
Waddesdon
Ivinghoe
DUNSTABLE DOWNS
Whipsnade
Kimpton
HERTFORDSHIRE
Bletchingdon
Kidlington
Yarnton
Islip
AYLESBURY
Markyate
Harpenden
Welwyn Garden City
Ware
OXFORD
Eynsham
Stanton St. John
Brill
Cuddington
Stone
Stoke Mandeville
Tring
Wheathampstead
Sawbridgeworth
Long Crendon
Haddenham
HEMEL HEMPSTEAD
Redbourn
ST. ALBANS
HERTFORD
HATFIELD
HARLOW
Botley
Wheatley
Thame
Berkhamsted
Wendover
London Colney
Hoddesdon
Kennington
Tetsworth
Princes Risborough
Great Missenden
Chesham
Kings Langley
Potters Bar
Cheshunt
Sandleigh
Radley
Chinnor
Prestwood
Cuffley
Waltham Abbey
Epping
Abingdon
Stadhampton
Chalgrove
CHILTERNS
AMERSHAM
Chorleywood
Radlett
Borehamwood
Loughton
Dorchester
Sutton Courtenay
Watlington
Stokenchurch
HIGH WYCOMBE
Hazlemere
Rickmansworth
WATFORD
Barnet
Benson
Chalfont St. Giles
Bushey
Enfield
Chingford
Epping Forest
Chigwell
Harwell
Didcot
Wallingford
BEACONSFIELD
Northwood
Finchley
Waltham Forest
Blewbury
Cholsey
Nettlebed
Marlow
Bourne End
Gerrards Cross
Harrow
Ruislip
GREATER
Haringey
Redbridge
East Ilsley
Henley-on-Thames
Cookham
Burnham
Stoke Poges
Brent
Islington
Hackney
Streatley
Woodcote
Sonning Common
MAIDENHEAD
SLOUGH
Hillingdon
LONDON
Camden
Tower Hamlets
Newham
Compton
Goring
Lower Shiplake
Bray
Hammersmith & Fulham
CITY
Westminster
Hampstead Norreys
Pangbourne
Purley
Wargrave
Twyford
Eton
Ealing
WEST END
BLACKWALL TUNNEL
Southwark
Woolwich
Hermitage
READING
Sonning
Woodley
Windsor
Hounslow
KEW BR.
Kensington & Chelsea
Lambeth
Greenwich
Bexley
WEST BERKSHIRE
Theale
HEATHROW AIRPORT
RICHMOND
Wandsworth
Lewisham
Dartford
Shinfield
BRACKNELL
Ascot
Egham
STAINES
LONDON
Thatcham
NEWBURY
Burghfield Common
Wokingham
Sunninghill
Virginia Water
Merton
Bromley
Swanley
Aldermaston
Crowthorne
Chertsey
Walton-on-Thames
KINGSTON
Burghclere
Heath End
Tadley
Sandhurst
Bagshot
Chobham
Weybridge
ESHER
SUTTON
CROYDON
Orpington
HAMPSHIRE
Kingsclere
Sherfield on Lodden
Camberley
WOKING
Byfleet
Epsom
Ewell
Purley
Biggin Hill
Hannington
Sherborne St. John
Hartley Wintney
Frimley
Ripley
Cobham
Banstead
Pirbright
Leatherhead
Hook
BASINGSTOKE
Fleet
Farnborough
East Horsley
SURREY
Overton
Old Basing
Odiham
Aldershot
Caterham
Westerham
Whitchurch
East Oakley
Crondall
Ash
GUILDFORD
Westcott
Oxted
Godstone
South Warnborough
Bentley
FARNHAM
Puttenham
Shalford
Shere
DORKING
REIGATE
Redhill
Wonersh
SURREY HILLS
Elstead
Godalming
LEITH HILL
GATWICK AIRPORT
Edenbridge
Micheldever
Preston Candover
ALTON
Frensham
Milford
Ewhurst
Newdigate
Horley
Penshurst
Wonston
Medstead
Kingsley
Headley
Hindhead
Witley
Ockley
Capel
Charlwood
Lingfield
Bordon
Cranleigh
CRAWLEY
Copthorne
EAST GRINSTEAD
Worthy
New Alresford
Selborne
Grayshott
Shottermill
Chiddingfold
Forest Row
Hartfield
WINCHESTER
Haslemere
Loxwood
HORSHAM
Cheriton
EAST
Liphook
BLACKDOWN HILL
Northchapel
Handcross
Balcombe
Ashdown Forest
Liss
Fernhurst
Wisborough Green
Billingshurst
Ardingly
Horsted Keynes
Nutley
Twyford
West Meon
PETERSFIELD
Rogate
Lower Beeding
Shawford
HAMPSHIRE
Coolham
Cuckfield
Bolney
Eastleigh
Meonstoke
Easebourne
Petworth
Haywards Heath
Maresfield
Bishopstoke
Bishop's Waltham
Clanfield
South Harting
Midhurst
Pulborough
West Grinstead
Cowfold
Wivelsfield
Newick
Uckfield
WEST SUSSEX
Hurstpierpoint
Burgess Hill
Hambledon
Singleton
Henfield
Hassocks
Keymer
Halland
Hedge End
Horndean
Compton
Storrington
Ditchling
Wickham
Cowplain
Waterlooville
Goodwood
Washington
Steyning
SUSSEX
DITCHLING BEACON
Ringmer
HAVANT
Mid Lavant
SOUTH DOWNS
LEWES
FAREHAM
Cosham
Westbourne
Tangmere
Arundel
Findon
Shoreham by Sea
Falmer
Glynde
Titchfield
Stubbington
Emsworth
Angmering
Lancing
Portslade
BRIGHTON
Fawley
Lee-on-the-Solent
Gosport
South Hayling
West Thorney
Bosham
CHICHESTER
Southwick
Hove
Rottingdean
Berwick
Sidlesham
Aldwick
Littlehampton
Goring-by-Sea
WORTHING
Peacehaven
Alfriston
PORTSMOUTH
Middleton-on-Sea
BOGNOR REGIS
Newhaven
East Cowes
East Wittering
Bracklesham
Seaford
Fishbourne
Ryde
Selsey
Selsey Bill
Wootton Bridge
Newport
Brading
ISLE OF WIGHT
Arreton
Bembridge
Sandown
Godshill
Shanklin
Whitwell
Bonchurch
Ventnor
Niton
CAEN CHERBOURG LE HAVRE ST MALO
BILBAO
21
22
23
24

HARWICH
COLCHESTER
Braintree
Witham
CHELMSFORD
Maldon
Brentwood
Billericay
Wickford
Rayleigh
BASILDON
SOUTHEND-ON-SEA
Shoeburyness
Canvey
Foulness Island
Burnham-on-Crouch
Bradwell-on-Sea
Mersea Is.
Brightlingsea
CLACTON-ON-SEA
Walton-on-the-Naze
Frinton-on-Sea
The Naze
ESBJERG
HAMBURG
HOOK OF HOLLAND
Thames Estuary
MEDWAY
Gravesend
Rochester
GILLINGHAM
Chatham
Sheerness
I. of Sheppey
Sittingbourne
Faversham
Whitstable
Herne Bay
MARGATE
Broadstairs
RAMSGATE
North Foreland
I. of Thanet
CANTERBURY
Sandwich
Deal
DOVER
South Foreland
FOLKESTONE
Hythe
CHANNEL TUNNEL
ASHFORD
MAIDSTONE
Tenterden
Romney Marsh
New Romney
Dungeness
Rye
Rye Bay
Winchelsea
Battle
HASTINGS
Bexhill
EASTBOURNE
K E N T
S U S S E X
WEALD
Strait of Dover
CALAIS
OSTEND
BOULOGNE
Sangatte
C. Gris-Nez
Wimereux
Boulogne-sur-Mer
Le Portel
Outreau
St.-Étienne-au-Mont
Marquise
Rinxent
Desvres
Samer
Camiers
Le Touquet-Paris-Plage
Étaples
U
V
W
24
25
26
27

13
14
15
16
17
R
S
T
The Skerries
Wylfa Hd.
Carmel Hd.
Cemaes
Amlwch
Llanfechell
Penysarn
Dulas Bay
128 PARYS MT.
ISLE OF ANGLESEY
Llanfaethlu
Holyhead Bay
Moelfre
Llanerchymedd
DUBLIN DUN LAOGHAIRE
HOLYHEAD
220
Holy I.
Bodedern
Benllech
Red Wharf Bay
Valley
Pentraeth
Gwalchmai
Llangefni
Menai Bridge
Beaumaris
Bangor
Rhosneigr
Gaerwen
Llanfairpwllgwyngyll
Aberffraw
Brynsiencyn
Newborough
Malltraeth Bay
Menai Strait
Y Felinheli
Llanrug
Caernarfon
Llanberis
Waunfawr
Caernarfon Bay
Rhostryfan
Penygroes
Talysarn
Rhyd-Ddu
1085 SNOWDON
Clynnog-fawr
Llanllyfni
Beddgelert
Llanaelhaiarn
Llithfaen
Rhoslan
Nefyn
Llanystumdwy
Tremadog
Porthmadog
Chwilog
Criccieth
TOLL
Tudweiliog
Llannor
Pwllheli
Lleyn Peninsula
Llanbedrog
Botwnnog
Abersoch
Aberdaron
Rhiw
Porth Neigwl
St. Tudwal's Is.
Braich-y-pwll
LLEYN PENINSULA
Bardsey Sd.
Bardsey I.
Trwyn Cilan
Tremadog Bay
Cardigan
Puffin I.
Great Ormes Head
LLANDUDNO
Conwy Bay
Llangoed
Penmaenmawr
Deganwy
CONWY
Rhos-on-Sea
Colwyn Bay
Old Colwyn
Llanddulas
Llanfairfechan
Abergwyngregyn
Ty'n-y-groes
Bethesda
CARNEDD LLEWELYN 1062
Dolgarrog
Trefriw
Gwydyr Forest Park
Capel Curig
SNOWDONIA NATIONAL PARK
Betws-y-Coed
Llanrwst
Dolwyddelan
Penmachno
Llanfair Talhaiarn
Llangernyw
Gwytherin
CONWY
Llansannan
Pentrefoelas
Cerrigydrudion
Ysbyty Ifan
Blaenau Ffestiniog
Maentwrog
Ffestiniog
Penrhyndeudraeth
Talsarnau
Trawsfynydd
853 ARENIG FAWR
Coed y Brenin Forest Park
Harlech
Llanbedr
GWYNEDD
Llanenddwyn
754 LLETHR
Llanelltyd
Dolgellau
Llanaber
Barmouth
CADER IDRIS 892
Fairbourne
Llwyngwril
Tal-y-llyn
Corris
Llangelynin
Abergynolwyn
Cemmaes Road
Bryncrug
Cwrt
Tywyn
Machynlleth
Aberdyfi
Dyfi
Borth
Talybont
Dinas Mawddwy
905 ARAN FAWDDWY
Mallwyd
Bala
L. Bala
Llanuwchllyn
Frongoch
Llandrillo
Celyn
BERWYN MTS
827 MOEL SYCH
Kinmel Bay
Rhyl
Rhuddlan
Abergele
St. Asaph
Henllan
Trefnant
Denbigh
Bylchau
L. Brenig
Ruthin
Llanarmon
Rhewl
DENBIGHSHIRE
Llanelidan
Gwyddelwern
Druid
Corwen
Llangwm
Glyndyfrdwy
Llangollen
Glyn Ceiriog
Chirk
Llanarmon Dyffryn Ceiriog
Llanrhaeadr-ym-Mochnant
Oswestry
Llanyblodwel
Llangynog
Penybontfawr
L. Vyrnwy
Llanwddyn
Llanfechain
Llanfyllin
Meifod
Dolanog
Foel
Llangadfan
Llanerfyl
Guilsfield
Welshpool
Llanfair Caereinion
Manafon
Berriew
Forden
Tregynon
Montgomery
Llanbrynmair
Carno
Trefeglwys
Caersws
Newtown
Llandinam
Kerry
Dolfor
Pt. of Ayr
Prestatyn
Dyserth
Hoylake
West Kirby
Heswall
Mostyn
Holywell
Bagillt
Neston
Flint
Nannerch
Northop
Mynydd Isa
Mold
Buckley
Llandyrnog
CLWYDIAN RANGE
FLINTSHIRE
Treuddyn
Caergwrle
Brymbo
Minera
Rhosllanerchrugog
Ruabon
WIRRAL
15
10
A5
A55
A470
A487
A494
A458
A489
A483
A5025
A4080
A4085
A4086
A499
A497
A498
A4212
A496
A493
A543
A544
A548
A525
A541
A542
A5104
A5151
A490
A495
B5109
B5111
B5112
B5420
B4419
B4422
B4366
B4418
B4417
B4354
B4415
B4413
B5106
B5113
B5384
B5382
B5381
B5429
B5105
B4501
B4407
B4391
B4401
B4402
B4403
B4500
B4580
B4396
B4393
B4395
B4382
B4392
B4385
B4390
B4389
B4518
B4569
B4405
B4353

POWYS
CEREDIGION
CAMBRIAN
CARMARTHENSHIRE
PEMBROKESHIRE
SWANSEA
GOWER
MYNYDD PRESCELLY
MYNYDD EPPYNT
MYNYDD DU
Mynydd Bach
BRECON BEACONS
NATIONAL PARK
PEMBROKESHIRE COAST NATIONAL PARK
BLACK MOUNTAIN
VALE OF GLAMORGAN
ROSSLARE
Devil's Bridge
St. Harmon
Llanbister
Llangunllo
Ysbyty Ystwyth
Llanilar
Lledrod
Llanrhystyd
Rhayader
Radnor Forest
660
Pontrhydfendigaid
Elan Valley Reservoirs
Elan Village
Penybont
Llandrindod Wells
New Radnor
Old Radnor
Gladestry
Llanon
Aberarth
Aberaeron
Tregaron
DRYGARN FAWR
645
Newbridge on Wye
New Quay
Llangeitho
Llanafan-fawr
Hundred House
Llanarth
Llangybi
Llanddewi-Brefi
Newchurch
Llangranog
Mydroilyn
Bettws Bledrws
Beulah
Builth Wells
Aberporth
Sarnau
L. Brianne
Painscastle
Cemaes Hd.
Gwbert-on-Sea
Lampeter
Llanwrtyd Wells
Cardigan
Cwmann
Llangammarch Wells
Clyro
St. Dogmaels
Llandygwydd
Llanwenog
Cilgerran
Llanybydder
Dinas Hd.
Strumble Hd.
Nevern
Newport
Llandyfriog
Llandysul
Llanfihangel-ar-arth
Pumpsaint
Cilycwm
Upper Chapel
Llyswen
Glasbury
Cenarth
Newcastle Emlyn
Goodwick
Eglwyswrw
Pencader
Llansawel
Landovery
Fishguard
Crymych
Talley
Llanwrda
Talgarth
536
Greenway
Brechfa
Myddfai
Trecastle
Sennybridge
BRECON
Llangorse
Mathry
Llanrhian
Letterston
Trelech
Llanpumsaint
Llangadog
Llanfrynach
St. David's Hd.
Wolf's Castle
Cynwyl Elfed
Crai
Tretower
St. David's
Solva
Spittal
Llandissilio
CARMARTHEN
Llandeilo
886
BRECON BEACONS
Crickhowell
Newgale
Meidrim
Abergwili
Fforest Fawr
Llangynidr
Ramsey I.
Llanarthney
St. Brides Bay
Camrose
Whitland
St. Clears
Llandybie
Brynamman
Gilwern
Gorslas
Glanaman
Abercrave
Tredegar
Brynmawr
Haverfordwest
Cross Hands
Penygroes
Gwaun-Cae-Gurwen
Beaufort
Ebbw Vale
Broad Haven
Narberth
Ammanford
Ystradgynlais
Penderyn
Rhymney
Blaina
Llanstephan
Pontyberem
Seven Sisters
Templeton
Laugharne
Ystalyfera
MERTHYR TYDFIL
Skomer I.
MILFORD HAVEN
Johnston
Rosemarket
Ferryside
Glyn Neath
Hirwaun
New Tredegar
Pontyates
Pendine
Herbrandston
Cresselly
Begelly
Kidwelly
Pontardulais
Pontardawe
600
CEFNFFORD
Aberdare
Bargoed
Neyland
Saundersfoot
Skokholm I.
Dale
Pembroke Dock
Sageston
Llangennech
Clydach
Resolven
Glyncorrwg
Mountain Ash
Oakdale
Pembrey
Treorchy
Trehams
Angle
Pembroke
Tenby
Burry Port
LLANELLI
Gorseinon
Birchgrove
Aberdulais
St. Ann's Hd.
Loughor
NEATH
RHONDDA
Tylorstown
Blackwood
Milford Haven
Castlemartin
Penally
Manorbier
Carmarthen Bay
Cymmer
Hengoed
Caldey I.
Briton Ferry
Cwmafan
Gowerton
Llanrhidian
Pontycymer
Porth
Pontypridd
Bedwas
Machen
Linney Hd.
Stackpole Hd.
SWANSEA
PORT TALBOT
Maesteg
Tonyrefail
Caerphilly
Rhossili B.
St. Govan's Hd.
Rhossili
Bishopston
The Mumbles
Church Village
Worms Hd.
Margam
Betws
Mumbles Hd.
Pyle
Tondu
Pencoed
Llantrisant
Port Eynon
Oxwich Pt.
Swansea Bay
Port Eynon Pt.
BRIDGEND
Radyr
CARDIFF
Porthcawl
St. Bride's Major
Cowbridge
Bonvilston
Wenvoe
T
U
V
13
14
15
16
17

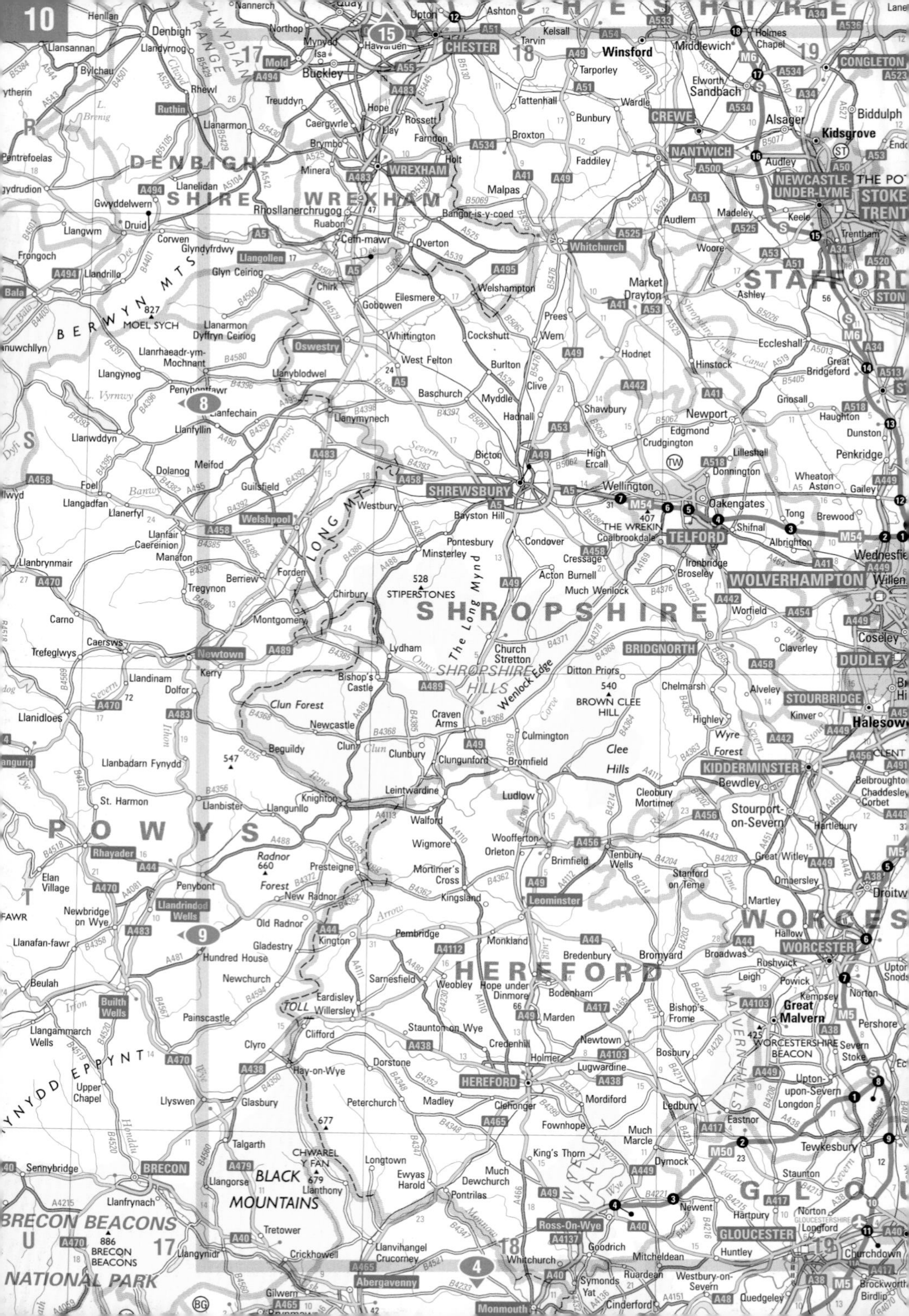
CHESHIRE
CHESTER
Winsford
Middlewich
Holmes Chapel
CONGLETON
Sandbach
CREWE
Alsager
Biddulph
Kidsgrove
NANTWICH
NEWCASTLE-UNDER-LYME
STOKE
TRENT
Denbigh
Mold
Buckley
Hawarden
Ruthin
DENBIGH-SHIRE
WREXHAM
CLWYDIAN RANGE
Llangollen
Corwen
Bala
Whitchurch
Malpas
Market Drayton
STAFFORD
BERWYN MTS
MOEL SYCH
Oswestry
Ellesmere
Wem
Newport
Eccleshall
Penkridge
Welshpool
LONG MT
SHREWSBURY
Wellington
TELFORD
Oakengates
Shifnal
THE WREKIN
Coalbrookdale
Ironbridge
WOLVERHAMPTON
STIPERSTONES
The Long Mynd
SHROPSHIRE
Church Stretton
Much Wenlock
BRIDGNORTH
DUDLEY
Newtown
SHROPSHIRE HILLS
Wenlock Edge
Bishop's Castle
Craven Arms
Clun Forest
BROWN CLEE HILL
Clee Hills
Wyre Forest
STOURBRIDGE
Halesowen
KIDDERMINSTER
Bewdley
Ludlow
Knighton
Llanidloes
POWYS
Rhayader
Radnor Forest
Presteigne
Tenbury Wells
Stourport-on-Severn
Leominster
Llandrindod Wells
Kington
Builth Wells
HEREFORD
Bromyard
WORCESTER
Droitwich
Great Malvern
MALVERN HILLS
WORCESTERSHIRE BEACON
Hay-on-Wye
HEREFORD
Ledbury
Tewkesbury
BRECON
BLACK MOUNTAINS
CHWAREL Y FAN
Abergavenny
Ross-On-Wye
WYE VALLEY
GLOUCESTER
Monmouth
BRECON BEACONS
BRECON BEACONS NATIONAL PARK
Crickhowell
Cinderford
Newent
Pershore
Upton-upon-Severn
Cheltenham
Churchdown

NOTTS
DERBYSHIRE
LEICESTERSHIRE
NORTHAMPTONSHIRE
WARWICKSHIRE
OXFORDSHIRE
BUCKS
BEDS
RUTLAND
CHESTERFIELD
MATLOCK
MANSFIELD
DERBY
NOTTINGHAM
NEWARK-ON-TRENT
LINCOLN
GRANTHAM
LOUGHBOROUGH
MELTON MOWBRAY
BURTON UPON TRENT
LEICESTER
HINCKLEY
NUNEATON
COVENTRY
RUGBY
MARKET HARBOROUGH
KETTERING
CORBY
STAMFORD
TAMWORTH
LICHFIELD
RUGELEY
SUTTON COLDFIELD
BIRMINGHAM
SOLIHULL
REDDITCH
WARWICK
ROYAL LEAMINGTON SPA
STRATFORD-UPON-AVON
EVESHAM
BANBURY
WELLINGBOROUGH
NORTHAMPTON
MILTON KEYNES
BEDFORD
AYLESBURY
DUNSTABLE
LUTON
Sherwood Forest
Vale of Belvoir
Charnwood Forest
Rockingham Forest
COTSWOLDS
EDGE HILL 226
ARBURY HILL 224
ILMINGTON DOWNS 260
DUNSTABLE DOWNS 243
M1
M6
M40
M42
M45
M69
A1
A6
A5
A14
A43
A46
A47
A52
A38
12
17
5
20
21
22

NOTTS
LINCOLN
Washingborough
Bardney
Horncastle
Hagworthingham
Partney
Chapel St
Ingoldmells
Sutton-on-Trent
Laxton
Branston
North Hykeham
Bracebridge Heath
Metheringham
Woodhall Spa
Spilsby
Old Bolingbroke
Mareham le Fen
Burgh le Marsh
SKEGNESS
Collingham
Waddington
Scopwick
Digby
Walcott
Coningsby
Stickford
Wainfleet All Saints
Eakring
Rainworth
Blidworth
Ravenshead
Navenby
Billinghay
Stickney
West Fen
East Fen
Gibraltar Pt.
NEWARK-ON-TRENT
Southwell
Balderton
Welbourn
Leadenham
Cranwell
Ruskington
Sibsey
Wrangle
Old Leake
Calverton
Arnold
Carlton
Lowdham
Elston
Claypole
Caythorpe
Leasingham
Sleaford
Brothertoft
East Bridgford
Long Bennington
Ancaster
Holland Fen
Benington
NOTTINGHAM
Radcliffe on Trent
Cotgrave
West Bridgford
Bingham
Whatton
Bottesford
Honington
Heckington
BOSTON
Osbournby
Helpringham
Swineshead
Fishtoft
Wyberton
Kirton
Redmile
Vale of Belvoir
GRANTHAM
Ropsley
Donington
Sutterton
Keyworth
Denton
Harby
Eaton
Aslackby
Billingborough
Quadring
Gosberton
Holbeach Marsh
Croxton Kerrial
Long Clawson
Waltham on the Wolds
LINCOLNSHIRE
Colsterworth
Corby Glen
Dunsby
Morton
Pinchbeck
SPALDING
MELTON MOWBRAY
Bourne
Twenty
Moulton
Holbeach
Gedney
Long Sutton
Sutton Bridge
Terrington St. Clement
Quorndon
Asfordby
Wymondham
Thurlby
Fen
Deeping Fen
Cowbit
Tydd St. Mary
Walpole
Whissendine
Cottesmore
Somerby
Stretton
Deeping St. Nicholas
Whaplode
Tydd St. Giles
Syston
Thurmaston
Langham
Exton
RUTLAND
Baston
Langtoft
Twyford
Empingham
Ryhall
Crowland
Market Deeping
WISBECH
Walsoken
Watlington
Oakham
STAMFORD
Rutland Water
Glinton
Wisbech St. Mary
LEICESTER
Billesdon
Manton
Ketton
Easton
PETERBOROUGH
Eye
Thorney
Friday Bridge
Outwell
Oadby
Wigston
East Norton
Uppingham
Duddington
Castor
Nordelph
Countesthorpe
Wansford
Whittlesey
LEICESTERSHIRE
King's Cliffe
Fotheringhay
Old Fletton
MARCH
Christchurch
Welney
Southery
Kibworth Beauchamp
Gretton
Rockingham
Yaxley
Wimblington
MARKET HARBOROUGH
Stoke Albany
CORBY
Rockingham Forest
Weldon
Oundle
Lutton
Stilton
Benwick
Doddington
Manea
Brigstock
Husbands Bosworth
Clipston
Desborough
Great Gidding
Sawtry
Ramsey
Chatteris
Downham
Littleport
Rothwell
Geddington
Welford
Naseby
KETTERING
Thrapston
Hamerton
CAMBRIDGESHIRE
Warboys
Somersham
Sutton
ELY
Crick
West Haddon
Broughton
Burton Latimer
Raunds
Great Staunton
Little Stukeley
Pidley
Earith
Witchford
Haddenham
Stretham
Soham
Brixworth
Finedon
Irthlingborough
Spaldwick
Huntingdon
St. Ives
Needingworth
NORTHAMPTONSHIRE
WELLINGBOROUGH
Higham Ferrers
Grafham Water
Brampton
Godmanchester
Wicken
Moulton
Rushden
Kimbolton
Buckden
Offord D'Arcy
Over
Cottenham
Burwell
Irchester
Earls Barton
Wollaston
Histon
Waterbeach
NORTHAMPTON
Sharnbrook
Keysoe
Papworth Everard
Bar Hill
Girton
Weedon Bec
Hardingstone
Bozeat
Eaton Socon
St. Neots
Bottisham
Bugbrooke
Yardley Hastings
Harrold
CAMBRIDGE
Blisworth
Horton
Lavendon
Turvey
Clapham
Great Barford
Comberton
Trumpington
Fulbourn
Dullingham
Olney
MILTON KEYNES
Bromham
Gamlingay
Great Shelford
Roade
Towcester
BEDFORD
Willington
Sandy
Potton
Harston
Little Shelford
Sawston
Whittlesford
Balsham
Kempston
Cardington
Linton
Silverstone
Whittlebury
Newport Pagnell
Biggleswade
Melbourn
Potterspury
Syresham
Akeley
Wolverton
BEDFORDSHIRE
Royston
Great Chesterford
Haverhill
Stony Stratford
Ampthill
Clophill
Henlow
Ashwell
Barley
Saffron Walden
Shefford
Buckingham
Bletchley
Woburn Sands
Woburn
Flitwick
Shillington
Stotfold
Tingewick
Great Horwood
Fenny Stratford
Letchworth
Baldock
Barkway
Newport
BUCKS
Winslow
Toddington
Hitchin
Barton-le-Clay
Cottered
Buntingford
Clavering
Thaxted
Finchingfield
Steeple Claydon
Hockliffe
Leighton Buzzard
Houghton Regis
STEVENAGE
Stansted Mountfitchet
Elsenham
Bicester
Linslade
Whitchurch
Wing
DUNSTABLE
LUTON
STANSTED AIRPORT
Bishop's Stortford
Quainton
Arncott
Waddesdon
Dunstable Downs
Whipsnade
Kimpton
Knebworth
HERTS
Ivinghoe
Markyate
AYLESBURY
Harpenden
Welwyn Garden City
Ware
Hatfield Heath
Brill
The Wash
THE FENS
Great Ouse
Old Bedford R.
New Bedford R.
22
23
24
17
11
6

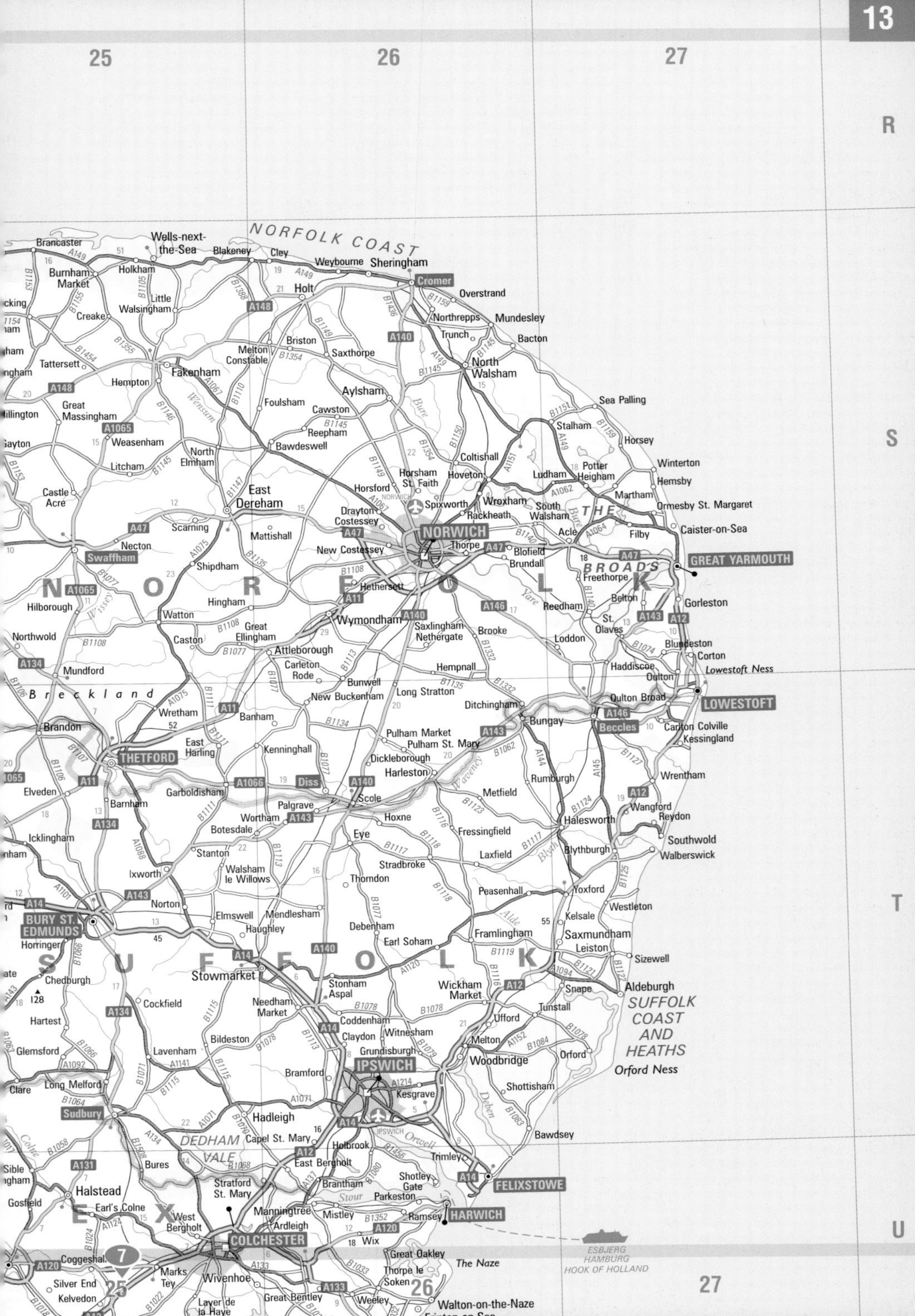
25
26
27
R
S
T
U
NORFOLK COAST
Brancaster
Wells-next-the-Sea
Blakeney
Cley
Weybourne
Sheringham
Cromer
Overstrand
Burnham Market
Holkham
Holt
Little Walsingham
Creake
Northrepps
Mundesley
Trunch
Bacton
Briston
Melton Constable
Saxthorpe
North Walsham
Tattersett
Fakenham
Hempton
Aylsham
Foulsham
Cawston
Reepham
Great Massingham
Weasenham
Bawdeswell
Sea Palling
Stalham
Horsey
Winterton
Hemsby
Potter Heigham
Ludham
Coltishall
Hoveton
Horsham St. Faith
Horsford
Litcham
North Elmham
Castle Acre
East Dereham
Spixworth
Wroxham
South Walsham
Martham
Ormesby St. Margaret
Caister-on-Sea
Drayton
Costessey
Rackheath
Scarning
Mattishall
NORWICH
Thorpe
Acle
Filby
Necton
Swaffham
New Costessey
Blofield
Brundall
GREAT YARMOUTH
THE BROADS
Shipdham
Freethorpe
NORFOLK
Hethersett
Hilborough
Hingham
Reedham
Belton
Gorleston
Watton
Wymondham
Saxlingham Nethergate
Brooke
St. Olaves
Northwold
Caston
Great Ellingham
Loddon
Blundeston
Corton
Attleborough
Mundford
Carleton Rode
Hempnall
Haddiscoe
Oulton
Lowestoft Ness
Breckland
Bunwell
Long Stratton
New Buckenham
Ditchingham
Oulton Broad
LOWESTOFT
Wretham
Banham
Bungay
Beccles
Carlton Colville
Kessingland
Brandon
Pulham Market
Pulham St. Mary
East Harling
Kenninghall
THETFORD
Dickleborough
Harleston
Wrentham
Elveden
Garboldisham
Diss
Rumburgh
Metfield
Scole
Barnham
Palgrave
Wangford
Reydon
Wortham
Hoxne
Halesworth
Botesdale
Fressingfield
Icklingham
Eye
Southwold
Walberswick
Stanton
Stradbroke
Laxfield
Blythburgh
Walsham le Willows
Ixworth
Thorndon
Peasenhall
Yoxford
Norton
Westleton
BURY ST. EDMUNDS
Elmswell
Mendlesham
Kelsale
Haughley
Debenham
Framlingham
Saxmundham
Horringer
Earl Soham
Leiston
SUFFOLK
Sizewell
Stowmarket
Chedburgh
Stonham Aspal
Wickham Market
Aldeburgh
Snape
Cockfield
Needham Market
SUFFOLK COAST AND HEATHS
Tunstall
Hartest
Coddenham
Witnesham
Ufford
Bildeston
Claydon
Glemsford
Lavenham
Grundisburgh
Melton
Woodbridge
Orford
IPSWICH
Orford Ness
Bramford
Clare
Long Melford
Kesgrave
Shottisham
Sudbury
Hadleigh
Bawdsey
DEDHAM VALE
Capel St. Mary
Holbrook
Trimley
Bures
East Bergholt
Shotley Gate
FELIXSTOWE
Brantham
Stratford St. Mary
Halstead
Parkeston
Gosfield
Earl's Colne
Manningtree
Mistley
Ramsey
HARWICH
West Bergholt
Ardleigh
COLCHESTER
Wix
Great Oakley
ESBJERG
HAMBURG
HOOK OF HOLLAND
Coggeshall
The Naze
Marks Tey
Silver End
Wivenhoe
Thorpe le Soken
Kelvedon
Layer de la Haye
Great Bentley
Weeley
Walton-on-the-Naze
Frinton-on-Sea
ESSEX

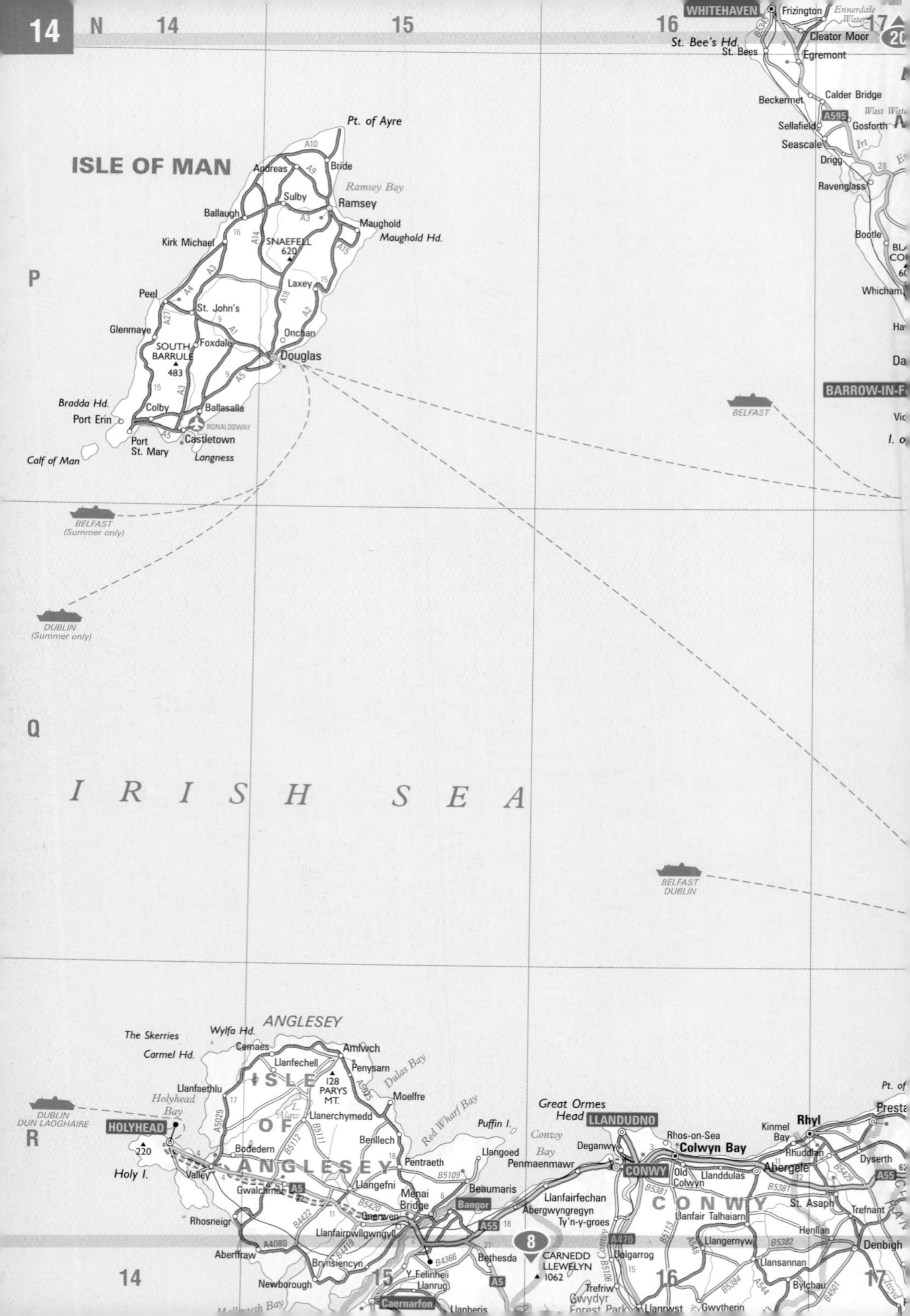
ISLE OF MAN
Pt. of Ayre
Andreas
Bride
Ramsey Bay
Sulby
Ramsey
Ballaugh
Maughold
Maughold Hd.
Kirk Michael
SNAEFELL
620
Laxey
Peel
St. John's
Glenmaye
Onchan
SOUTH
BARRULE
483
Foxdale
Douglas
Bradda Hd.
Colby
Ballasalla
Port Erin
RONALDSWAY
Port
St. Mary
Castletown
Calf of Man
Langness
BELFAST
(Summer only)
DUBLIN
(Summer only)
BELFAST
BELFAST
DUBLIN
I R I S H S E A
WHITEHAVEN
Frizington
Ennerdale Water
Cleator Moor
St. Bee's Hd.
St. Bees
Egremont
Beckermet
Calder Bridge
Sellafield
Gosforth
Seascale
Drigg
Ravenglass
Bootle
Whicham
BARROW-IN-F
ANGLESEY
The Skerries
Wylfa Hd.
Carmel Hd.
Cemaes
Amlwch
Llanfechell
Penysarn
Dulas Bay
128
PARYS
MT.
Llanfaethlu
ISLE
OF
ANGLESEY
Moelfre
Holyhead
Bay
Llanerchymedd
Red Wharf Bay
DUBLIN
DUN LAOGHAIRE
HOLYHEAD
Benllech
Puffin I.
Great Ormes
Head
LLANDUDNO
220
Bodedern
Pentraeth
Llangoed
Conwy
Bay
Deganwy
Rhos-on-Sea
Colwyn Bay
Kinmel
Bay
Rhyl
Prestatyn
Holy I.
Valley
Llangefni
Beaumaris
Penmaenmawr
CONWY
Old
Colwyn
Llanddulas
Abergele
Rhuddlan
Dyserth
Gwalchmai
Menai
Bridge
Bangor
Llanfairfechan
Abergwyngregyn
Ty'n-y-groes
CONWY
St. Asaph
Trefnant
Rhosneigr
Gaerwen
Llanfairpwllgwyngyll
Llanfair Talhaiarn
Henllan
Aberffraw
Brynsiencyn
Bethesda
8
CARNEDD
LLEWELYN
1062
Dolgarrog
Llangernyw
Llansannan
Denbigh
Y Felinheli
Llanrug
Newborough
Caernarfon
Llanberis
Trefriw
Gwydyr
Forest Park
Llanrwst
Gwytherin
Bylchau
Malltraeth Bay
N
P
Q
R
14
15
16
17
A10
A9
A3
A14
A15
A18
A2
A4
A27
A1
A5
A595
A5025
B5112
B5111
B5109
B5420
B4422
B4419
A4080
A55
B4366
A470
B5381
B5113
A548
B5382
A544
B5384
B5106
B5429
B4501

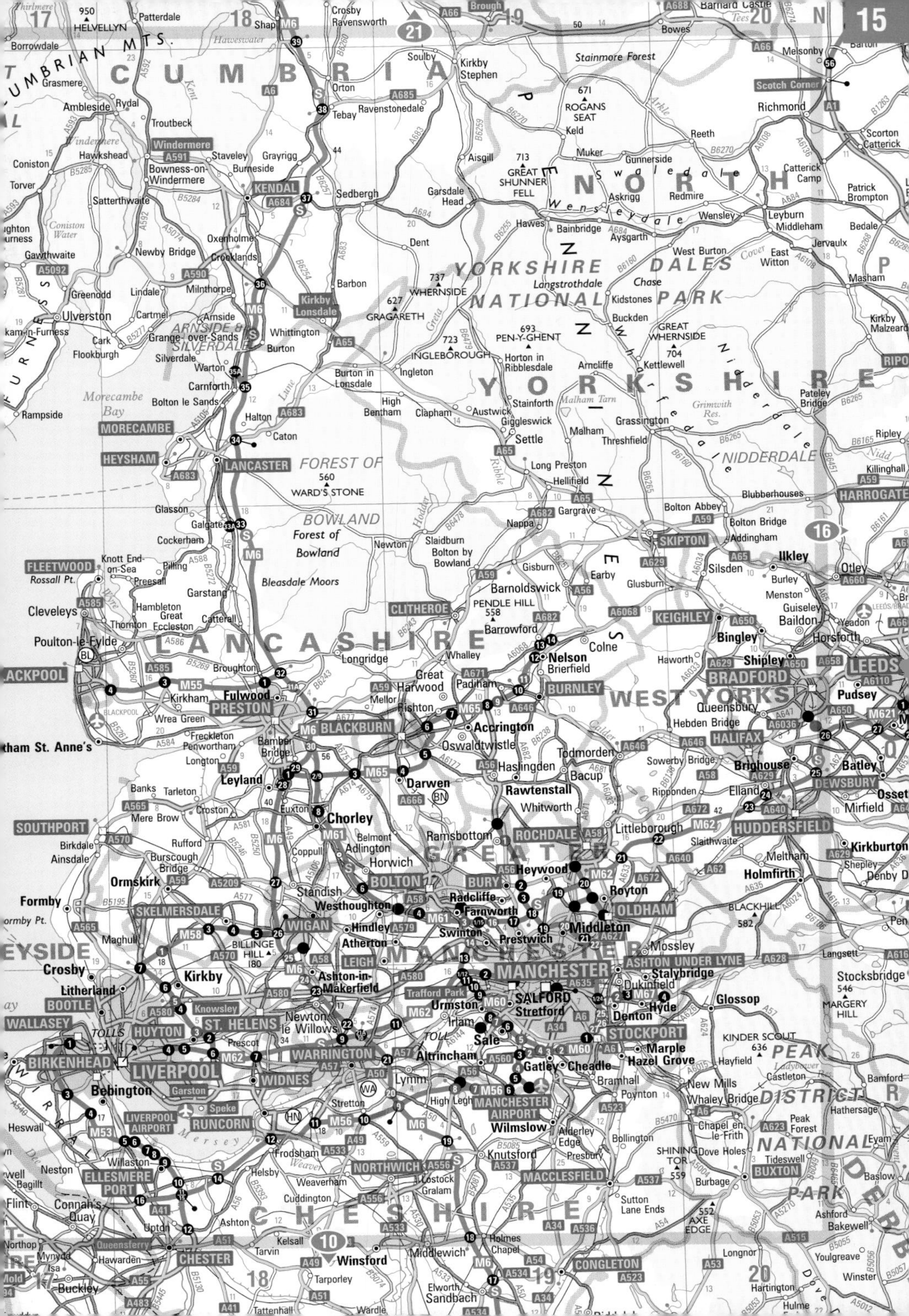
CUMBRIA
CUMBRIAN MTS.
HELVELLYN
Patterdale
Shap
Crosby Ravensworth
Brough
Barnard Castle
Bowes
Stainmore Forest
Melsonby
Scotch Corner
Richmond
Scorton
Catterick
Catterick Camp
Borrowdale
Grasmere
Ambleside
Rydal
Troutbeck
Windermere
Hawkshead
Coniston
Staveley
Grayrigg
Burneside
Bowness-on-Windermere
Torver
Satterthwaite
KENDAL
Sedbergh
Soulby
Kirkby Stephen
Orton
Tebay
Ravenstonedale
ROGANS SEAT
Keld
Muker
Gunnerside
Reeth
Swaledale
NORTH
Aisgill
GREAT SHUNNER FELL
Askrigg
Redmire
Garsdale Head
Hawes
Bainbridge
Wensleydale
Wensley
Leyburn
Middleham
Patrick Brompton
Bedale
Aysgarth
West Burton
East Witton
Jervaulx
Masham
Oxenholme
Crooklands
Newby Bridge
Gawthwaite
Dent
YORKSHIRE DALES NATIONAL PARK
Langstrothdale
Chase
Kidstones
Buckden
GREAT WHERNSIDE
Kettlewell
Kirkby Malzeard
Milnthorpe
Lindale
Greenodd
Ulverston
Cartmel
Arnside
ARNSIDE & SILVERDALE
Grange-over-Sands
Cark
Flookburgh
Barrow-in-Furness
FURNESS
Barbon
Kirkby Lonsdale
WHERNSIDE
GRAGARETH
Whittington
Burton
INGLEBOROUGH
PEN-Y-GHENT
Horton in Ribblesdale
Arncliffe
Silverdale
Warton
Carnforth
Burton in Lonsdale
Ingleton
YORKSHIRE
Nidderdale
Pateley Bridge
RIPON
Morecambe Bay
Bolton le Sands
Rampside
High Bentham
Clapham
Austwick
Stainforth
Malham Tarn
Grimwith Res.
MORECAMBE
Halton
Caton
Giggleswick
Settle
Malham
Threshfield
Grassington
Ripley
HEYSHAM
LANCASTER
FOREST OF BOWLAND
WARD'S STONE
Long Preston
Hellifield
NIDDERDALE
Killinghall
Blubberhouses
HARROGATE
Glasson
Galgate
Cockerham
BOWLAND
Forest of Bowland
Newton
Slaidburn
Bolton by Bowland
Nappa
Gargrave
Bolton Abbey
Bolton Bridge
Addingham
SKIPTON
FLEETWOOD
Rossall Pt.
Knott End-on-Sea
Pilling
Preesall
Garstang
Bleasdale Moors
Gisburn
Earby
Barnoldswick
Glusburn
Silsden
Ilkley
Otley
Burley
Menston
Guiseley
Yeadon
Baildon
Horsforth
LEEDS/BRADFORD
Cleveleys
Hambleton
Great Eccleston
Thornton
Catterall
CLITHEROE
PENDLE HILL
Barrowford
Nelson
Colne
Brierfield
KEIGHLEY
Bingley
Shipley
Haworth
Poulton-le-Fylde
LANCASHIRE
Longridge
Whalley
Great Harwood
Padiham
BURNLEY
WEST YORKS
BRADFORD
LEEDS
Pudsey
Queensbury
BLACKPOOL
Kirkham
Broughton
Fulwood
PRESTON
Wrea Green
Freckleton
Penwortham
Lytham St. Anne's
Mellor
Rishton
BLACKBURN
Accrington
Oswaldtwistle
Hebden Bridge
HALIFAX
Brighouse
Batley
Longton
Bamber Bridge
Leyland
Darwen
Haslingden
Todmorden
Bacup
Rawtenstall
Sowerby Bridge
Ripponden
Elland
DEWSBURY
Ossett
Mirfield
Banks
Tarleton
Croston
Mere Brow
Euxton
Chorley
Whitworth
ROCHDALE
Littleborough
HUDDERSFIELD
SOUTHPORT
Birkdale
Ainsdale
Rufford
Burscough Bridge
Coppull
Belmont
Adlington
Horwich
Ramsbottom
GREATER
Heywood
Slaithwaite
Meltham
Holmfirth
Kirkburton
Shepley
Denby Dale
Ormskirk
Standish
BOLTON
BURY
Radcliffe
Farnworth
Royton
OLDHAM
Formby
Formby Pt.
SKELMERSDALE
Westhoughton
WIGAN
Hindley
Atherton
LEIGH
Swinton
Prestwich
Middleton
Maghull
BILLINGE HILL
MANCHESTER
Mossley
Langsett
Stocksbridge
MARGERY HILL
MERSEYSIDE
Crosby
Litherland
BOOTLE
Kirkby
Knowsley
Ashton-in-Makerfield
Trafford Park
SALFORD
Stretford
ASHTON UNDER LYNE
Stalybridge
Dukinfield
Hyde
Denton
Glossop
WALLASEY
HUYTON
ST. HELENS
Newton le Willows
Urmston
Irlam
Sale
STOCKPORT
KINDER SCOUT
PEAK
BIRKENHEAD
LIVERPOOL
Prescot
WARRINGTON
Altrincham
Gatley
Cheadle
Marple
Hazel Grove
Hayfield
Castleton
Bamford
Bebington
Garston
WIDNES
Lymm
High Legh
MANCHESTER AIRPORT
Bramhall
Poynton
New Mills
Whaley Bridge
PEAK DISTRICT NATIONAL PARK
Hathersage
Heswall
LIVERPOOL AIRPORT
Speke
RUNCORN
Mersey
Stretton
Wilmslow
Alderley Edge
Chapel en le Frith
Peak Forest
Eyam
WIRRAL
Neston
Willaston
ELLESMERE PORT
Frodsham
Helsby
NORTHWICH
Weaverham
Knutsford
MACCLESFIELD
Bollington
Prestbury
SHINING TOR
Dove Holes
Tideswell
BUXTON
Baslow
Flint
Bagillt
Connah's Quay
Cuddington
Lostock Gralam
Sutton Lane Ends
Burbage
AXE EDGE
Ashford
Bakewell
CHESHIRE
Upton
Ashton
CHESTER
Queensferry
Northop
Mynydd Isa
Hawarden
Buckley
Mold
Kelsall
Tarvin
Winsford
Tarporley
Middlewich
Holmes Chapel
Elworth
Sandbach
CONGLETON
Longnor
Hartington
Hulme
Youlgreave
Winster
Tattenhall
Wardle
Dove
DERBYSHIRE

Appleby-in-Westmorland
MICKLE FELL
Mickleton
Balderhead Res.
Staindrop
Newton Aycliffe
Heighington
Billingham
Eston
Hoff
Cotherstone
Gainford
STOCKTON-ON-TEES
MIDDLESBROUGH
Crosby Ravensworth
Brough
Barnard Castle
Winston
Thornaby on Tees
DARLINGTON
Shap
Bowes
Tees
Hurworth-on-Tees
TEESSIDE
Stainton
Eaglescliffe
Yarm
Soulby
Kirkby Stephen
Stainmore Forest
Melsonby
Barton
Stokesley
Great
Orton
Dalton
Hutton Rudby
Scotch Corner
Tebay
Ravenstonedale
671 ROGANS SEAT
Keld
East Cowton
Great Broughton
Richmond
Wiske
CLEVELAND
Grayrigg
Aisgill
713 GREAT SHUNNER FELL
Muker
Reeth
Gunnerside
Scorton
Catterick
Osmotherley
Swaledale
Catterick Camp
Brompton
KENDAL
Sedbergh
Garsdale Head
Askrigg
Redmire
NORTH
Patrick Brompton
Leeming Bar
Northallerton
HAMBLETON HILLS
Wensleydale
Hawes
Bainbridge
Aysgarth
Wensley
Leyburn
Middleham
Bedale
South Otterington
Knayton
Hawnby
Dent
YORKSHIRE DALES NATIONAL PARK
West Burton
East Witton
Jervaulx
VALE OF YORK
Barbon
737 WHERNSIDE
627 GRAGARETH
Langstrothdale
Chase
Cover
Masham
Carlton Miniott
Thirsk
Sutton-under-Whitestonecliffe
Helmsley
Kirkby Lonsdale
Kidstones
Buckden
Sowerby
Whittington
Burton
Greta
693 PEN-Y-GHENT
723 INGLEBOROUGH
GREAT WHERNSIDE 704
Kirkby Malzeard
Topcliffe
Ampleforth
Burton in Lonsdale
Ingleton
Horton in Ribblesdale
Arncliffe
Kettlewell
Nidderdale
YORKSHIRE
RIPON
Lune
High Bentham
Clapham
Austwick
Stainforth
Malham Tarn
Wharfedale
Helperby
Easingwold
Caton
Giggleswick
Settle
Malham
Grimwith Res.
Pateley Bridge
Boroughbridge
Aldborough
Grassington
Threshfield
Bishop Monkton
FOREST OF 560 WARD'S STONE
Long Preston
NIDDERDALE
Ripley
Nidd
Whixley
Hellifield
Killinghall
Knaresborough
BOWLAND
Forest of Bowland
Nappa
Gargrave
Bolton Abbey
Blubberhouses
HARROGATE
Green Hammerton
Upper Poppleton
Rawcliffe
Newton
Slaidburn
Bolton by Bowland
SKIPTON
Bolton Bridge
Addingham
Marston Moor
Acomb
Fulford
Gisburn
Earby
Silsden
Ilkley
Spofforth
Wetherby
dale Moors
Barnoldswick
Glusburn
Burley
Otley
Wharfe
Collingham
Boston Spa
CLITHEROE
PENDLE HILL 558
Menston
Bramhope
Harewood
Tadcaster
Barrowford
Guiseley
LEEDS/BRADFORD
KEIGHLEY
Bingley
Baildon
Yeadon
Longridge
Whalley
Nelson
Colne
Brierfield
Haworth
Horsforth
WEST
Cawood
Riccall
Great Harwood
Padiham
Shipley
PRESTON
Mellor
BURNLEY
BRADFORD
LEEDS
Garforth
Sherburn in Elmet
SELBY
Rishton
Pudsey
Kippax
Hambleton
BLACKBURN
Accrington
Queensbury
Oswaldtwistle
Hebden Bridge
HALIFAX
Morley
Rothwell
Haslingden
Todmorden
Calder
Castleford
Knottingley
Darwen
Bacup
Sowerby Bridge
Brighouse
Batley
Normanton
Rawtenstall
Ripponden
Elland
DEWSBURY
Ossett
WAKEFIELD
PONTEFRACT
Chorley
Whitworth
Mirfield
Belmont
Adlington
Ramsbottom
ROCHDALE
Littleborough
HUDDERSFIELD
YORKSHIRE
Hemsworth
Horwich
GREATER
Slaithwaite
Heywood
Meltham
Kirkburton
Askern
Standish
BOLTON
BURY
Holmfirth
Shepley
Darton
Cudworth
South Kirkby
Adwick le Street
Westhoughton
Radcliffe
Royton
Denby Dale
Royston
Bentley
Hindley
Farnworth
OLDHAM
BLACKHILL 582
BARNSLEY
Atherton
Swinton
Prestwich
Middleton
Penistone
Worsbrough
Wombwell
Dearne
LEIGH
MANCHESTER
Mossley
SOUTH
Mexborough
New Edlington
Ashton-in-Makerfield
ASHTON UNDER LYNE
Stalybridge
Langsett
Wath upon Dearne
Trafford Park
Dukinfield
Stocksbridge
Chapeltown
Rawmarsh
Swinton
Conisbrough
Urmston
SALFORD
Stretford
Hyde
Glossop
546 MARGERY HILL
Irlam
Denton
ROTHERHAM
Tickhill
TOLL
Sale
STOCKPORT
KINDER SCOUT 636
SHEFFIELD
Maltby
ARRINGTON
Altrincham
Marple
Hazel Grove
PEAK
Gatley
Cheadle
Hayfield
Thurcroft
Lymm
Bramhall
Ladybower Res.
Castleton
Dinnington
Stretton
High Legh
MANCHESTER AIRPORT
New Mills
Bamford
Woodhouse
Carlton-in-Lindrick
Poynton
Whaley Bridge
DISTRICT
Beighton
South Anston
Wilmslow
Hathersage
Alderley Edge
Chapel en le Frith
Peak Forest
Totley
Killamarsh
WORKSOP
NORTHWICH
Knutsford
Bollington
SHINING TOR 559
Dove Holes
NAT.
Eyam
Dronfield
Eckington
Lostock Gralam
Prestbury
Tideswell
Whittington
Barlborough
MACCLESFIELD
BUXTON
DERBYSHIRE
Baslow
Staveley
Clowne
CHESHIRE
Burbage
PARK
Sutton Lane Ends
552 AXE EDGE
CHESTERFIELD
Bolsover
Market Warsop
Holmes Chapel
Ashford
Bakewell
Shirebrook
Winsford
Middlewich
Ollerton

22
23
24
N
P
Q
R
Brotton
Loftus
Staithes
Kettle Ness
Hinderwell
Lythe
WHITBY
Sneaton
Hawsker
Egton
Sleights
Robin Hood's Bay
Fylingdales Moor
Goathland
Staintondale
Rosedale Abbey
Cloughton
Burniston
Lockton
Scalby
SCARBOROUGH
Thornton Dale
Ebberston
Ayton
Eastfield
Pickering
Seamer
Snainton
Filey
The Carrs
Sherburn
Staxton
Hunmanby
Filey Bay
Malton
Norton
Rillington
Burton Fleming
Flamborough
Flamborough Hd.
Weaverthorpe
Rudston
Langtoft
BRIDLINGTON
Acklam
Sledmere
Kilham
Burton Agnes
Fridaythorpe
Garton-on-the-Wolds
Bridlington Bay
Nafferton
Wetwang
Driffield
Lissett
Stamford Bridge
EAST RIDING OF YORKSHIRE
YORKSHIRE WOLDS
Beeford
Skipsea
Bainton
Hutton Cranswick
North Frodingham
Barmby Moor
Pocklington
Middleton on the Wolds
Hornsea
Hayton
Leven
Market Weighton
Beverley
Skirlaugh
Holme-on-Spalding-moor
Aldbrough
Bubwith
North Newbald
HOLDERNESS
South Cave
Cottingham
Sproatley
Marfleet
Preston
KINGSTON UPON HULL
Hedon
Withernsea
Howden
Brough
Hessle
Burstwick
Paull
Hollym
GOOLE
North Ferriby
HUMBER BRIDGE
Keyingham
Swinefleet
New Holland
Patrington
Burton upon Stather
Barton-upon-Humber
Barrow upon Humber
Easington
Winterton
Humber
NORTH LINCOLNSHIRE
Roxby
Bonby
Sunk Island
Thorne
Ulceby
Immingham
Kilnsea
Crowle
Stallingborough
SCUNTHORPE
GRIMSBY
Spurn Hd.
Althorpe
Broughton
Keelby
Cleethorpes
Belton
Brigg
Barnetby le Wold
Laceby
Humberston
ROTTERDAM
ZEEBRUGGE
Isle of Axholme
Epworth
Hibaldstow
Waltham
Mouth of the Humber
Messingham
Grasby
New Waltham
Scotter
Tetney
Haxey
Kirton in Lindsey
South Kelsey
Caistor
Marshchapel
Donna Nook
Owston Ferry
Nettleton
Grainthorpe
North Somercotes
North Thoresby
Misterton
Blyton
Ludborough
Saltfleet
Waddingham
Normanby le Wold
Walkeringham
Usselby
Binbrook
Beckingham
Corringham
Caenby Corner
Market Rasen
Saltfleetby
GAINSBOROUGH
Louth
West Rasen
Ludford
South Elkington
Lea
Kexby
Manby
Faldingworth
Wheatley
Hainton
LINCOLNSHIRE WOLDS
Legbourne
Mablethorpe
Retford
Marton
Sturton
Welton
Stainton
Wragby
Withern
Sutton-on-Sea
Maltby le Marsh
Scamblesby
Saxilby
LINCOLNSHIRE
Huttoft
TOLL
Belchford
Alford
Nettleham
Ulceby Cross
Chapel St. Leonards
East Markham
Skellingthorpe
Washingborough
Willoughby
LINCOLN
Bardney
Horncastle
Hagworthingham
Partney
Ingoldmells
Ingoldmells Pt.
Sutton-on-Trent
Branston
Burgh le
12

Oronsay
Passage of Oronsay
Ardlussa
Lochgilphead
Ardrishaig
Otter Ferry
Ardentinny
Coulport
Cove
Rubh a' Mhail
L. Tarbert
Lagg
Keillmore
Kilfinan
Sandbank
Strone
Gourock
Dunoon
Glenstriven
Colintraive
Rhubodach
Kyles of Bute
Innellan
Tighnabruaich
Kames
Portavadie
Kilmory
PAPS OF JURA
784
JURA
KNAPDALE
561
Loch Fyne
Ardnave Pt.
Ardnave
Bunnahabhain
Sanaigmore
L. Gruinart
Port Askaig
Feolin Ferry
Sound of Islay
Sound of Jura
L. Caolisport
Craighouse
Tarbert
Port Bannatyne
Rothesay
Craigmore
Wemyss Bay
Skelmorlie
Ballygrant
ISLAY
ARGYLL
AND BUTE
Kilberry
Kennacraig
Whitehouse
Bruichladdich
Bridgend
Port Charlotte
Bowmore
L. Indaal
490
BEN BHEIGEIR
Inchmarnock
Sound of Bute
BUTE
Kingarth
Kilchattan
Great Cumbrae Is.
Millport
Hunterston
Claonaig
Skipness
Clachan
Gigha
Lochranza
Little Cumbrae Is.
Portnahaven
ISLAY (GLENEGADALE)
Laggan B.
Ardmore Pt.
KINTYRE
NORTH AYRSHIRE
Pirnmill
Corrie
Tayinloan
874
GOAT FELL
Ardrossan
Saltcoats
Port Ellen
Ardbeg
The Oa
Killean
Lower Killeyan
Mull of Oa
Kilbrannan Sound
Carradale
ARRAN
Brodick
Glenbarr
Saddell
B880
Lamlash
Holy I.
Firth of Clyde
Blackwaterfoot
Kilchenzie
MACHRIHANISH
Machrihanish Bay
Dippen
Pladda
Campbeltown
Machrihanish
Earadale Pt.
446
CNOC MOY
Johnston's Pt.
Southend
Rathlin Island
Mull of Kintyre
Turnberry
Sanda I.
Ailsa Craig
334
Ballintoy
Ballycastle B.
Fair Hd.
Ballycastle
Ballinlea
Ballyvoy
Girvan
North Channel
Carrowreagh
517
KNOCKLAYD
Loughran
Runabay Hd.
Armoy
Cushendun
Lendalfoot
Bennane Hd.
Dervock
Mullarts
Colmonell
Drumdallagh
Cushendall
Ballantrae
Red B.
MOUNTAINS OF ANTRIM
Glenariff
554
TROSTAN
Loughguile
Garron Pt.
439
BENERAIRD
Newtown Crommelin
Carnlough
Milleur Pt.
Corsewall Pt.
Cullinane
Glenarm
Clogh
Islandtown
436
Kirkcolm
Cairnryan
ANTRIM
Parkview
Milltown
TROON
Leswalt
L. Ryan
Innermessan
Teeshan
The Sheddings
THE RHINS
STRANRAER
Broughshane
Carncastle
Lochans
Ballymena
Ahoghill
AGNEWS HILL
476
Larne
Larne Lough
Dunragit
Moorfields
Glynn
Portpatrick
Stoneykirk
Kells
Connor
Glenoe
I. Magee
Sandhead
Moneyglass
Ballycarry
Black Hd.
Randalstown
Ballyclare
Ballynure
Ardwell
Luce Bay
Doagh
Whitehead
Antrim
Templepatrick
Eden
Mossley
Greenisland
Carrickfergus
Port Logan
LIVERPOOL HEYSHAM DOUGLAS (Summer Only)
Drummore
Glengormley
Belfast Lough
BELFAST INTERNATIONAL
Bangor
Groomsport
Copeland I.
Newtownabbey
Nutts Corner
Crumlin
Holywood
Donaghadee

Fintry
Killearn 578
Campsie Fells
Lennox Hills
Carron Valley Res.
Balloch
Jamestown
Bonhill
Strathblane
Lennoxtown
Kilsyth
Denny
Dunipace
Plean
Larbert
Stenhousemuir
KINCARDINE BRIDGE
Grangemouth
Bo'ness
Falkirk
Bonnybridge
Rosyth
Inverkeithing
N. Queensferry
S. Queensferry
FORTH ROAD BRIDGE
Aberdour
Inchkeith
Leith
Prestonpans
Musselburgh
EDINBURGH
Kirkliston
Linlithgow
Broxburn
Dumbarton
Milngavie
Bearsden
Kirkintilloch
Cumbernauld
Slamannan
ERSKINE BRIDGE
Clydebank
Bishopbriggs
Muirhead
Airdrie
Caldercruix
Armadale
Bathgate
Livingston
Colinton
Currie
Loanhead
Lasswade
Dalkeith
Bonnyrigg
Roslin
Pentland Hills Regional Park
East Calder
West Calder
Erskine
Renfrew
GLASGOW
PAISLEY
Bridge of Weir
Coatbridge
Blackridge
Whitburn
Harthill
Fauldhouse
Shotts
Johnstone
Barrhead
Lochwinnoch
Rutherglen
Uddingston
Bellshill
Motherwell
Wishaw
Hamilton
Newton Mearns
EAST KILBRIDE
Neilston
Beith
Eaglesham
Larkhall
Carluke
Forth
Auchengray
Kilcadzow
Penicuik
MID LOTHIAN
Carlops
West Linton
Pentland Hills
Leadburn
Moorfoot Hills
651 BLACKHOPE SCAR
562
Lugton
Dunlop
Stewarton
Fenwick
Chapeltown
Stonehouse
Strathaven
Blackwood
Lesmahagow
Lanark
Carstairs
Carnwath
Dunsyre
Newbigging
Dolphinton
Blyth Bridge
Peebles
Clydesdale
Kilmaurs
KILMARNOCK
Dreghorn
Newmilns
Darvel
Galston
Greenholm
Hurlford
Dundonald
SOUTH LANARKSHIRE
Coalburn
Douglas
Rigside
Symington
Biggar
Stobo
Broughton
Innerleithen
SCOTTISH BORDERS
Yarrow
Ettrick Forest
KYLE
Monkton
PRESTWICK
Tarbolton
Mauchline
Catrine
Sorn
Muirkirk
Crawfordjohn
Abington
CULTER FELL 748
Tweedsmuir
840 BROAD LAW
Talla Res.
Megget Res.
St. Mary's L.
Fruid Res.
Tweedshaws
WHITE COOMB 822
Ramseycleuch
EAST AYRSHIRE
Auchinleck
Logan
Cumnock
Ochiltree
Coylton
Drongan
593 CAIRN TABLE
Crawford
Elvanfoot
Leadhills
733 GREEN LOWTHER
Lowther Hills
SOUTHERN UPLANDS
Dalrymple
Connel Park
New Cumnock
Kirkconnel
Sanquhar
Mennock
Enterkinfoot
Patna
Kirkmichael
Maybole
Crosshill
Straiton
Dalleagles
Dalmellington
Bellsbank
L. Doon
Daer Res.
Moffat
Beattock
Annandale
Howpasley
Davington
Eskdalemuir
Carronbridge
Thornhill
Closeburn
Penpont
796
The Glenkens
Nithsdale
Drumjohn
Carsphairn
Moniaive
Kirkland
St. Ann's
Boreland
Eskdale
CARRICK
844 MERRICK
Galloway
Rhinns of Kells
Dunscore
DUMFRIES & GALLOWAY
Locharbriggs
Torthorwald
Lochmaben
Lockerbie
Hightae
Dalry
Balmaclellan
Corsock
DUMFRIES
Collin
Dalton
Ecclefechan
Eaglesfield
Glentrool Village
Forest Park
Clatteringshaws L.
New Galloway
Bargrennan
GALLOWAY
Kirkpatrick Durham
Crocketford
Beeswing
Mouswald
Kirkpatrick Fleming
Gretna Green
Gretna
Haugh of Urr
Crossmichael
Glencaple
Bankend
Ruthwell
Cummertrees
Annan
Bowness-on-Solway
Port Carlisle
710 CAIRNSMORE OF FLEET
Minnigaff
Newton Stewart
Laurieston
L. Ken
New Abbey
569 CRIFFELL
Kirkbean
Dalbeattie
Castle Douglas
SOLWAY COAST
Burgh-by-Sands
Kirkcowan
Creetown
Ringford
Gatehouse of Fleet
Palnackie
Rockcliffe
Caulkerbush
Skinburness
Kirkbride
Newton Arlosh
Silloth
Thursby
Wigtown
THE MACHARS
Culmazie
Kirkinner
Kirkcudbright
Auchencairn
Beckfoot
Abbey Town
Wigton
Red Dial
Whauphill
Garlieston
Borgue
Dundrennan
Sorbie
Wigtown Bay
Kirkcudbright Bay
Solway Firth
Allonby
Aspatria
Mealsgate
Port William
Crosby
Bothel
CUMBRIA
Maryport
Fothergill
Dearham
HIGH PIKE 658
Whithorn
Glasserton
Isle of Whithorn
Flimby
Broughton
Seaton
Cockermouth
Derwent
931 SKIDDAW
Burrow Hd.
WORKINGTON
Great Clifton
Bassenthwaite L.
Threlkeld
M8
M9
M80
M77
M74
A74(M)
A75
A76
A77
A70
A71
A702
A701
24
20
14
15
16
17

Bearsden
Clydebank
Bishopbriggs
Muirhead
Airdrie
Armadale
Bathgate
Livingston
Colinton
Dalkeith
Ormiston
Renfrew
Coatbridge
Whitburn
Harthill
East Calder
Currie
Loanhead
Lasswade
Bonnyrigg
Newtongrange
Pathhead
GLASGOW
Fauldhouse
West Calder
Pentland Hills
Regional Park
MIDLOTHIAN
Roslin
Penicuik
Gorebridge
Fala
Uddingston
Rutherglen
Bellshill
Shotts
Barrhead
Motherwell
Wishaw
Newton Mearns
EAST KILBRIDE
Hamilton
Forth
Auchengray
Pentland Hills
Carlops
Leadburn
Heriot
West Linton
Moorfoot Hills
Eaglesham
Larkhall
Carluke
Kilcadzow
Dunsyre
651 BLACKHOPE SCAR
Fountainhall
Chapeltown
Stonehouse
Carnwath
Newbigging
Dolphinton
Stewarton
Strathaven
Carstairs
Blyth Bridge
Clydesdale
Fenwick
Blackwood
Lanark
Peebles
Lesmahagow
Walkerburn
KILMARNOCK
Newmilns
Darvel
Galston
Greenholm
SOUTH LANARKSHIRE
Biggar
Stobo
Broughton
Innerleithen
Clovenfords
Hurlford
Coalburn
Rigside
Symington
SOUTHERN UPLANDS
Douglas
CULTER FELL 748
Yarrow
Selkirk
Mauchline
Catrine
Tarbolton
Sorn
Muirkirk
593 CAIRN TABLE
Crawfordjohn
Abington
Tweedsmuir
840 BROAD LAW
SCOTTISH BORDERS
Ettrick Forest
EAST AYRSHIRE
Annbank
Auchinleck
Logan
Crawford
Talla Res.
Megget Res.
St. Mary's L.
Ochiltree
Cumnock
Elvanfoot
Fruid Res.
Tweedshaws
WHITE COOMB 822
Leadhills
733 GREEN LOWTHER
Ramseycleuch
Roberton
Connel Park
Kirkconnel
New Cumnock
Sanquhar
Lowther Hills
Dalleagles
Mennock
Moffat
Howpasley
Teviot
Dalmellington
Enterkinfoot
Daer Res.
Beattock
Teviothead
Bellsbank
L. Doon
Davington
Eskdalemuir
The Glenkens
796
Carronbridge
Thornhill
Annandale
Drumjohn
Penpont
Closeburn
St. Ann's
Nithsdale
Carsphairn
Moniaive
Kirkland
Boreland
Eskdale
Dunscore
DUMFRIES & GALLOWAY
Langholm
Rhinns of Kells
Locharbriggs
Lochmaben
Lockerbie
Dalry
Balmaclellan
Torthorwald
Hightae
Corsock
DUMFRIES
Collin
Canonbie
Rowanburn
New Galloway
Clatteringshaws L.
Dalton
Ecclefechan
Eaglesfield
GALLOWAY
Crocketford
Mouswald
Kirkpatrick Fleming
Longtown
Kirkpatrick Durham
Beeswing
Bankend
Gretna Green
Haugh of Urr
Glencaple
Gretna
710 CAIRNSMORE OF FLEET
Laurieston
L. Ken
Crossmichael
New Abbey
Ruthwell
Cummertrees
Annan
Bowness-on-Solway
Port Carlisle
Rockcliffe
Blackford
Smithfield
Castle Douglas
Dalbeattie
569 CRIFFELL
Kirkbean
SOLWAY COAST
Burgh-by-Sands
Houghton
Stanwix
Creetown
Ringford
Gatehouse of Fleet
Caulkerbush
Skinburness
Kirkbride
Wigtown
Palnackie
Silloth
Newton Arlosh
CARLISLE
Rockcliffe
Thursby
Kirkinner
Kirkcudbright
Auchencairn
Beckfoot
Abbey Town
Wigton
Dalston
Borgue
Dundrennan
Red Dial
Garlieston
Wigtown Bay
Kirkcudbright Bay
Solway Firth
Allonby
Aspatria
Mealsgate
Sebergham
Crosby
Bothel
Whithorn
Maryport
Fothergill
Dearham
Caldbeck
HIGH PIKE 658
Skelton
Isle of Whithorn
Flimby
Broughton
Derwent
CUMBRIA
Burrow Hd.
Seaton
Cockermouth
Greystoke
WORKINGTON
Great Clifton
Bassenthwaite L.
931 SKIDDAW
LAKE DISTRICT NATIONAL PARK
Threlkeld
Harrington
Thornthwaite
Pooley Bridge
Distington
Dockray
Parton
Keswick
Derwent Water
Ullswater
WHITEHAVEN
Crummock Water
Buttermere
Frizington
Ennerdale Water
Thirlmere
Patterdale
St. Bee's Hd.
Cleator Moor
950 HELVELLYN
15
16
17
18
19
24
14

LOTHIAN
Cockburnspath
St. Abb's Head
St. Abb's
Ecclaw
A1107
25
Coldingham
Eyemouth
18
19
20
21
L
M
N
Grantshouse
Reston
Ayton
Burnmouth
535
MEIKLE
SAYS LAW
LAMMERMUIR HILLS
Preston
Longformacus
Chirnside
Foulden
Duns
A6105
BERWICK-UPON-TWEED
Tweedmouth
Scremerston
Westruther
Polwarth
Whitsome
Greenlaw
Swinton
Norham
MERSE
Gordon
Leitholm
Ancroft
A1
Goswick
Holy I.
Coldstream
Cornhill on Tweed
Barmoor Castle
Lowick
Ross
Budle Bay
Farne Is.
Stichill
Crookham
Flodden
Bamburgh
Smailholm
Kelso
Maxwellheugh
Belford
Seahouses
North Sunderland
Roxburgh
A697
Doddington
Lucker
Chathill
Beadnell
Kirknewton
Wooler
Chatton
Town Yetholm
Brunton
Ancrum
Morebattle
North Charlton
Embleton
Jedburgh
Ilderton
816
THE CHEVIOT
Wooperton
Rennington
Denholm
A68
Oxnam
Longhoughton
Ingram
Breamish
Glanton
Aln
Alnwick
Lesbury
Alnmouth
Bonchester Bridge
CHEVIOT HILLS
Upper Hindhope
NORTHUMBERLAND COAST
Shilbottle
Netherton
Alwinton
Warkworth
Amble
Coquet
Coquet I.
Huntford
Catcleugh
Catcleugh Res.
Longframlington
Rothbury Forest
Felton
Broomhill
602
PEEL FELL
NORTHUMBERLAND NATIONAL PARK
Rochester
Rothbury
441
SIMONSIDE
Weldon
Druridge Bay
Widdrington
A1068
Kielder Forest Park
Kielder
Elishaw
Otterburn
Elsdon
Longhorsley
Ellington
NORTHUMBERLAND
ASHINGTON
Newbiggin-by-the-Sea
Falstone
Kielder Res.
North Tyne
West Woodburn
Cambo
Hartburn
Pegswood
MORPETH
Bedlington
Cowpen
Blyth
Kirkwhelpington
Wansbeck
Whalton
Ridsdale
Bellingham
Park
519
SIGHTY CRAG
Redesmouth
A696
Stannington
Belsay
Birtley
Blyth
Cramlington
Hartley
Seaton Delaval
STAVANGER HAUGESUND BERGEN
Wark
Colwell
Earsdon
Whitley Bay
Ryal
KRISTIANSAND GOTHENBURG
Bewcastle
Ponteland
Chollerton
Stamfordham
NEWCASTLE
Wide Open
Longbenton
TYNEMOUTH
Humshaugh
Brunton
Irthing
Wallsend
NEWCASTLE-UPON-TYNE
SOUTH SHIELDS
AMSTERDAM
Newbrough
Haydon Bridge
Gilsland
Haltwhistle
A69
Newburn
TOLL
Jarrow
TYNE & WEAR
Greenhead
Hexham
Corbridge
Tyne
Blaydon
Hebburn
Boldon
Allen
Prudhoe
Whickham
GATESHEAD
Painshawfield
Broomhaugh
Rowlands Gill
SUNDERLAND
Lambley
Catton
Slaley
Birtley
Washington
Derwent Res.
Annfield Plain
Stanley
Penshaw
Ryhope
622
COLD FELL
South Tyne
Allendale Town
Chester-le-Street
A1018
Blanchland
Leadgate
CONSETT
Houghton-le-Spring
Croglin
PENNINES
Derwent
Edmundbyers
Delves
Sacriston
Seaham
Alston
Castleside
Lanchester
Hetton-le-Hole
Murton
Allenheads
Easington Colliery
Nenthead
COLLIER LAW
516
Esh Winning
DURHAM
Easington
Haswell
Peterlee
Horden
Kirkoswald
Brandon
Wheatley Hill
NORTH PENNINES
Wearhead
Stanhope
Tow Law
Lazonby
Melmerby
Weardale
Crook
Willington
Wingate
893
CROSS FELL
St. Johns Chapel
Wolsingham
Spennymoor
Trimdon
HARTLEPOOL
Langwathby
DURHAM
Ferryhill
Chilton
Sedgefield
Tees Bay
PENRITH
Culgaith
Cow Green Res.
Teesdale
BISHOP AUCKLAND
Greatham
Shildon
Wolviston
Teesside
West Auckland
REDCAR
Temple Sowerby
Kirkby Thore
Middleton in Teesdale
Newton Aycliffe
Billingham
TOLL
790
MICKLE FELL
Cockfield
Eston
Appleby-in-Westmorland
Mickleton
Staindrop
Heighington
STOCKTON-ON-TEES
Baldersdale
Balderhead Res.
Cotherstone
Gainford
MIDDLESBROUGH
Hoff
Thornaby on Tees
15
Winston
16
Crosby Ravensworth
Brough
Barnard Castle
DARLINGTON
Stainton
Tees
Hurworth-on-Tees
Egglescliffe
TEESSIDE
Yarm
Bowes
M6

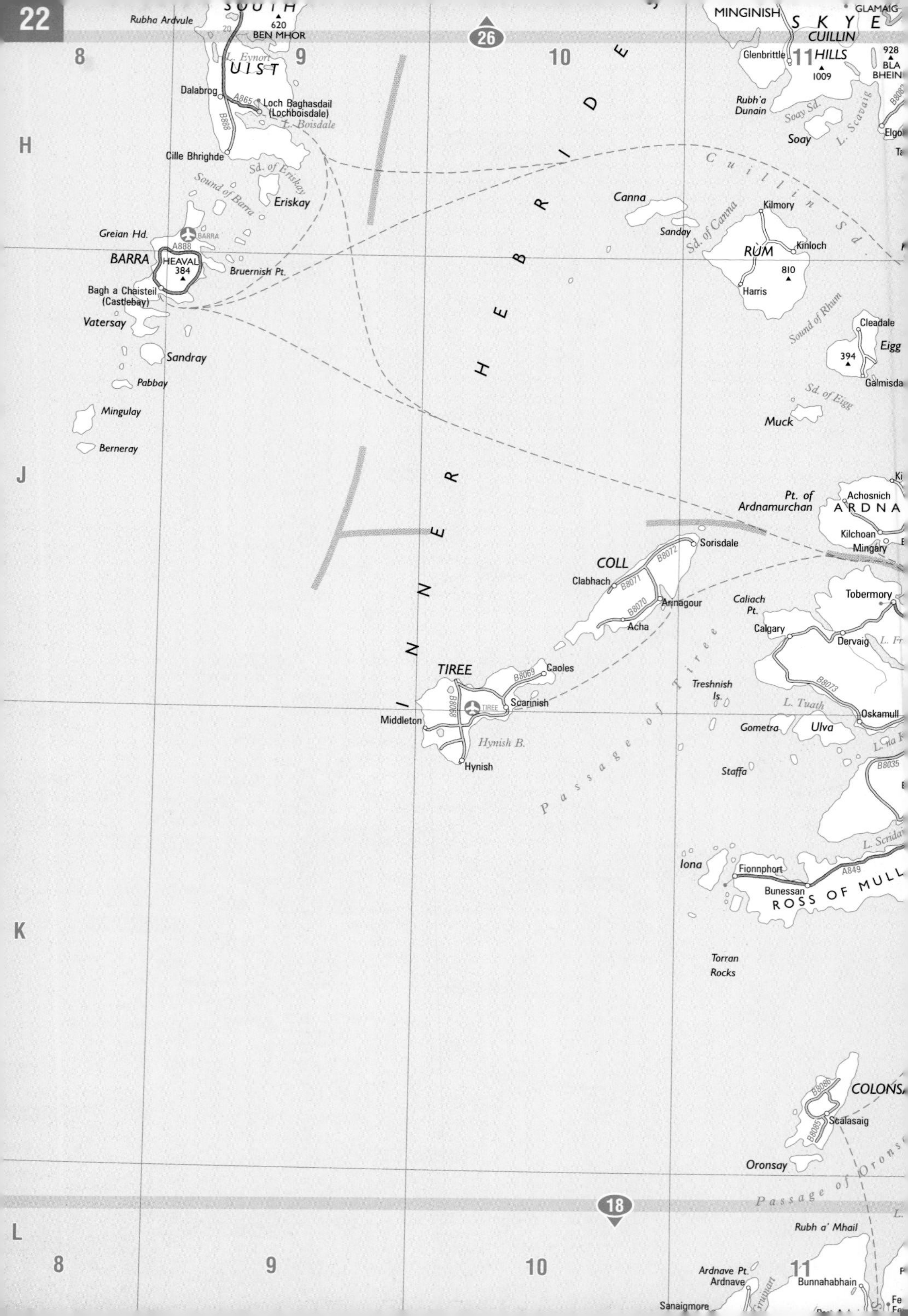
SOUTH
UIST
Rubha Ardvule
620
BEN MHOR
L. Eynort
Dalabrog
A865
Loch Baghasdail
(Lochboisdale)
L. Boisdale
B888
Cille Bhrighde
Sd. of Eriskay
Sound of Barra
Eriskay
Greian Hd.
BARRA
A888
BARRA
HEAVAL
384
Bruernish Pt.
Bagh a Chaisteil
(Castlebay)
Vatersay
Sandray
Pabbay
Mingulay
Berneray
INNER HEBRIDES
MINGINISH
SKYE
CUILLIN
HILLS
1009
928
BLA
BHEIN
Glenbrittle
Rubh'a
Dunain
Soay Sd.
Soay
L. Scavaig
Elgol
Cuillin Sd.
Canna
Sanday
Sd. of Canna
Kilmory
RUM
Kinloch
810
Harris
Sound of Rhum
Cleadale
Eigg
394
Galmisdale
Sd. of Eigg
Muck
Pt. of
Ardnamurchan
Achosnich
ARDNA
Kilchoan
Mingary
Sorisdale
COLL
B8072
Clabhach
B8071
B8070
Arinagour
Acha
Caliach
Pt.
Tobermory
Calgary
Dervaig
B8073
Treshnish
Is.
L. Tuath
Oskamull
Gometra
Ulva
Staffa
B8035
TIREE
B8069
Caoles
B8068
TIREE
Scarinish
Middleton
Hynish B.
Hynish
Passage of Tiree
L. Scridain
Iona
Fionnphort
A849
Bunessan
ROSS OF MULL
Torran
Rocks
B8086
COLONSAY
Scalasaig
B8085
Oronsay
Passage of Oronsay
Rubh a' Mhail
Ardnave Pt.
Ardnave
Gruinart
Bunnahabhain
Sanaigmore
H
J
K
L
8
9
10
11
26
18

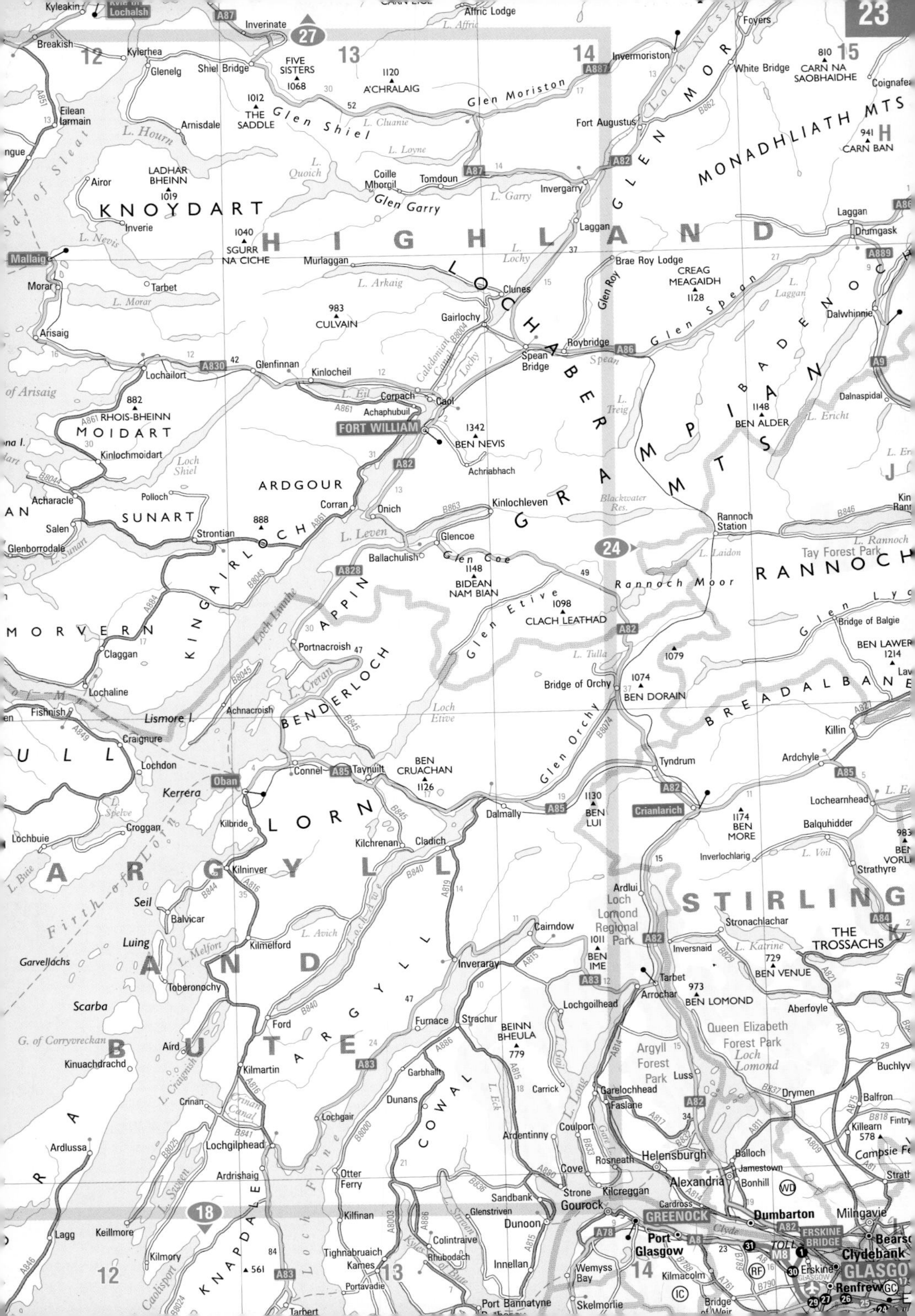
Kyleakin
Lochalsh
A87
Affric Lodge
L. Affric
Foyers
Inverinate
27
Breakish
12
Kylerhea
13
14
Invermoriston
15
Glenelg
Shiel Bridge
FIVE SISTERS
1068
1120
A'CHRALAIG
A887
White Bridge
810
CARN NA SAOBHAIDHE
Coignafearn
Glen Moriston
Loch Ness
GLEN MOR
B862
A851
Eilean Iarmain
1012
THE SADDLE
Glen Shiel
L. Cluanie
Fort Augustus
MONADHLIATH MTS
Arnisdale
L. Hourn
L. Loyne
941
CARN BAN
H
L. Quoich
A82
Airor
LADHAR BHEINN
1019
Coille Mhorgil
Tomdoun
A87
Glen Garry
L. Garry
Invergarry
KNOYDART
Inverie
L. Nevis
1040
SGURR NA CICHE
HIGHLAND
Laggan
Laggan
Drumgask
A86
Mallaig
Murlaggan
L. Lochy
Brae Roy Lodge
CREAG MEAGAIDH
1128
A889
Morar
Tarbet
L. Morar
L. Arkaig
Clunes
Glen Roy
Glen Spean
L. Laggan
Dalwhinnie
LOCHABER
983
CULVAIN
Gairlochy
Caledonian Canal
B8004
Arisaig
Roybridge
A86
Spean Bridge
Spean
A9
A830
Glenfinnan
Kinlocheil
Lochailort
L. Eil
Corpach
Caol
of Arisaig
882
RHOIS-BHEINN
A861
Achaphubuil
L. Treig
1148
BEN ALDER
Dalnaspidal
L. Ericht
FORT WILLIAM
1342
BEN NEVIS
MOIDART
GRAMPIAN MTS
Kinlochmoidart
Loch Shiel
A82
Achriabhach
B8044
ARDGOUR
Acharacle
Polloch
Corran
Onich
B863
Kinlochleven
Blackwater Res.
SUNART
888
Rannoch Station
B846
Salen
Strontian
L. Leven
Glencoe
L. Sunart
Glenborrodale
Ballachulish
Glen Coe
24
L. Laidon
L. Rannoch
Tay Forest Park
RANNOCH
KINGAIRLOCH
A828
1148
BIDEAN NAM BIAN
49
Rannoch Moor
APPIN
B8043
Glen Etive
1098
CLACH LEATHAD
A884
Glen Lyon
Bridge of Balgie
MORVERN
Loch Linnhe
A82
Portnacroish
Claggan
L. Tulla
1079
BEN LAWERS
1214
B8045
L. Creran
BENDERLOCH
1074
BEN DORAIN
Bridge of Orchy
BREADALBANE
Lochaline
Loch Etive
Fishnish
Achnacroish
Lismore I.
B845
Glen Orchy
B8074
A849
Craignure
Killin
MULL
Lochdon
Tyndrum
Ardchyle
Connel
A85
Taynuilt
BEN CRUACHAN
1126
A85
Oban
Kerrera
1130
BEN LUI
Dalmally
A85
A82
Crianlarich
Lochearnhead
LORN
B845
1174
BEN MORE
Balquhidder
L. Spelve
Croggan
Kilbride
Kilchrenan
Cladich
Lochbuie
Inverlochlarig
L. Voil
ARGYLL AND BUTE
Kilninver
B840
A819
Strathyre
L. Buie
Firth of Lorn
A816
Ardlui
Loch Lomond Regional Park
STIRLING
Seil
B844
Balvicar
Loch Awe
Cairndow
Stronachlachar
A84
Luing
Kilmelford
L. Melfort
L. Avich
1011
BEN IME
A82
Inversnaid
L. Katrine
THE TROSSACHS
Garvellachs
Inveraray
A815
729
BEN VENUE
A821
Toberonochy
A83
Tarbet
Arrochar
973
BEN LOMOND
B829
Scarba
Lochgoilhead
Aberfoyle
B840
Ford
Furnace
Strachur
BEINN BHEULA
779
Queen Elizabeth Forest Park
Loch Lomond
A81
G. of Corryvreckan
Aird
Argyll Forest Park
Kinuachdrachd
Kilmartin
A83
A886
A815
L. Goil
A814
Luss
Buchlyvie
L. Craignish
Garbhallt
COWAL
L. Eck
Carrick
Garelochhead
B837
Drymen
A816
Crinan
Crinan Canal
Dunans
Faslane
Gare L.
A82
Balfron
Lochgair
B8000
A817
A875
B818
Fintry
Killearn
578
Ardlussa
B8025
B841
Lochgilphead
Ardentinny
Coulport
B833
B832
A811
A809
Campsie Fells
Ardrishaig
L. Sween
Otter Ferry
Loch Fyne
A880
Cove
Rosneath
Helensburgh
Balloch
Jamestown
Bonhill
Strathblane
18
B836
Sandbank
Strone
Kilcreggan
Alexandria
A814
Cardross
Gourock
GREENOCK
Dumbarton
Milngavie
Lagg
Keillmore
Kilfinan
A8003
A886
Glenstriven
Loch Striven
Dunoon
A78
A815
Port Glasgow
A8
Clyde
A82
ERSKINE BRIDGE
TOLL
M8
Bearsden
Clydebank
Kilmory
KNAPDALE
84
Tighnabruaich
Colintraive
Kyles of Bute
Rhubodach
Erskine
A846
12
561
A83
Kames
13
Innellan
14
Wemyss Bay
Kilmacolm
B789
A761
B790
GLASGOW
Renfrew
Caolisport
B8024
Portavadie
Skelmorlie
Bridge of Weir
Tarbert
Port Bannatyne

HIGHLAND
GRAMPIAN MOUNTAINS
MONADHLIATH MTS.
CAIRNGORM MTS.
GLEN MORE
STRATHSPEY
BADENOCH
LOCHABER
PERTH AND KINROSS
RANNOCH
BREADALBANE
STIRLING
THE TROSSACHS
OCHIL HILLS
Fort Augustus
Invermoriston
Foyers
White Bridge
Aviemore
Boat of Garten
Nethy Bridge
Kingussie
Newtonmore
Dalwhinnie
Blair Atholl
Pitlochry
Aberfeldy
Kenmore
Killin
Tyndrum
Crianlarich
Callander
Crieff
Comrie
Dunblane
Bridge of Allan
STIRLING
Alloa
Dunfermline
Falkirk
Grangemouth
Denny
Kilsyth
Cumbernauld
Dumbarton
Helensburgh
GREENOCK
Port Glasgow
Clydebank
Bearsden
Milngavie
Kirkintilloch
Airdrie
Coatbridge
GLASGOW
PAISLEY
Renfrew
Livingston
Bathgate
Linlithgow
Dunkeld
Blairgowrie
PERTH
Braemar
Kinross
Auchterarder
Gleneagles
1214 BEN LAWERS
1148 BEN ALDER
1344 BEN NEVIS
1081 SCHIEHALLION
973 BEN LOMOND
1245 CAIRN GORM
1309 BEN MACDHUI
Forest of Atholl
Rannoch Moor
Loch Lomond Regional Park
Queen Elizabeth Forest Park
Argyll Forest Park
Campsie Fells
Lennox Hills
Glen More Forest Park

Badenyon
Lumsden
Tullynessle
Alford
29
Monymusk
Kemnay
Kintore
Newmachar
Dyce
Balmedie
Strathdon
MAR
Don
Ordhead
Dunecht
Westhill
Bankhead
Bucksburn
Bridge of Don
ABERDEEN
LERWICK
STROMNESS
Girdle Ness
ABERDEEN CITY
872
MORVEN
Tarland
Lumphanan
Echt
Torphins
Peterculter
Cults
Cove Bay
Ordie
Aboyne
Dee
Ballater
Marywell
Banchory
Portlethen
Cammachmore
Newtonhill
Muchalls
Strachan
Ballochan
E E N S H I R E
938
MT. KEEN
Stonehaven
KINCARDINE
Spittal of Glenmuick
S OF ANGUS
Auchronie
Auchenblae
Glen Esk
N. Esk
HOWE OF THE MEARNS
Todhead Point
Clova
Waterhead
Fettercairn
Inverbervie
Laurencekirk
Gourdon
Johnshaven
Glenprosen Lodge
Rottal
Edzell
N G U S
Marykirk
St. Cyrus
Dykehead
Tannadice
Brechin
Montrose
S. Esk
Kirriemuir
Strathmore
Lunan B.
FORFAR
Friockheim
Inverkeilor
Glamis
Inverarity
Marywell
Meigle
Carmyllie
IDLAW HILLS
455
Monikie
Arbroath
Muirdrum
Barry
Carnoustie
DUNDEE
Monifieth
Broughty Ferry
Invergowrie
TAY BRIDGE
TOLL
Buddon Ness
Inchture
Tayport
Inchcape Rock
Wormit
Newport-on-Tay
Firth of Tay
Leuchars
Kilmany
Guard Bridge
St. Andrews
Eden
Cupar
Kingsbarns
Ladybank
Ceres
Dunino
Fife Ness
F
E
Crail
Freuchie
Kirkton of Largo
Kilrenny
Anstruther
Markinch
Windygates
Pittenweem
Leven
Methil
Earlsferry
Elie
St. Monance
I. of May
Buckhaven
East Wemyss
Dysart
Firth of Forth
KIRKCALDY
Bass Rock
North Berwick
Kinghorn
Burntisland
Inchkeith
Dirleton
Gullane
Whitekirk
Aberlady
Drem
EAST
Dunbar
Barns Ness
Leith
Prestonpans
Cockenzie
Tyne
East Linton
Musselburgh
Tranent
Haddington
Spott
Esk
Macmerry
Garvald
Cockburnspath
St. Abb's Head
St. Abb's
Ormiston
LOTHIAN
Dalkeith
Lasswade
Ecclaw
Gifford
21
Grantshouse
Coldingham
Eyemouth
Bonnyrigg
Newtongrange
Roslin
Pathhead
Reston
535
H
J
K
L
17
18
19
20
A90
A96
A93
A92
A94
A1
A68
A720
A921
A915
A911
A914
A916
A917
A913
A91
A919
A933
A932
A934
A935
A937
A957
A956
A944
A980
A97
A939
A947
A198
A6137
A6093
A1107
B976
B9119
B993
B977
B9125
B9077
B979
B974
B967
B966
B9120
B955
B957
B9134
B965
B9127
B978
B961
B954
B939
B940
B9131
B9171
B942
B937
B1347
B1377
B6370
B6368
B6355
B6371
B999
B994

8
9
10
11
E
F
G
H
Butt of Le
Dail bho Dhe
Borgh
Barabhas
Siabost
Carlabhagh
291
BEN
MHOLACH
Flannan Is.
Gallan Hd.
Great
Bernera
Aird
Uig
Calanais
Gearraidh
na h-Aibhne
Stornoway
L. Roag
Aird Brenish
Breanais
575
MEALISVAL
Giosla
LEWIS
Crosbost
Cromor
Baile Ailein
Kintarvie
L. Langavat
Grabhair
Scarp
Leumrabhagh
NORTH
Aird a
Mhulaidh
571
BEINN MHOR
Husinish
Husinish Pt.
HARRIS
799
CLISHAM
WESTERN
West L. Tarbert
Ardhasig
Taransay
Aird Asaig
Tairbeart
(Tarbert)
Sd. of Shiant
Sd. of Taransay
Scalpay
Toe Hd.
Sgarasta Mhor
SOUTH
HARRIS
Caolas
Stocinis
East L. Tarbert
Taobh Tuath
Pabbay
An t-Ob
Sd. of Pabbay
Sound of Harris
Berneray
Roghadal
Renish Pt.
Haskeir Is.
Rubha Hunish
OUTER HEBRIDES
ISLES
Griminish Pt.
Solas
NORTH UIST
Loch nam Madadh
(Lochmaddy)
Vaternish Pt.
Little Minch
Paibeil
Sound of Monach
Geary
L. Snizort
Clachan
na Luib
L. Eport
347
EAVAL
Dunvegan
Hd.
Stein
Lusta
Monach Is.
Baleshare
Cairinis
Grimsay
Claigan
BENBECULA
Gramsdal
Ronay
Milovaig
Lephin
Dunvegan
Roskhill
BENBECULA
Neist Pt.
488
HEALAVAL
BHEAG
Creag
Ghoraidh
Wiay
Ardivachar Pt.
Bagh nam
Faoileann
Bracadale
Coillore
L. Bracadale
Tobha Mor
HECLA
605
Fernilea
Carbost
SOUTH UIST
22
MINGINISH
Rubha Ardvule
620
BEN MHOR
A857
A858
A859
B8011
B8060
B887
A865
A867
B893
B894
B892
B891
B890
A850
A863
B884
B885
B8009
A855
A87
L. Seaforth
L. Shell
L. Erisort
L. Harport

C. Wrath
Faraid Hd.
Durness
Whiten Hd.
Achiemore
Strathan
Heilam
Tongue
Sheigra
Kinlochbervie
Eriboll
Rhiconich
908
FOINAVEN
927
BEN HOPE
763
BEN LOYAL
Handa I.
Scourie
Laxford Bridge
Reay Forest
721
BEN STACK
Strathmore
Eddrachillis Bay
Kylestrome
Unapool
Kinloch
873
BEN HEE
Altnaharra
Pt. of Stoer
Drumbeg
Culkein
809
QUINAG
ASSYNT
Stoer
SUTHERLAND
Inchnadamph
961
BEN KLIBRECK
Lochinver
998
BEN MORE ASSYNT
Enard B.
Inverkirkaig
847
CANISP
Duchally
Rubha Coigeach
Glen Oykel
Ledmore
Elphin
Reiff
Summer Is.
Achiltibuie
Sallachy
Cromalt Hills
Achavraie
COIGACH
Strathkanaird
Lubcroy
Rosehall
Altass
Oykel Bridge
Inveran
Culrain
Greenstone Pt.
Ullapool
Alt na h'Airbhe
Croick
Badrallach
Ardessie
Freevater Forest
Cove
Mellon Charles
Laide
Aultbea
Ardcharnich
Melvaig
1062
AN TEALLACH
EASTER ROSS
1081
BEN DEARG
Braemore
Poolewe
Longa I.
Gairloch
Kerrysdale
Port Henderson
1109
SGURR MOR
1045
BEN WYVIS
981
SLIOCH
Talladale
Red Point
WESTER ROSS
Kinlochewe
Garve
Achanalt
Strathpeffer
Diabaig
LIATHACH
1053
Achnasheen
Rona
Fasag
Torridon
Milton
Contin
Shieldaig
Scardoy
Muir of Ord
Glen Orrin
Achnashellach
Beauly
HIGHLAND
Applecross Forest
Monar Forest
1052
SGURR A' CHOIRE GHLAIS
1083
Coulags
Brochel
Applecross
Monar Lodge
Struy
THE AIRD
RAASAY
Toscaig
Ardarroch
Lochcarron
SGURR NA LAPAICH
1150
Stromemore
Clachan
Crowlin Is.
Plockton
Liatrie
Cannich
Drumnadrochit
Stromeferry
Scalpay
Lewiston
Scalpay
Sconser
Kyle of Lochalsh
Auchtertyre
Dornie
1182
CARN EIGE
MEALFUARVONIE
696
775
GLAMAIG
Kyleakin
Glen Affric
Affric Lodge
Inverinate
Foyers
Nis
Cellar Hd.
Tolsta Hd.
Tiumpan Hd.
Port Nan Giuran
EYE PENINSULA
The Minch
Sound of Raasay
Inner Sound
28
23

C. Wrath
Kyle of Durness
Faraid Hd.
14
15
16
17
Strathy Pt.
Holborn Hd.
STROMNESS
Dunnet B.
Whiten Hd.
Durness
Achiemore
Strathan
Kyle of Tongue
Portskerra
Dounreay
Scrabster
Thurso
Melvich
Reay
Strathy
Bettyhill
Sordale
L. Calder
Halkirk
Heilam
L. Eriboll
Eriboll
Tongue
Craigtown
Strath Halladale
Kinlochbervie
Olgrinmore
Dalhalvaig
Mybster
Rhiconich
908 FOINAVEN
L. Hope
927 BEN HOPE
763 BEN LOYAL
Borgie
Strath Naver
Forsinain
CAITHNE
Laxford Bridge
Reay Forest
Strathmore
L. Loyal
Forsinard
Achav
721 BEN STACK
L. More
873 BEN HEE
Altnaharra
L. Naver
L. nan Clar
Kylestrome
Unapool
Kinloch
Kinbrace
705 MORVEN
Braemore
Dunbeath
809 QUINAG
961 BEN KLIBRECK
L. Choire
Strath of Kildonan
Altanduino
SUTHERLAND
Inchnadamph
Assynt
Kildonan
Berriedale
HIGHLAND
998 BEN MORE ASSYNT
847 CANISP
Black Water
103 Ousdale
Ord of Caithness
Helmsdale
628 BEN DHORAIN
Duchally
Loch Shin
Dalnessie
Ledmore
Glen Oykel
Elphin
27
Langwell
Brora
L. Brora
Cromalt Hills
Sallachy
Lairg
Rogart
Torroble
Lubcroy
Rosehall
Altass
Fleet
Golspie
Oykel Bridge
Inveran
Culrain
Bonarbridge
Embo
Freevater Forest
Croick
Ardgay
Kincardine
Clashmore
Dornoch
KIRKWALL
Ardcharnich
Carron
Dornoch Firth
Tarbat Ness
EASTER ROSS
Edderton
Tain
Portmahomack
1081 BEN DEARG
Braemore
710 BEN THARSUINN
Moray Firth
Fearn
Balintore
L. Glas
Alness
Kilmuir
Nigg B.
1109 SGURR MOR
L. Glascarnoch
1045 BEN WYVIS
Invergordon
Balnapaling
Branderburgh
Burghead
Hopeman
Burghead B.
L. Fannich
Evanton
Cromarty Firth
Balblair
Cromarty
Findhorn
WESTER ROSS
Cullicudden
BLACK ISLE
Kinloss
Achanalt
Garve
Strathpeffer
Dingwall
Rosemarkie
Nairn
Barnhill
Forres
Achnasheen
L. Luichart
Contin
Cononbridge
Fortrose
Avoch
Ardersier
Auldearn
Milton
Findhorn
Kellas
Dallas
Strathconon
Munlochy
INVERNESS
Littlemill
Scardoy
Glen Orrin
Muir of Ord
North Kessock
Cawdor
Beauly Firth
Culloden
Balloch
Beauly
INVERNESS
Ferness
Archiestown
SGURR A' CHOIRE GHLAIS 1083
THE AIRD
Monar Lodge
Struy
Craggie
Strath Glass
Caledonian Canal
Lettoch
Liatrie
Dores
Moy
Cannich
Drumnadrochit
Farr
659 CARN GLAS-CHOIRE
Grantown-on-Spey
Hills of Cromdale
Lewiston
L. Duntelchaig
Tomatin
Affric
Torness
Dulnain Bridge
Strath Avon
Affric Lodge
MEALFUARVONIE 696
Errogie
Carrbridge
L. Affric
Loch Ness
24
Foyers
Dulnain
Nethy Bridge
Boat of Garten
Tomir

18
19
20
E
F
G
H
Duncansby Head
Duncansby
Freswick
Nybster
Keiss
Sinclair's B.
Reiss
Noss Hd.
Staxigoe
Wick
Thrumster
Ulbster
Troup Hd.
Kinnairds Hd.
FRASERBURGH
Rosehearty
Pennan
Gardenstown
Inverallochy
St. Combs
Rathen
New Aberdour
Rattray Hd.
Crimond
Strichen
St. Fergus
PETERHEAD
Mintlaw
Longside
Buchan Ness
Boddam
Findochty
Portknockie
Cullen
Portsoy
Spey B.
Buckie
Portgordon
Fordyce
Banff
Macduff
Craibstone
Fochabers
Weachyburn
Newbyth
New Pitsligo
Newmill
Aberchirder
Cuminestown
Mulben
Keith
Turriff
BUCHAN
Maud
New Deer
Old Deer
Fortrie
Craigellachie
ABERDEENSHIRE
Huntly
Badenscoth
Methlick
Fyvie
Hatton
Cruden Bay
Laggan
STRATHBOGIE
Rothienorman
Tarves
Ellon
Colpy
FORMARTINE
Ardwell
Kennethmont
Insch
GARIOCH
Oldmeldrum
Hackley Head
Newburgh
Cabrach
Rhynie
722 THE BUCK
Lumsden
Tullynessle
Inverurie
Newmachar
Badenyon
Kemnay
Balmedie
Deveron
Ythan
Ugie
Urie
Isla
Spey
17
25

16
17
18
19
D
E
F
ORKNEY
Mull Head
Papa
Westray
WESTRAY
PAPA WESTRAY
Papa Sd.
NORTH RONALDSAY
Dennis Hd.
Hollandstoun
N. Ronaldsay
N. Ronaldsay Firth
Noup Hd.
Pierowall
B9066
Westray
Midbea
Berst Ness
Rapness
The North Sound
Burness
SANDAY
B9068
B9069
Sanday
Start Pt.
Overbister
Kettletoft
B9070
Calfsound
Eday Sd.
Westray Firth
Sacquoy Hd.
Wasbister
Rousay
B9064
Brinyan
Egilsay
B9063
Eday
Veness
Store
Sanday Sound
STRONSAY
Papa Stronsay
Odie
Whitehall
Aith
B9061
B9060
Stronsay
Rothiesholm
Lamb Hd.
Eynhallow Sd.
Brough Hd.
The Barony
A966
30
Twatt
B9057
Redland
Wyre
Gairsay
B9056
A967
Dounby
A986
B9059
Stronsay Firth
L. of Harray
Balfour
Shapinsay
Auskerry
Voy
B9055
7
Finstown
Wide Firth
Shapinsay Sd.
L. of Stenness
A965
Stromness
LERWICK
Kirkwall
MAINLAND
KIRKWALL
Deer Sound
Mull Head
Deerness
INVERGORDON
Hoy Sd.
A964
17
Orphir
A961
A960
Gritley
SCRABSTER
ABERDEEN
Linksness
WARD HILL
Graemsay
B9052
Pt. of Ayre
Old Man of Hoy
St. Mary's
Copinsay
Rora Hd.
Rackwick
B9047
Scapa Flow
Rose Ness
Burray
Flotta
Hoy
Lyness
St. Margaret's Hope
20
Longhope
South Ronaldsay
Tor Ness
Hurliness
South Walls
A961
Cleat
Swona
Burwick
Pentland Firth
STROMNESS
Dunnet Hd.
Stroma
Muckle Skerries
John o' Groats
Brough
Duncansby Head
Holborn Hd.
Mey
A836
Canisbay
Duncansby
Strathy Pt.
Dunnet B.
Dunnet
Scrabster
Thurso
Portskerra
Dounreay
14
A836
19
Castletown
Freswick
A836
A9
Strathy
Melvich
Reay
B876
15
Nybster
Sordale
Sortat
Keiss
L. Calder
B874
Hastigrow
A99
Strath Halladale
Craigtown
Halkirk
B874
Sinclair's B.
Olgrinmore
B876
Reiss
A897
Thurso
Noss Hd.
Dalhalvaig
Wick
WICK
Staxigoe
B870
B870
Watten
21
Mybster
A882
Forsinain
Wick
CAITHNESS
A9
Forsinard
Thrumster
23
Achavanich
Ulbster
A99
16
Halberry Head
36
Lybster
Latheron
Kinbrace
705
MORVEN
Braemore
Dunbeath
A9
17
anduino
Berriedale
Kildonan
A897
Ousdale

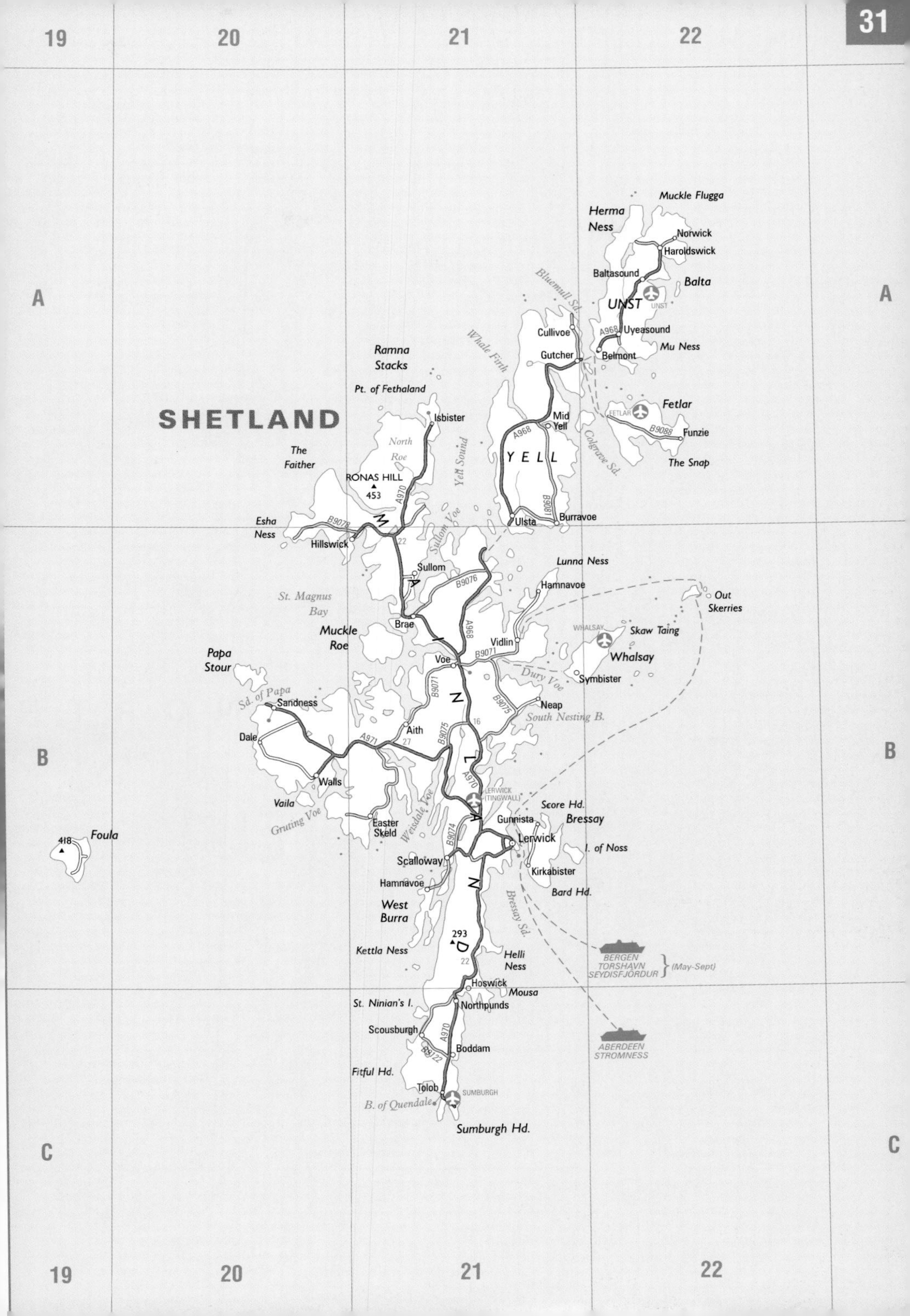
19
20
21
22
A
B
C
SHETLAND
Muckle Flugga
Herma Ness
Norwick
Haroldswick
Baltasound
Balta
UNST
UNST
Bluemull Sd.
Cullivoe
A968
Uyeasound
Mu Ness
Belmont
Gutcher
Whale Firth
Fetlar
FETLAR
B9088
Funzie
The Snap
Mid Yell
A968
YELL
Colgrave Sd.
B9081
Burravoe
Ulsta
Yell Sound
Ramna Stacks
Pt. of Fethaland
Isbister
North Roe
The Faither
RONAS HILL
453
A970
Esha Ness
B9078
Hillswick
MAINLAND
22
Sullom Voe
Sullom
B9076
Lunna Ness
Hamnavoe
Out Skerries
St. Magnus Bay
Brae
A968
Muckle Roe
WHALSAY
Skaw Taing
Vidlin
Whalsay
B9071
Papa Stour
Voe
Dury Voe
Symbister
Sd. of Papa
Sandness
B9071
B9075
Neap
South Nesting B.
16
Aith
Dale
A971
27
B9075
A970
Walls
LERWICK (TINGWALL)
Vaila
Gruting Voe
Weisdale Voe
Easter Skeld
Score Hd.
Gunnista
Bressay
Foula
418
B9074
Lerwick
I. of Noss
Scalloway
Kirkabister
Hamnavoe
Bard Hd.
West Burra
Bressay Sd.
293
Kettla Ness
22
Helli Ness
BERGEN
TORSHAVN
SEYDISFJÖRDUR
(May-Sept)
Hoswick
Mousa
St. Ninian's I.
Northpunds
Scousburgh
A970
B9122
Boddam
ABERDEEN
STROMNESS
Fitful Hd.
Tolob
SUMBURGH
B. of Quendale
Sumburgh Hd.
19
20
21
22

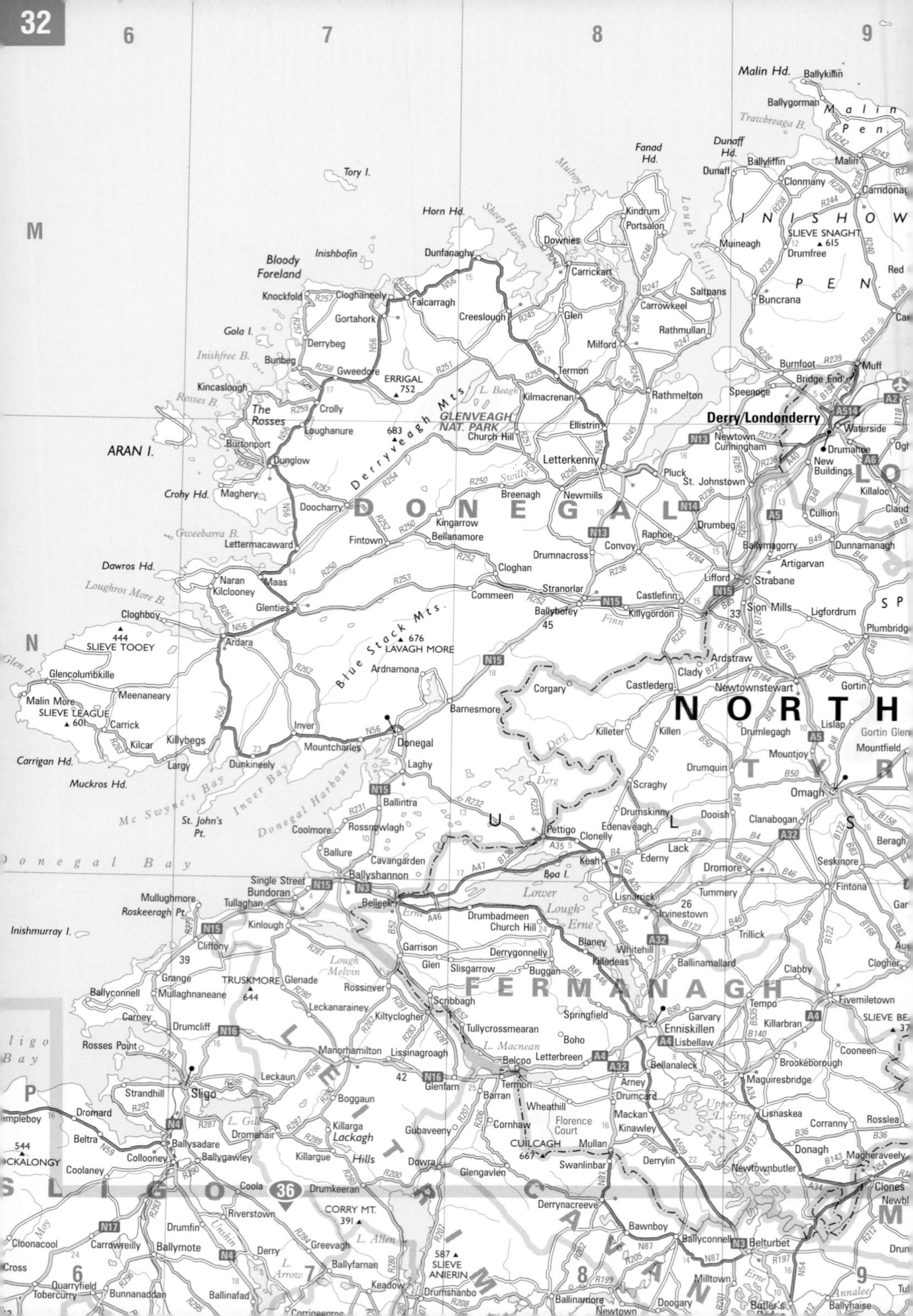
6
7
8
9
Malin Hd.
Ballykillin
Ballygorman
Malin
Pen.
Trawbreaga B.
Fanad Hd.
Dunaff Hd.
Tory I.
Mulroy B.
Lough Swilly
Dunaff
Ballyliffin
Malin
Clonmany
Carndonagh
Horn Hd.
Sheep Haven
Kindrum
Portsalon
INISHOWEN
SLIEVE SNAGHT 615
M
Downies
Muineagh
Drumfree
Bloody Foreland
Inishbofin
Dunfanaghy
Carrickart
Red
PEN.
Knockfold
Cloghaneely
Falcarragh
Creeslough
Carrowkeel
Saltpans
Buncrana
Gortahork
Glen
Gola I.
Rathmullan
Derrybeg
Milford
Inishfree B.
Bunbeg
Gweedore
ERRIGAL 752
Termon
Burnfoot
Muff
Bridge End
Kincasslough
L. Beagh
Kilmacrenan
Rathmelton
Speenoge
Rosses B.
The Rosses
Crolly
Derryveagh Mts.
GLENVEAGH NAT. PARK
Loughanure
683
Church Hill
Ellistrin
Derry/Londonderry
Waterside
Newtown Cunningham
Burtonport
ARAN I.
Drumahoe
Dunglow
Letterkenny
New Buildings
Pluck
St. Johnstown
Crohy Hd.
Maghery
Breenagh
Newmills
Killaloo
Foyle
DONEGAL
Doocharry
Kingarrow
Cullion
Gweebarra B.
Bellanamore
Raphoe
Drumbeg
Lettermacaward
Fintown
Convoy
Ballymagorry
Dunnamanagh
Drumnacross
Artigarvan
Dawros Hd.
Cloghan
Lifford
Strabane
Naran
Maas
Stranorlar
Castlefinn
Loughros More B.
Kilclooney
Commeen
Glenties
Ballybofey
Killygordon
Sion Mills
Ligfordrum
Cloghboy
Finn
Plumbridge
444 SLIEVE TOOEY
Blue Stack Mts.
676 LAVAGH MORE
N
Ardara
Ardstraw
Glen B.
Ardnamona
Clady
Glencolumbkille
Corgary
Castlederg
Newtownstewart
Gortin
Malin More
Meenaneary
SLIEVE LEAGUE 601
Barnesmore
NORTH
Carrick
Inver
Killeter
Killen
Lislap
Gortin Glen
Kilcar
Killybegs
Mountcharles
Donegal
Derg
Drumlegagh
Mountfield
Carrigan Hd.
Largy
Dunkineely
Laghy
Mountjoy
Muckros Hd.
Inver Bay
L. Derg
Drumquin
TYR
Mc Swyne's Bay
Donegal Harbour
Ballintra
Scraghy
Omagh
St. John's Pt.
Rossnowlagh
Drumskinny
Dooish
Coolmore
Pettigo
Edenaveagh
Clanabogan
Ballure
Clonelly
Lack
Beragh
Cavangarden
Kesh
Ederny
Donegal Bay
Ballyshannon
Boa I.
Dromore
Seskinore
Single Street
Bundoran
Mullughmore
Belleek
Lower Lough Erne
Lisnarrick
Fintona
Tullaghan
Tummery
Roskeeragh Pt.
Drumbadmeen
Church Hill
Irvinestown
Inishmurray I.
Kinlough
Trillick
Cliffony
Garrison
Blaney
Whitehill
Lough Melvin
Derrygonnelly
Killadeas
Ballinamallard
Clogher
Grange
Glen
Slisgarrow
Buggan
Clabby
TRUSKMORE 644
Glenade
FERMANAGH
Ballyconnell
Mullaghnaneane
Rossinver
Tempo
Fivemiletown
Leckanarainey
Scribbagh
Springfield
Garvary
Carney
Kiltyclogher
Killarbran
SLIEVE BEA
Drumcliff
Tullycrossmearan
Enniskillen
Boho
Lisbellaw
Sligo Bay
Rosses Point
Manorhamilton
Lissinagroagh
L. Macnean
Letterbreen
Cooneen
Belcoo
Bellanaleck
Brookeborough
LEITRIM
Leckaun
Glenfarn
Termon
Arney
Maguiresbridge
Sligo
Boggaun
Barran
Drumcard
Strandhill
P
Dromard
Wheathill
Mackan
Lisnaskea
L. Gill
Florence Court
Upper L. Erne
Rosslea
Beltra
Dromahair
Killarga
Cornhaw
Kinawley
Corranny
Lackagh Hills
Gubaveeny
Ballysadare
CUILCAGH 667
Mullan
Donagh
544
Collooney
Ballygawley
Killargue
Dowra
Swanlinbar
Derrylin
Magheraveely
Coolaney
Glengavlen
Newtownbutler
Clones
SLIGO
Coola
36
Drumkeeran
CAVAN
Riverstown
CORRY MT. 391
Derrynacreeve
Drumfin
Bawnboy
Cloonacool
Carrowreilly
Ballymote
Greevagh
L. Allen
Ballyconnell
Belturbet
Derry
587 SLIEVE ANIERIN
Cross
L. Arrow
Ballyfarnan
Quarryfield
Tobercurry
Bunnanaddan
Ballinafad
Keadew
Drumshanbo
Milltown
Erne
Annalee
Ballinamore
Newtown
Doogary
Butler's
Ballyhaise

33
Campbeltown
10
11
12
13
M
N
P
Machrihanish Bay
Machrihanish
Earadale Pt.
446 CNOC MOY
Johnston's Pt.
Southend
Mull of Kintyre
Sanda I.
North Channel
Rathlin Island
Ballycastle B.
Fair Hd.
Benbane Hd.
Giants Causeway
Ballintroohan
Inishowen Hd.
Stroove
Magilligan Pt.
The Skerries
Portballintrae
Portrush
Portstewart
Bushmills
Ballintoy
Ballycastle
Ballyvoy
Ballinlea
Downhill
Castlerock
Carrowreagh
517 KNOCKLAYD
Moss-side
Derrykeighan
Loughran
Runabay Hd.
Articlave
Coleraine
Ballybogy
Armoy
Dervock
Cushendun
Mullarts
Cushendall
Red B.
Garron Pt.
Eargantea
Dirtagh
Bolea
Macosquin
Drumdallagh
Crindle
Ballymoney
Milltown
Glenariff
554 TROSTAN
Limavady
Drumramer
Ringsend
Loughguile
MOUNTAINS OF ANTRIM
Drumsurn
Killykergan
Ardreagh
Finvoy
Dunloy
Newtown Crommelin
Carnlough
Glenarm
Drumaduff
Garvagh
Cullinane
Gortnacross
Drumsaragh
Rasharkin
Clogh
436 Islandtown
Kilrea
Parkview
LONDONDERRY
ANTRIM
Milltown
Dungiven
CAIRNRYAN
The Sheddings
Teeshan
Swatragh
Carncastle
Fincarn
Broughshane
Inishrush
Portglenone
Ballymena
Larne
Larne Lough
AGNEWS HILL 476
554
Maghera
Ahoghill
Gulladuff
Lisnamusk
Moorfields
Glynn
683 SAWEL MT.
Tobermore
Connor
I. Magee
Glenoe
Moneyneany
Bellaghy
Kells
L. Beg
Ballycarry
Black Hd.
Sperrin
Draperstown
Castledawson
Desertmartin
Labby
Moneyglass
Ballyclare
Ballynure
Whitehead
Toome
Randalstown
Magherafelt
Doagh
DOUGLAS (Summer only) LIVERPOOL HEYSHAM STRANRAER TROON
Eden
Broughderg
The Loup
Ballyronan
Antrim
Carrickfergus
Davagh
Moneymore
Mossley
Greenisland
Creeve
Templepatrick
Belfast Lough
Groomsport
Copeland I.
Bangor
NORTHERN IRELAND
Glengormly
Newtownabbey
Cookstown
Coagh
BELFAST INTERNATIONAL
Nutts Corner
Holywood
Donaghadee
Creggan
Drum Manor
Arboe
Crumlin
Dundrod
Legoniel
Conlig
Millisle
BELFAST
Dundonald
Newtownards
Lough Neagh
Tullaghoge
Glenavy
Pomeroy
Stewartstown
Newtownbreda
Comber
Ballywalter
Coalisland
Ballinderry Upr.
Dunmurry
Greyabbey
Killeen
Aghalee
Drumbeg
Carryduff
Lisbane
Donaghmore
Magheragall
Lisburn
Ballyhalbert
Parkanaur
Maghery
Derrytrasna
Ballygowan
Kircubbin
Glastry
Dungannon
Granville
The Temple
Moira
Cabragh
39
Saintfield
Portavogie
Hillsborough
Ballygawley
Eglish
Moy
Charlemont
Craigavon
Lurgan
Ardkeen
Derryboy
Waringstown
Annahilt
Cloghy
Shrigley
Benburb
Portadown
Ballynahinch
Crossgar
Aughnacloy
Dromore
Killyleagh
Portaferry
Dyan
Loughall
Strangford Lough
Strangford
Drumsallan
Rich Hill
Gilford
Lawrencetown
Mount Ida
Dromara
DOWN
Annacloy
Caledon
Garvaghy
Killylea
Armagh
Tandragee
Banbridge
Finnis
Frankville
Emyvale
Tynan
Millford
Hamiltonsbawn
Scarva
Downpatrick
Tobermoney
Ballyquintin
Glaslough
Loughbrickland
Katesbridge
Killard Pt.
ARMAGH
Acton
Castlewellan
Ballyhornan
Markethill
Poyntz Pass
Ballyward
Ballydugan
Clough
Tedavnet
Middletown
Clady Milltown
Diamond
Ballyroney
Castlewellan
Dundrum
Ardglass
Killough
Silverstream
Mountnorris
Keady
Beech Hill
Square
Dundrum Bay
St. John's Pt.
Drumbear
Darkley
Whitecross
Rathfriland
Kilcoo
Tollymore
Newtown Hamilton
Ardahy
Milltown
Bessbrook
Hilltown
Newcastle
Scotch Corner
Belleek
Camlough
Newry
Mayo Bridge
852 SLIEVE DONARD
Corvoy
Creaghanroe
MOURNE MTS.
Glasdrumman
Tullymacreeve
Lislea
Cullyhanna
Burren
744
Meigh
577 SLIEVE GULLION
Ballybay
Rostrevor
Annalong
Castleblaney
Attical
Moyad
Warrenpoint
Killowen
Ballymartin
Crossmaglen
Forkill
Omeath
Broomfield
Cullaville
Drumbilla
Ravensdale
Carlingford
Lisnacree
Kilkeel
Greencastle
Shantonagh
590 SLIEVE FOYE
Kilcurry

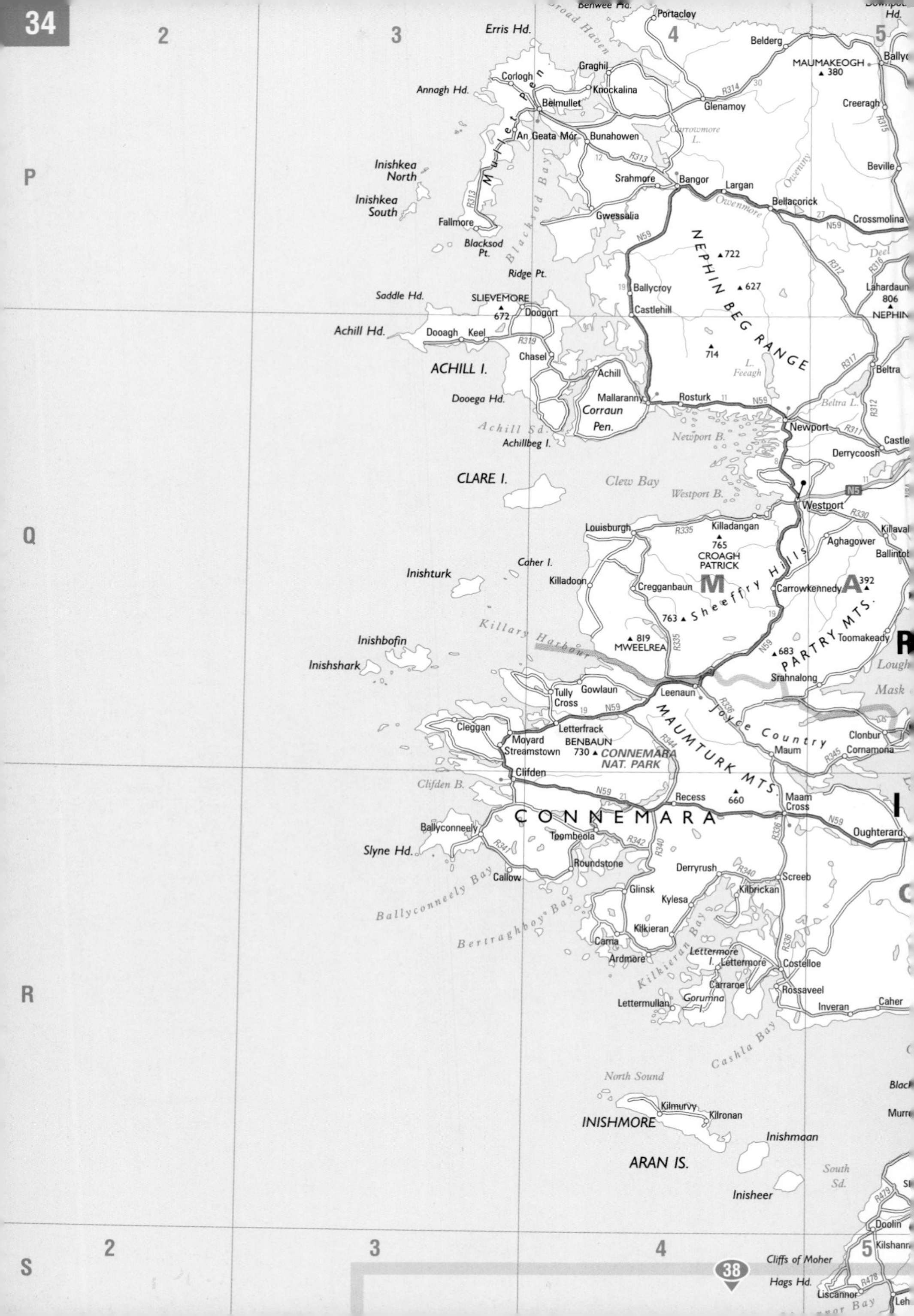
2
3
4
5
P
Q
R
S
Erris Hd.
Portacloy
Belderg
MAUMAKEOGH 380
Broad Haven
Graghil
Corlogh
Annagh Hd.
Knockalina
Belmullet
Glenamoy
Creeragh
Mullet Pen.
An Geata Mór
Bunahowen
Carrowmore L.
Inishkea North
Inishkea South
Srahmore
Bangor
Largan
Owenmore
Oweniny
Bellacorick
Beville
Crossmolina
Gwessalia
Fallmore
Blacksod Pt.
Blacksod Bay
NEPHIN BEG RANGE
722
627
714
Ridge Pt.
Ballycroy
Castlehill
Saddle Hd.
SLIEVEMORE 672
Doogort
Lahardaun
806
NEPHIN
Achill Hd.
Dooagh
Keel
Chasel
ACHILL I.
Achill
L. Feeagh
Beltra
Beltra L.
Dooega Hd.
Mallaranny
Corraun Pen.
Rosturk
Newport
Achill Sd.
Achillbeg I.
Newport B.
Castle
Derrycoosh
CLARE I.
Clew Bay
Westport B.
Westport
Louisburgh
Killadangan
765
CROAGH PATRICK
Aghagower
Killavally
Ballintober
Caher I.
Inishturk
Killadoon
Cregganbaun
Sheeffry Hills
Carrowkennedy
392
PARTRY MTS.
Toomakeady
763
Killary Harbour
819
MWEELREA
683
Inishbofin
Inishshark
Srahnalong
Lough Mask
Tully Cross
Gowlaun
Leenaun
Cleggan
Letterfrack
Moyard
Streamstown
BENBAUN 730
CONNEMARA NAT. PARK
MAUMTURK MTS.
Joyce Country
Maum
Clonbur
Cornamona
Clifden
Clifden B.
Recess
660
Maam Cross
CONNEMARA
Ballyconneely
Toombeola
Oughterard
Slyne Hd.
Roundstone
Callow
Derryrush
Screeb
Ballyconneely Bay
Bertraghboy Bay
Glinsk
Kylesa
Kilbrickan
Kilkieran
Carna
Ardmore
Kilkieran Bay
Lettermore I.
Lettermore
Costelloe
Carraroe
Rossaveel
Lettermullan
Gorumna I.
Inveran
Caher
Cashla Bay
North Sound
Kilmurvy
Kilronan
INISHMORE
Inishmaan
ARAN IS.
South Sd.
Inisheer
Doolin
Kilshanny
Cliffs of Moher
Hags Hd.
Liscannor
38

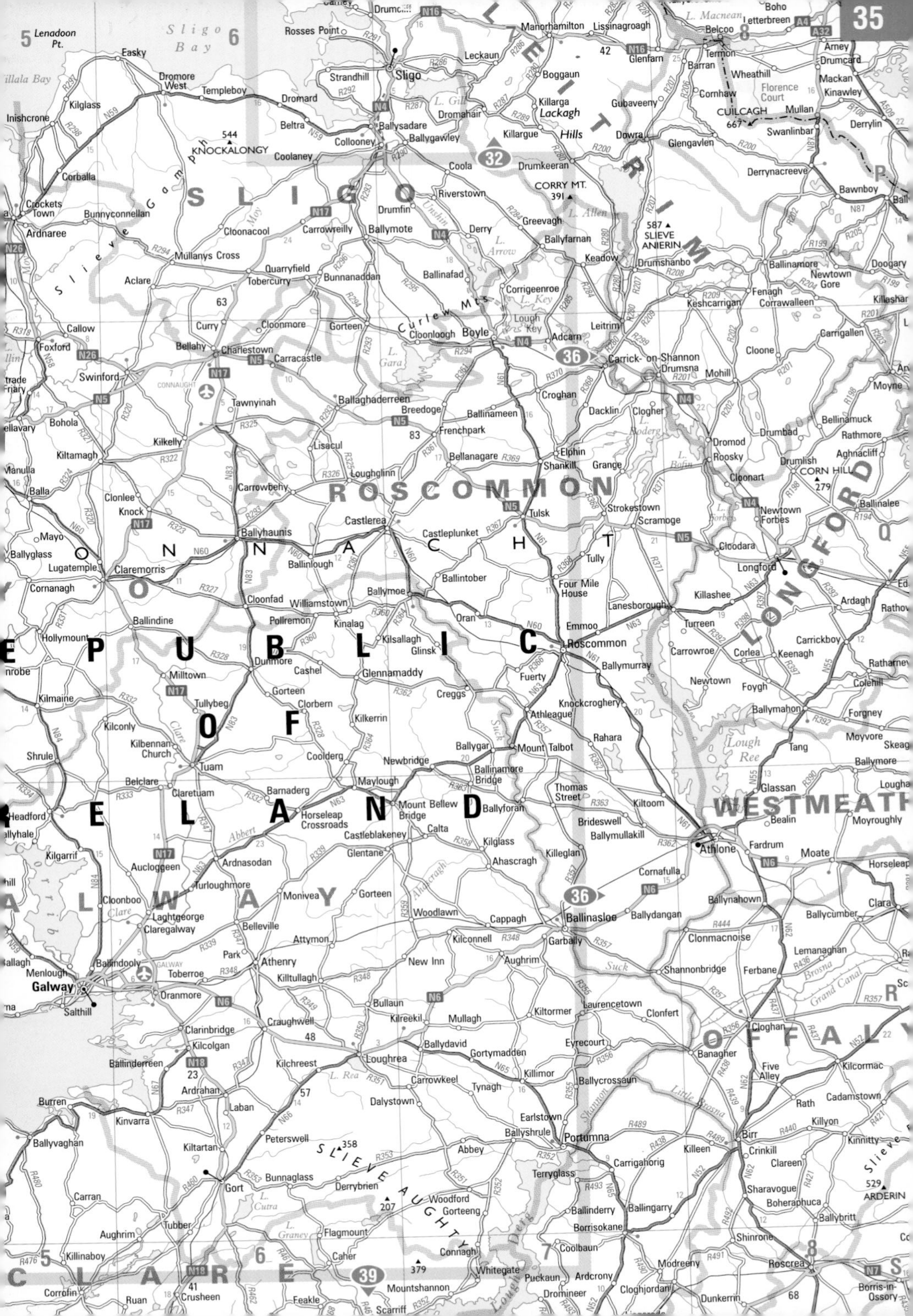
Sligo Bay
Lenadoon Pt.
Killala Bay
Rosses Point
Drumcliff
Manorhamilton
Lissinagroagh
L. Macnean
Boho
Belcoo
Letterbreen
Easky
Dromore West
Templeboy
Strandhill
Sligo
Leckaun
Boggaun
Glenfarn
Termon
Barran
Arney
Drumcard
Kilglass
Inishcrone
Dromard
L. Gill
Dromahair
Killarga
Lackagh Hills
Gubaveeny
Wheathill
Cornhaw
Florence Court
Mackan
Kinawley
Beltra
Ballysadare
Collooney
Ballygawley
Killargue
Dowra
CUILCAGH 667
Mullan
Swanlinbar
Derrylin
544 KNOCKALONGY
Coolaney
Glengavlen
Corballa
Coola
Drumkeeran
CORRY MT. 391
Derrynacreeve
Bawnboy
SLIGO
LEITRIM
Crockets Town
Bunnyconnellan
Riverstown
Drumfin
Unshin
L. Allen
587 SLIEVE ANIERIN
Ardnaree
Cloonacool
Carrowreilly
Ballymote
Derry
Greevagh
Ballyfarnan
L. Arrow
Slieve Gamph
Mullanys Cross
Keadow
Drumshanbo
Ballinamore
Doogary
Aclare
Quarryfield
Tobercurry
Bunnanaddan
Ballinafad
Newtown Gore
63
Corrigeenroe
L. Key
Fenagh
Keshcarrigan
Corrawalleen
Killashandra
Curlew Mts
Lough Key
Callow
Curry
Cloonmore
Gorteen
Cloonlough
Boyle
Adcarn
Leitrim
Carrigallen
Foxford
Bellahy
Charlestown
Carracastle
L. Gara
Carrick-on-Shannon
Cloone
Drumsna
Mohill
Swinford
CONNAUGHT
Croghan
Moyne
Strade
Friary
Tawnyinah
Ballaghaderreen
Breedoge
Ballinameen
Dacklin
Clogher
Ballavary
Bohola
Frenchpark
83
L. Roderg
Drumbad
Ballinamuck
Kilkelly
Lisacul
Bellanagare
Elphin
Dromod
Rathmore
Kiltamagh
Loughglinn
Shankill
Grange
L. Bofin
Roosky
Drumlish
Aghnacliff
Manulla
CORN HILL 279
Balla
Clonlee
Carrowbehy
ROSCOMMON
Cloonart
Knock
Tulsk
Strokestown
Scramoge
Newtown Forbes
L. Forbes
Ballinalee
LONGFORD
Mayo
Ballyhaunis
Castlerea
Castleplunket
Cloodara
Ballyglass
CONNACHT
Ballinlough
Tully
Longford
Lugatemple
Claremorris
Ballintober
Four Mile House
Cornanagh
Ballymoe
Lanesborough
Killashee
Ardagh
Cloonfad
Williamstown
Rathowen
Ballindine
Pollremon
Kinalag
Oran
Emmoo
Turreen
Hollymount
Kilsallagh
Glinsk
Roscommon
Carrickboy
REPUBLIC OF IRELAND
Carrowroe
Corlea
Keenagh
Ballinrobe
Dunmore
Cashel
Ballymurray
Milltown
Glennamaddy
Fuerty
Newtown
Foygh
Ratharney
Coleill
Kilmaine
Tullybeg
Gorteen
Clorbern
Creggs
Knockcroghery
Athleague
Ballymahon
Forgney
Kilconly
Kilkerrin
Rahara
Moyvore
Shrule
Kilbennan Church
Clare
Tuam
Coolderg
Ballygar
Mount Talbot
Tang
Lough Ree
Skeagh
Newbridge
Ballinamore Bridge
Ballymore
Belclare
Claretuam
Barnaderg
Maylough
Thomas Street
Glassan
Loughanavally
Headford
Horseleap Crossroads
Mount Bellew Bridge
Ballyforan
Kiltoom
WESTMEATH
Bealin
Moyroughly
Abbert
Calta
Brideswell
Ballymullakill
Castleblakeney
Kilglass
Athlone
Fardrum
Moate
Kilgarriff
Auclogeen
Ardnasodan
Glentane
Ahascragh
Killeglan
Horseleap
Turloughmore
Cornafulla
Monivea
Gorteen
GALWAY
Cloonboo
Woodlawn
Ballinasloe
Ballydangan
Ballynahown
Clara
Laghtgeorge
Claregalway
Cappagh
Ballycumber
Belleville
Attymon
Kilconnell
Garbally
Clonmacnoise
Lemanaghan
Park
Athenry
New Inn
Aughrim
Ballagh
Menlough
Ballindooly
Toberroe
Killtullagh
Shannonbridge
Ferbane
Brosna
Grand Canal
Galway
Salthill
Oranmore
Bullaun
Kilreekil
Mullagh
Kiltormer
Laurencetown
Clonfert
Clarinbridge
Craughwell
48
Eyrecourt
Cloghan
OFFALY
Kilcolgan
Loughrea
Ballydavid
Gortymadden
Banagher
Ballinderreen
Kilchreest
L. Rea
Carrowkeel
Killimor
Five Alley
Kilcormac
23
Ardrahan
Tynagh
Ballycrossaun
Little Brosna
Burren
Kinvarra
Laban
57
Dalystown
Rath
Cadamstown
Earlstown
Ballyvaghan
Killyon
Peterswell
358
Ballyshrule
Portumna
Birr
Kinnitty
Kiltartan
SLIEVE AUGHTY
Abbey
Carrigahorig
Killeen
Crinkill
Clareen
Gort
Bunnaglass
Derrybrien
Terryglass
Sharavogue
Slieve Bloom
Carran
L. Cutra
207
Woodford
Gorteeng
Ballinderry
Ballingarry
Boheraphuca
529 ARDERIN
Tubber
Aughrim
L. Graney
Flagmount
Borrisokane
Ballybritt
Shinrone
Killinaboy
Caher
Connagh
Coolbaun
Modreeny
Roscrea
CLARE
379
Whitegate
Puckaun
Ardcrony
Lough Derg
Corrofin
41
Crusheen
Mountshannon
Dromineer
Cloghjordan
Dunkerrin
68
Borris-in-Ossory
Ruan
Feakle
Scarriff
N16
N4
N17
N26
N5
N60
N61
N63
N83
N84
N6
N18
N62
N65
N55
N52
N7
N87
A4
A32
32
36
39

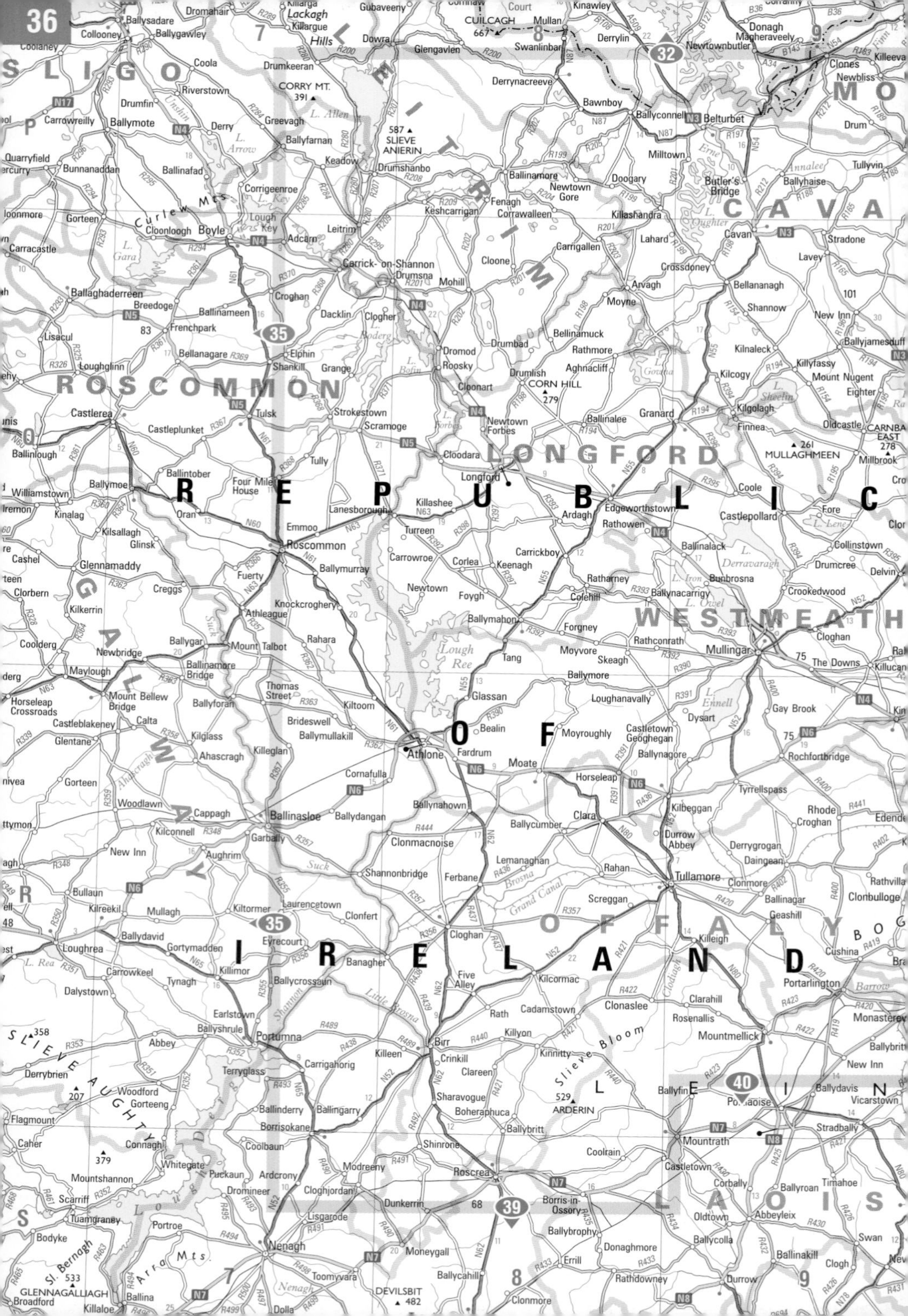

Dromahair
Lackagh
Killargue
Hills
Gubaveeny
Court
CUILCAGH
667
Mullan
Kinawley
Donagh
Magheraveely
Ballysadare
Ballygawley
Collooney
Coolaney
7
8
9
Dowra
Glengavlen
Swanlinbar
Derrylin
32
Newtownbutler
Clones
Killeevan
Newbliss
SLIGO
LEITRIM
Coola
Drumkeeran
CORRY MT.
391
Derrynacreeve
Riverstown
Drumfin
Unshin
L. Allen
Bawnboy
Ballyconnell
Belturbet
Drum
MO
Carrowreilly
Ballymote
Derry
Greevagh
587
SLIEVE
ANIERIN
Milltown
Erne
L. Arrow
Ballyfarnan
Quarryfield
Bunnanaddan
Keadow
Drumshanbo
Ballinamore
Doogary
Tullyvin
Ballinafad
Corrigeenroe
L. Key
Newtown
Gore
Butler's
Bridge
Annalee
Ballyhaise
Curlew Mts.
Fenagh
Keshcarrigan
Corrawalleen
Killashandra
CAVAN
Loonmore
Gorteen
Lough
Key
L. Gara
Cloonloogh
Boyle
Adcarn
Leitrim
Lahard
L. Oughter
Cavan
Stradone
Carracastle
Carrick-on-Shannon
Carrigallen
Cloone
Crossdoney
Lavey
Drumsna
Mohill
Arvagh
Bellananagh
101
Ballaghaderreen
Croghan
Breedoge
Ballinameen
Dacklin
Clogher
L. Boderg
Moyne
Shannow
New Inn
Lisacul
Frenchpark
83
35
Bellinamuck
Ballyjamesduff
Dromod
Drumbad
Rathmore
Kilnaleck
Bellanagare
Elphin
Loughglinn
Shankill
Grange
L. Bofin
Roosky
Aghnacliff
L. Gowna
Killyfassy
Kilcogy
Mount Nugent
Drumlish
CORN HILL
279
Eighter
L. Sheelin
ROSCOMMON
Cloonart
Castlerea
Tulsk
Strokestown
Scramoge
L. Forbes
Newtown
Forbes
Granard
Kilgolagh
Castleplunket
Ballinalee
Finnea
Oldcastle
CARNBANE
EAST
278
LONGFORD
Ballinlough
Tully
Cloodara
MULLAGHMEEN
261
Millbrook
Ballintober
Four Mile
House
Longford
Coole
Williamstown
Ballymoe
REPUBLIC
Killashee
Edgeworthstown
Fore
Kinalag
Oran
Lanesborough
Ardagh
Castlepollard
L. Lene
Emmoo
Turreen
Rathowen
Kilsallagh
Glinsk
Roscommon
Carrickboy
Ballinalack
Collinstown
Cashel
Carrowroe
Corlea
Keenagh
L. Derravaragh
Drumcree
Delvin
Glennamaddy
Ballymurray
Fuerty
Creggs
Ratharney
Bunbrosna
L. Iron
Clorbern
Newtown
Foygh
Colehill
Ballynacarrigy
L. Owel
Crookedwood
Kilkerrin
Knockcroghery
Athleague
WESTMEATH
Ballymahon
GALWAY
Forgney
Rahara
Lough
Ree
Rathconrath
Cloghan
Coolderg
Ballygar
Mount Talbot
Moyvore
Mullingar
Newbridge
Tang
Skeagh
75
The Downs
Killucan
Ballinamore
Bridge
Maylough
Thomas
Street
Ballymore
Horseleap
Crossroads
Mount Bellew
Bridge
Glassan
Loughanavally
Ballyforan
Kiltoom
L. Ennell
Gay Brook
Castleblakeney
Calta
Brideswell
Bealin
Dysart
OF
Moyroughly
Castletown
Geoghegan
Glentane
Kilglass
Ballymullakill
Athlone
Fardrum
Ballynagore
Rochfortbridge
Ahascragh
Killeglan
Moate
Cornafulla
Horseleap
Gorteen
Tyrrellspass
Woodlawn
Ballynahown
Kilbeggan
Rhode
Cappagh
Ballinasloe
Ballydangan
Clara
Croghan
Edenderry
Kilconnell
Garbally
Ballycumber
Durrow
Abbey
Clonmacnoise
Derrygrogan
New Inn
Aughrim
Lemanaghan
Daingean
Suck
Shannonbridge
Ferbane
Brosna
Rahan
Tullamore
Clonmore
Rathvilla
Bullaun
Grand Canal
Ballinagar
Clonbullogue
Laurencetown
Scregan
Kilreekil
Mullagh
Kiltormer
Clonfert
Geashill
OFFALY
35
Ballydavid
Eyrecourt
Cloghan
Killeigh
Gortymadden
Loughrea
IRELAND
L. Rea
Cushina
Carrowkeel
Killimor
Banagher
Five
Alley
Kilcormac
Tynagh
Ballycrossaun
Portarlington
Dalystown
Clarahill
Little Brosna
Clonaslee
Rosenallis
Barrow
Shannon
Rath
Cadamstown
Monasterevin
Earlstown
358
Ballyshrule
Mountmellick
SLIEVE AUGHTY
Portumna
Abbey
Birr
Killyon
Slieve Bloom
Ballybrittas
Kinnitty
Terryglass
Carrigahorig
Killeen
Crinkill
Derrybrien
Clareen
New Inn
207
Woodford
529
ARDERIN
Ballyfin
40
Portlaoise
Ballydavis
Vicarstown
Gorteeng
Sharavogue
Boheraphuca
LEINSTER
Flagmount
Ballinderry
Ballingarry
Borrisokane
Ballybritt
Stradbally
Caher
Connagh
Coolbaun
Shinrone
Coolrain
Mountrath
379
Whitegate
Puckaun
Ardcrony
Modreeny
Roscrea
Castletown
Mountshannon
Dromineer
Cloghjordan
Corbally
Timahoe
Scarriff
Dunkerrin
68
39
Borris-in-Ossory
Ballyroan
LAOIS
Tuamgraney
Lough Derg
Lisgarode
Oldtown
Abbeyleix
Portroe
Bodyke
Nenagh
Moneygall
Ballybrophy
Ballycolla
Swan
Sl. Bernagh
Arra Mts.
Donaghmore
Ballinakill
533
GLENNAGALLIAGH
Toomyvara
Ballycahill
Erril
Clogh
Broadford
Ballina
Killaloe
Nenagh
DEVILSBIT
482
Rathdowney
Durrow
Clonmore
Dolla

Dundrum Bay
St. John's Pt.
Darkley
Whitecross
Newtown Hamilton
Milltown
Bessbrook
Rathfriland
Kilcoo
Tollymore
Newcastle
MOURNE MTS.
Belleek
Newry
Hilltown
Bridge
852 SLIEVE DONARD
Corvoy
Creaghanroe
Camlough
Burren
Glasdrumman
Cullyhanna
Tullymacreeve
Lislea
Meigh
744
Castleblaney
577 SLIEVE GULLION
Rostrevor
Attical
Moyad
Annalong
Warrenpoint
Killowen
Broomfield
Crossmaglen
Forkill
Omeath
Ballymartin
Cullaville
Drumbilla
Ravensdale
Carlingford
590 SLIEVE FOYE
Lisnacree
Kilkeel
Greencastle
Kilcurry
Greenore
Carlingford Lough
Cranfield Pt.
Lisgall
Inishkeen
Dundalk
Corvally
Rampark
Rathcor
Ballagan Pt.
Shercock
Essexford
Channonrock
Carrickmacross
Black Rock
Louth
LOUTH
Lurgangreen
Dundalk Bay
Bracklin
Drumbo
Tallanstown
Dromiskin
Kingscourt
Manfieldstown
Castlebellingham
Edmondstown
Gudderstown
Annagassan
Dunheeda
Killsaran
Salterstown
Ardee
Dunany Pt.
Drumcondra
Dromin
Togher
Nobber
Dunleer
Woodtown
Grangebellew
Ashville
Clogher Head
Clogher Hd.
Moynalty
Lobinstown
Collon
Kellystown
Castletown
Newtown Monasterboice
Ballymakenny
Termonfeckin
Carlanstown
Rathkenny
Mell
Baltray
Kells
Oristown
Slane
Drogheda
Mornington
Kilberry
Bettystown
Laytown
MEATH
Donore
Julianstown
Fordstown
Navan
Duleek
Kentstown
Balrath
Gormanstown
Balbriggan
Dunderry
Ardcath
Balrothery
Skerries
Garristown
Naul
Tara
Kildalkey
Trim
Dunsany
Lusk
Rush
Laracor
Ballyboghil
Dunshaughlin
Ashbourne
Cross Keys
Ratoath
Portrane
Lambay I.
Summerhill
Donabate
Rathmolyon
Batterstown
Malahide
Swords
Longwood
Mullagh
Cloghran
Portmarnock
Innfield
Dunboyne
Ward
Ireland's Eye
Cloncurry
Kilcock
Baldoyle
Clonee
Howth
Johnstown Bridge
Maynooth
Blanchardstown
Finglas
Glasnevin
Drumcondra
Clontarf
Howth Hd.
Baltracey
Leixlip
Lucan
DUBLIN
DOUGLAS (Summer Only)
HOLYHEAD
LIVERPOOL
Donadea
Celbridge
Timahoe
Clondalkin
Crumlin
Blackrock
Straffan
Dundrum
Dun Laoghaire
Dalkey
Prosperous
Clane
Rathcoole
Stillorgan
Allenwood
Saggart
Tallaght
Cabinteely
HOLYHEAD
Robertstown
Sallins
Kill
CUPIDSTOWN HILL 380
DUBLIN
Killiney
Kilmeage
Kilteel
Brittas
Kiltiernan
Allen
Carragh
Rathmore
Bray
Naas
Enniskerry
Newbridge
754 KIPPURE
Bray Hd.
Kildare
Blessington
Poulaphouca Res.
Greystones
Ballymore Eustace
Sally Gap
506 GREAT SUGAR LOAF
Kilcullen
Kilcoole
DARE
Hollywood
Newtown Mount Kennedy
Ballyshannon
Newcastle
Roundwood
Vartry Res.
Dunlavin
WICKLOW MOUNTAINS
Fontstown
Donard
Ashford
Laragh
Ballinalea
Ardscull
Ballitore
Rathnew
Wicklow
Glendalough
Moone
Timolin
LUGNAQUILLA 926
Glenealy
Wicklow Hd.
Kilkea
WICKLOW
Kilbride
Baltinglass
Aghavannagh
Rathdrum
Castledermot
Kiltegan
Rathvilly
Knockananna
Aughrim
Mizen Hd.
Carlow
Killerig
Hacketstown
Avoca
Clonmore
Woodenbridge
10
11
12
33
40
P
Q
R
S

3
4
34
C
5
L
S
T
U
2
3
4
5
Liscannor Bay
Lehinch
Inagh
Spanish Pt.
Milltown Malbay
SLIEVECALLEN
391
Mal Bay
Shanovogh
Kilmaley
Mutton I.
Quilty
Kilmurry
Creegh
Cahermurphy
Lissycasey
Donegal Pt.
Doonbeg
Kilmihil
Beelaha
Cooraclare
Knockalough
Kilkee
Moyasta
Kilfearagh
Tullagower
Killadysert
Breaghva
Kilrush
Knock
Labasheeda
Carrigaholt
Doonaha
Scattery I.
Lakyle
Loghill
Feeard
Shanagolden
Loop Hd.
Kilbaha
Astee
Tarbert
Glin
Ballyhahill
Mouth of the Shannon
Ballylongford
Ballybunion
Newtown Sands
Lisselton
Carrigkerry
Cashen
Athea
Newcastle West
Galey
Ballyduff
Listowel
Dreenagh
Kerry Hd.
Causeway
Feale
Six Crosses
Crataloe
Ballin Cloher
Lixnaw
Ballyheige
Abbeyfeale
Stacks Mts.
Glanaruddery Mts.
Lyracrumpane
Lerrig
Kilflynn
Kilkinlea
Seven Hogs
Abbeydorney
Mullaghareirk
Rough Pt.
Brandon Bay
Ardfert
Brandon Pt.
Tralee Bay
357
334
Rockchapel
Branden
Fenit
Spa
Tralee
BRANDON MT.
953
Castlegregory
Ballydavid Hd.
Smerwick Harbour
Cloghane
Stradbally
Derrymore
Castleisland
Cordal
Taur
827
853
Slieve Mish
Sybil Pt.
Ballydavid
Camp
Scartaglin
KERRY
Ballyferriter
Fybagh
Castlemaine
Farranfore
Kishkeam
Anascaul
Inishtooskert
Ventry
Milltown
Dingle
Inch
Boherboy
Lispole
Milltown
KERRY COUNTY
Knockagree
Castlemaine Harbour
Slea Hd.
Killorglin
Rathmore
Great Blasket I.
Beaufort
Killarney
Inishvickillane
Dingle Bay
Kilgobnet
Barraduff
Millstreet
L. Caragh
L. Leane
Muckross
Glenbeigh
Glencar
Glenfesk
THE PAPS
696
1041
835
DERRYNASAGGART MTS
CARRAUNTOOHILL
Clonkeen
650
Carriganimmy
Doulus Hd.
MACGILLYCUDDY'S REEKS
MANGERTON MT.
840
775
KILLARNEY NAT. PARK
Ballyvourney
Valencia Harbour
TEERMOYLE MT.
Caherciveen
VALENCIA I.
Lissatinnig Bridge
Inny
Derriana L.
Maulyneill
Bray Hd.
Portmagee
Sallahig
Cleady
Kenmare
Kilgarvan
Templenoe
Puffin I.
New Chapel Cross
Ballingeary
Inchigeelagh
Ballinskelligs
Waterville
L. Currane
Sneem
St. Finan's Bay
Parknasilla
575
Great Skellig
Ballinskelligs Bay
KNOCKBOY
707
Bolus Hd.
Ardkearagh
Caherdaniel
Bunaw
SHEHY MTS.
Hog's Hd.
Derrynane
Kenmare River
Togher
Lauragh
CAHA MTS.
Glengarriff
Kealkill
Scariff I.
Lamb's Hd.
Ardgroom
NOWEN HILL
537
Dunmanway
HUNGRY HILL
686
Adrigole
Coulagh Bay
Whiddy I.
Deelish
Kilronane
Slieve Miskish
Cods Hd.
Curryglass
Bantry
Drinagh
Ballydonegan Bay
491
Drimoleague
Allihies
Castletown Bearhaven
Ballydonegan
Aghaville
Carrigfadda
Durrus
Bear I.
Bantry Bay
Cahermore
Bunalunn
Dursey I.
Connonagh
Leap
Dursey Hd.
Crow Hd.
Kilcrohane
Ballydehob
Kilcoe
Glandore
Sheeps Hd.
Dunmanus Bay
Skibbereen
Toormore
Skull
Castletownshend

TIPPERARY
WATERFORD
CORK
Limerick
Nenagh
Scarriff
Glendree
Tuamgraney
Portroe
Lisgarode
Moneygall
Ballybrophy
Donaghmore
Spancelhill
Tulla
Bodyke
Sl. Bernagh
533
GLENNAGALLIAGH
Arra Mts.
Toomyvara
DEVILSBIT
482
Ballycahill
Erill
Rathdowney
Durrow
Moymore
Quin
Broadford
Ballina
Killaloe
Dolla
Silvermines
Clonmore
Templemore
Templetouhy
Galmoy
Kilkishen
Newmarket-on-Fergus
Kilmurry
O'briensbridge
Birdhill
SILVERMINE MTS.
694
KEEPER HILL
Templederry
Borrisoleigh
Loughmoe
Moyne
Johnstown
Gattabaun
Freshford
Sixmilebridge
Hurlers Cross
Bunratty
Ardnacrusha
Cloonlara
Castleconnell
Newport
Lackamore
Rear Cross
SLIEVEFELIM
465
Upperchurch
Bouladuff
Urlingford
Clomantagh
Manselstown
Thurles
Twomileborris
Anacotty
Lisnagry
Glenstal Abbey
Milestone
Rosmult
Holycross
Littleton
Ballysloe
Tullaroan
Pallaskenry
Mungret
Clarina
Kildimo
Abington
Cappamore
Doon
Cappagh White
Annacarty
Ballagh
Boherlahan
New Birmingham
Ballinunty
Ballingarry
Kilmanagh
Patrickswell
Ballyneety
Caherconlish
Dromkeen
Pallas Green
GOLDEN VALE
Dundrum
Ballinure
Killenaule
Callan
Adare
Fedamore
Kilteely
Oola
Donohill
Rathclogh
Cashel
Drangan
Mullinahone
Croom
Herbertstown
Cullen
36
Limerick Junction
Golden
Knockbrit
Kilamery
Holycross
Bruff
Hospital
Emly
Lattin
Tipperary
Kilfeakle
Rosegreen
Fethard
Cloneen
Ninemilehouse
Windgap
Ballingarry
Athlacca
Knocklong
Kilross
Newinn
Lisronagh
722
SLIEVENAMON
Rockhill
Bruree
Newtown
Ballyclerahan
Scogh
Ballyagran
Kilmallock
Galbally
Ballylanders
GALTY MTS.
Caher
Raheen
Kilsheelan
Carrick-on-Suir
Charleville
Newtownshandrum
Kilfinnane
920
GALTYMORE
Knocklofty
Clonmel
Ardpatrick
Milford
Ballyhaght
519
Dromina
Ballylooby
Ardfinnane
COMERAGH MTS.
Carrickbeg
Rathgormuck
Kilbeheny
BALLYHOURA MTS.
Funshion
Mitchelstown
Ballyporeen
Clogheen
Newcastle
Ballymacarbry
755
MONAVULLAGH MTS.
Clonea
792
Liscarroll
Buttevant
Kildorrery
302
Kilworth Mts.
KNOCKMEALDOWN MTS.
795
KNOCKMEALDOWN
Ballynamult
727
Kilmacthomas
Castlecor
Doneraile
Rockmills
Araglin
Kilbrien
Lemybrien
Ballylaneen
Glanworth
Kilworth
Millstreet
Ballyclogh
Castletownroche
Fermoy
Ballyduff
Cappoquin
Stradbally
Mallow
Killavullen
Ballyhooly
Lismore
Blackwater
Banteer
Gortroe
Nagles Mts.
Cappagh
Tallowbridge
Dungarvan
Dungarvan Harbour
Nad
Ballynamona
429
KNOCKNASKAGH
49
Castlelyons
Conna
Aghern
Curraglass
Tallow
Rathcormack
Ballyroe
Aglish
Helvick Hd.
Burnfoot
Bweeng
Glenville
Bride
Gorteen
Ringville
Watergrasshill
Rathduff
Ballincurrig
Clashmore
Inch
76
Mine Hd.
Donoughmore
Carrignavar
Clash
Dungourney
Sallybrook
Riverstown
Killeagh
Youghal
Ardmore
Ardmore Hd.
Blarney
Dripsey
Carrigtohill
Midleton
Castlemartyr
Ballymacoda
Youghal Bay
Coachford
Innishcarra Res.
Carrigadrohid Res.
Ballincollig
Douglas
Passage West
Cóbh
Ballynacorra
Ladysbridge
Garryvoe
Crookstown
Monkstown
Great I.
Rostellan
Cloyne
Churchtown
Ballinhassig
Ringaskiddy
Whitegate
Ballycotton
Bealnablath
Cross Barry
Carrigaline
Crosshaven
SWANSEA
Kilpatrick
Inishannon
Riverstick
Minane Bridge
Cork Harbour
ROSCOFF (Apr-Oct)
Enniskean
Bandon
Dunderrow
Belgooly
Nohaval
Ballinadee
Kinsale
Kilbrittain
Ballinspittle
Frower Pt.
Timoleague
Courtmacsherry
Kinsale Harbour
Butlerstown
Old Head of Kinsale
Barry's Pt.
Courtmacsherry Bay
Seven Heads
Clonakilty Bay
Galley Hd.
Bantry Bay
Kilcrohane
Bunalunn
Connonagh
Leap
Glandore
Ballydehob
Kilcoe
Skibbereen
Sheeps Hd.
Dunmanus Bay
Toormore
Skull
Castletownshend
Goleen
Long I.
Roaringwater Bay
Baltimore
Toe Hd.
Crookhaven
Mizen Hd.
Sherkin I.

Rochfortbridge
Moyvally
Innfield
Clonard
Kilcock
Dunboyne
Ward
Portmarnock
Baldoyle
Ireland's Eye
Howth
Tyrrellspass
Johnstown Bridge
Maynooth
Leixlip
Blanchardstown
Finglas
Glasnevin
Drumcondra
Clontarf
Howth Hd.
Kilbeggan
Rhode
Croghan
Edenderry
Carbury
Baltracey
Lucan
Celbridge
DUBLIN
Durrow Abbey
Derrygrogan
Daingean
Killane
Timahoe
Donadea
Straffan
Clondalkin
Crumlin
Blackrock
Dun Laoghaire
Dalkey
Tullamore
Clonmore
Rathvilla
Prosperous
Clane
Rathcoole
Saggart
Tallaght
Dundrum
Stillorgan
Cabinteely
Ballinagar
Clonbullogue
Allenwood
Robertstown
Kill
CUPIDSTOWN HILL
380
Killiney
OFFALY
BOG OF ALLEN
Kilmeage
Sallins
Kilteel
Brittas
DUBLIN
Geashill
Carragh
Rathmore
Kiltiernan
Killeigh
Cushina
Rathangan
Allen
Miltown
Naas
Enniskerry
Bray
Bracknagh
Bray Hd.
754 KIPPURE
Portarlington
Newbridge
Blessington
Clarahill
Monasterevin
Kildare
Kilcullen
Ballymore Eustace
Poulaphouca Res.
Sally Gap
506 GREAT SUGAR LOAF
Greystones
Rosenallis
Mountmellick
Ballybrittas
KILDARE
Hollywood
Newtown Mount Kennedy
Kilcoole
New Inn
Ballyshannon
Newcastle
Ballyfin
LEINSTER
Ballydavis
Boley
Cloney
Dunlavin
Roundwood
Vartry Res.
Portlaoise
Vicarstown
Fontstown
WICKLOW MOUNTAINS
Donard
Ashford
Ballinalea
Mountrath
Stradbally
Ardscull
Ballitore
Laragh
Rathnew
Wicklow
Castletown
Athy
Timolin
Moone
Glendalough
LUGNAQUILLA 926
Corbally
Ballyroan
Timahoe
Kilkea
Glenealy
WICKLOW
LAOIS
Ballylynan
Baltinglass
Kilbride
Oldtown
Abbeyleix
Castledermot
Aghavannagh
Rathdrum
Ballycolla
Swan
Arless
Kiltegan
Ballinakill
Clogh
Newtown
Ballickmoyler
Rathvilly
Knockananna
Aughrim
Durrow
Carlow
Killerig
Hacketstown
Avoca
Graigue
Clonmore
Woodenbridge
Mizen Hd.
Castlecomer
Tullow
Tinahely
CROGHAN MT. 607
Arklow
Ballyragget
Gattabaun
Damerstown
Oldleighlin
Nurney
Shillelagh
Coolgreany
Arklow Hd.
Freshford
Leighlinbridge
Ballon
Clomantagh
CARLOW
Kilmichael Pt.
Paulstown
Muine Bheag
Fennagh
Carnew
Myshall
Kildavin
Craanford
Gorey
Tullaroan
Kilkenny
Bunclody
Courtown
Riverchapel
Kilmanagh
Goresbridge
Gowran
MT. LEINSTER 796
Camolin
Ballingarry
Grange
Bennettsbridge
Borris
Ferns
Ballycanew
Killenagh
Ballymurphy
Ballycarney
Kiltealy
Ballindaggan
Ballygarrett
KILKENNY
Blackstairs Mts.
734 BLACKSTAIRS MT.
Cahore Pt.
Callan
Kells
Stonyford
Kilfane
Graiguenamanagh
Mullinahone
Thomastown
BRANDON 519
Glynn
Enniscorthy
Ford
Kilamery
Knocktopher
Inistioge
Rathnure
Kilmuckridge
Windgap
Kilmaganny
WEXFORD
Blackwater
Ballywilliam
Clonroche
Oilgate
Tullaghought
Listerlin
Scogh
Lukeswell
New Ross
Carrick-on-Suir
Piltown
Mullinavat
Old Ross
Killurin
Castlebridge
Ballynabola
Camross
Killinaspick
Carrickbeg
Fiddown
Wexford
Wexford Harbour
Rathgormuck
Kilmacow
Foulkesmill
Taghmon
Portlaw
Mooncoin
FISHGUARD PEMBROKE
Clonea
Campile
Waddington
Rosslare
Waterford
Arthurstown
Wellingtonbridge
Rosslare Harbour
Kilmeadan
Greenore Pt.
Passage East
Tintern Abbey
Killinick
Bridgetown
Kilmacthomas
Adamstown
Duncormick
Broadway
CHERBOURG ROSCOFF
Summer Only
Bannow
Kilmore
Tacumshin L.
Tuskar Rock
WATERFORD
Fethard
Bannow Bay
Churchtown
Ballylaneen
Kill
Tramore
Dunmore East
Lady's I. Lake
Crossfarnoge Pt.
Kilmore Quay
Carnsore Pt.
Baginbun Hd.
Stradbally
Bunmahon
Annestown
Tramore Bay
Hook Hd.
Saltee Is.
Waterford Harbour
Helvick Hd.
36
37
39
9
10
11

Key to Town Plan Symbols

Through Route(dual/single)	Abbey/Cathedral	Historic Ship	Tourist Information Centre
Secondary Road(dual/single)	Ancient Monument	House	open all year
Minor Road	Aquarium	House & Garden	summer only
Pedestrian Roads	Art Gallery	Museum	Other Place of Interest
Restricted Access Roads	Bird Garden	Preserved Railway	Hospital
Shopping Streets	Building of Public Interest	Railway Station	Parking
Railway	Castle	Roman Antiquity	Police Station
Railway/Bus Station	Church of Interest	Theatre	Post Office
Shopping Precinct	Cinema	Tramway	Shopmobility
Park	Garden	Zoo	Youth Hostel

Chesham
Kings Langley
Abbots Langley
Bricket Wood
London Colney
Radlett
Potters Bar
South Mimms
Chesham Bois
Latimer
Sarratt
Chenies
Aldenham
Borehamwood
Barnet
Little Chalfont
Chorleywood
Watford
Croxley Green
Rickmansworth
Oxhey
Bushey
Elstree
Arkley
Totteridge
Chalfont St. Giles
South Oxhey
Bushey Heath
Stanmore
Friern Barnet
Seer Green
Jordans
Chalfont Common
Maple Cross
Batchworth Heath
Eastbury
Edgware
Mill Hill
Finchley
Beaconsfield
Chalfont St. Peter
Harefield
Northwood
Hatch End
Harrow Weald
Wealdstone
Kingsbury
Pinner
Ruislip Common
Harrow
Hendon
Golders Green
Gerrards Cross
Denham Green
Hedgerley
Tatling End
Ruislip
Eastcote
Rayners Lane
Harrow on the Hill
Highgate
Hampstead
Denham
Fulmer
Ickenham
Wembley
Cricklewood
Willesden
Farnham Common
Stoke Poges
Uxbridge
Sudbury
Northolt
Alperton
Harlesden
Kilburn
Wexham Street
Iver Heath
Perivale
Farnham Royal
Stoke Green
Hillingdon
Greenford
Cowley
Yeading
George Green
Iver
Southall
Ealing
Acton
Paddington
Kensington
Slough
Yiewsley
Hayes
Hanwell
West Drayton
Richings Park
Langley
Upton
Chiswick
Eton
Eton Wick
Harmondsworth
Harlington
Heston
Brentford
Hammersmith
Chelsea
Sipson
Cranford
Kew
Fulham
Datchet
Colnbrook
Poyle
Longford
Isleworth
Mortlake
Putney
Windsor
Heathrow Airport
Horton
Stanwell
Hounslow
Richmond
Wandsworth
Old Windsor
Wraysbury
Stanwell Moor
West Bedfont
East Bedfont
Roehampton
Twickenham
Wimbledon Common
Feltham
Hythe End
Englefield Green
Egham
Staines
Ashford
Hanworth
Teddington
Ham
Kingston Vale
Woodside
Hampton
Bushy Park
Wimbledon
Merton
Laleham
Littleton
Sunbury-on-Thames
Kingston upon Thames
Haynes Park
Virginia Water
Thorpe
Morden
Sunninghill
West Molesey
East Molesey
Thames Ditton
New Malden
Sunningdale
Shepperton
Surbiton
Broomhall
Chertsey
Walton on Thames
Long Ditton
Tolworth
Worcester Park
St. Helier
Lyne
Carshalton
Addlestone
Hersham
Esher
Hook
Cheam
Sutton
Weybridge
Ottershaw
Claygate
Chessington
New Haw
Burrowhill
Lightwater
Ewell
Belmont
Chobham
Woodham
Byfleet
Whiteley Village
West End
Cobham
Oxshott
Epsom
Castle Green
West Byfleet
Wood Field
Knaphill
Cheapside
Wisley
Stoke D'Abernon
Banstead
Bisley
Horsell
Woking
Downside
Great Burgh
Pyrford
Leatherhead Common
Ashtead
Burgh Heath
Chipstead
St. John's
Old Woking
Ripley
Martyr's Green
Mayford
Ockham
Fetcham
Leatherhead
Tadworth
Hooley
Kingswood
Send Marsh
Send
Little Bookham
Walton on the Hill
Fox Corner
Burntcommon
Headley
Lower Kingswood
Sutton Green
Worplesdon
West Horsley
East Horsley
Effingham
Great Bookham
Mickleham
Pitch Place
Slyfield
Burpham
East Clandon
West Clandon
Westhumble
Merstham
Greater London
Surrey
M25
M1
M4
M40
M3

London

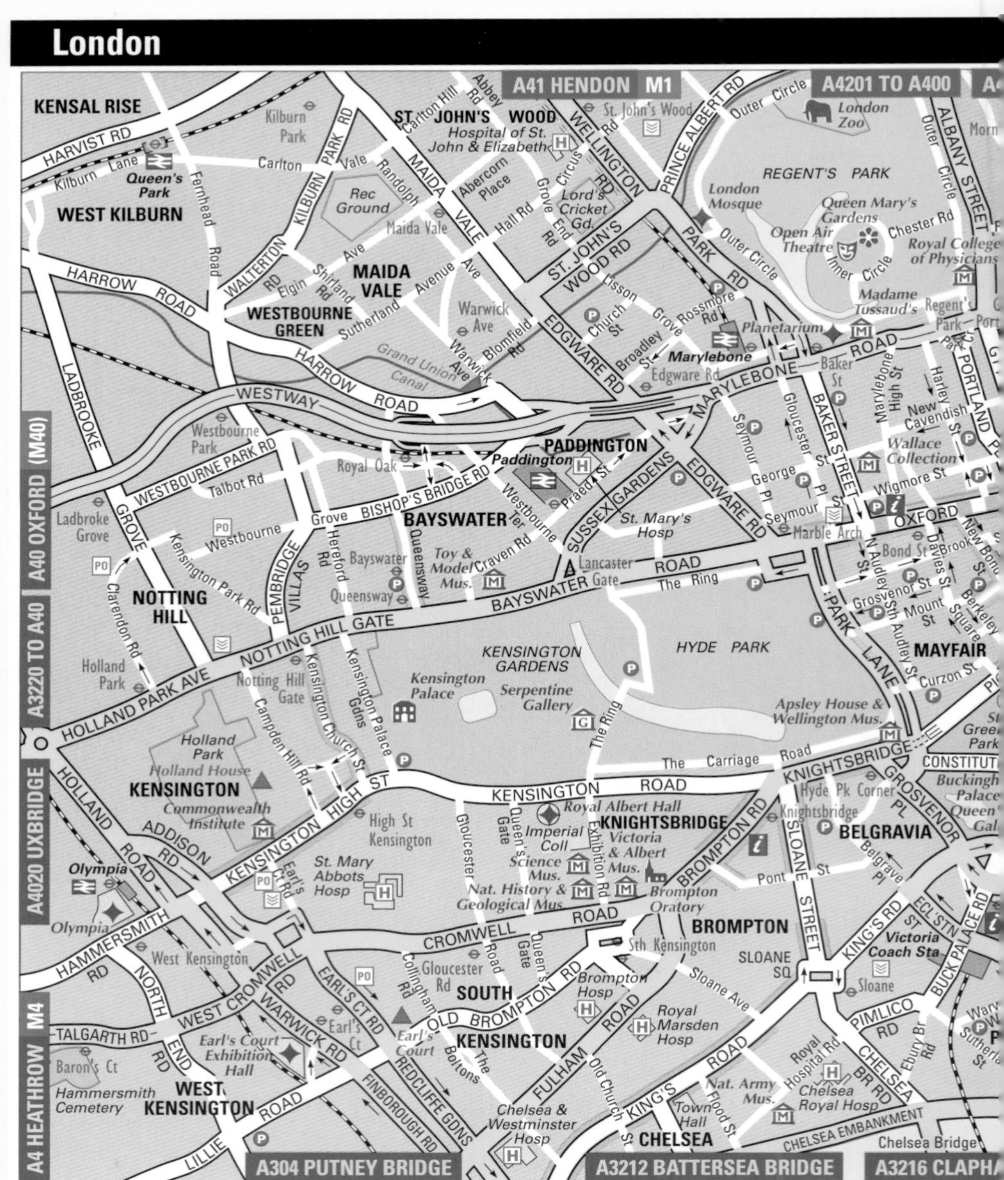
A41 HENDON M1
A4201 TO A400
A40 OXFORD (M40)
A3220 TO A40
A4020 UXBRIDGE
M4
A4 HEATHROW
A304 PUTNEY BRIDGE
A3212 BATTERSEA BRIDGE
KENSAL RISE
WEST KILBURN
ST. JOHN'S WOOD
MAIDA VALE
WESTBOURNE GREEN
REGENT'S PARK
PADDINGTON
BAYSWATER
NOTTING HILL
KENSINGTON GARDENS
HYDE PARK
MAYFAIR
KENSINGTON
KNIGHTSBRIDGE
BELGRAVIA
BROMPTON
SOUTH KENSINGTON
WEST KENSINGTON
CHELSEA
London Zoo
Lord's Cricket Gd.
Planetarium
Madame Tussaud's
Marylebone
Paddington
Kensington Palace
Serpentine Gallery
Apsley House & Wellington Mus.
Royal Albert Hall
Victoria & Albert Mus.
Science Mus.
Nat. History & Geological Mus.
Olympia
Earl's Court Exhibition Hall
Victoria Coach Sta
Nat. Army Mus.
Chelsea Royal Hosp
Chelsea & Westminster Hosp
Royal Marsden Hosp
Brompton Hosp
Chelsea Bridge

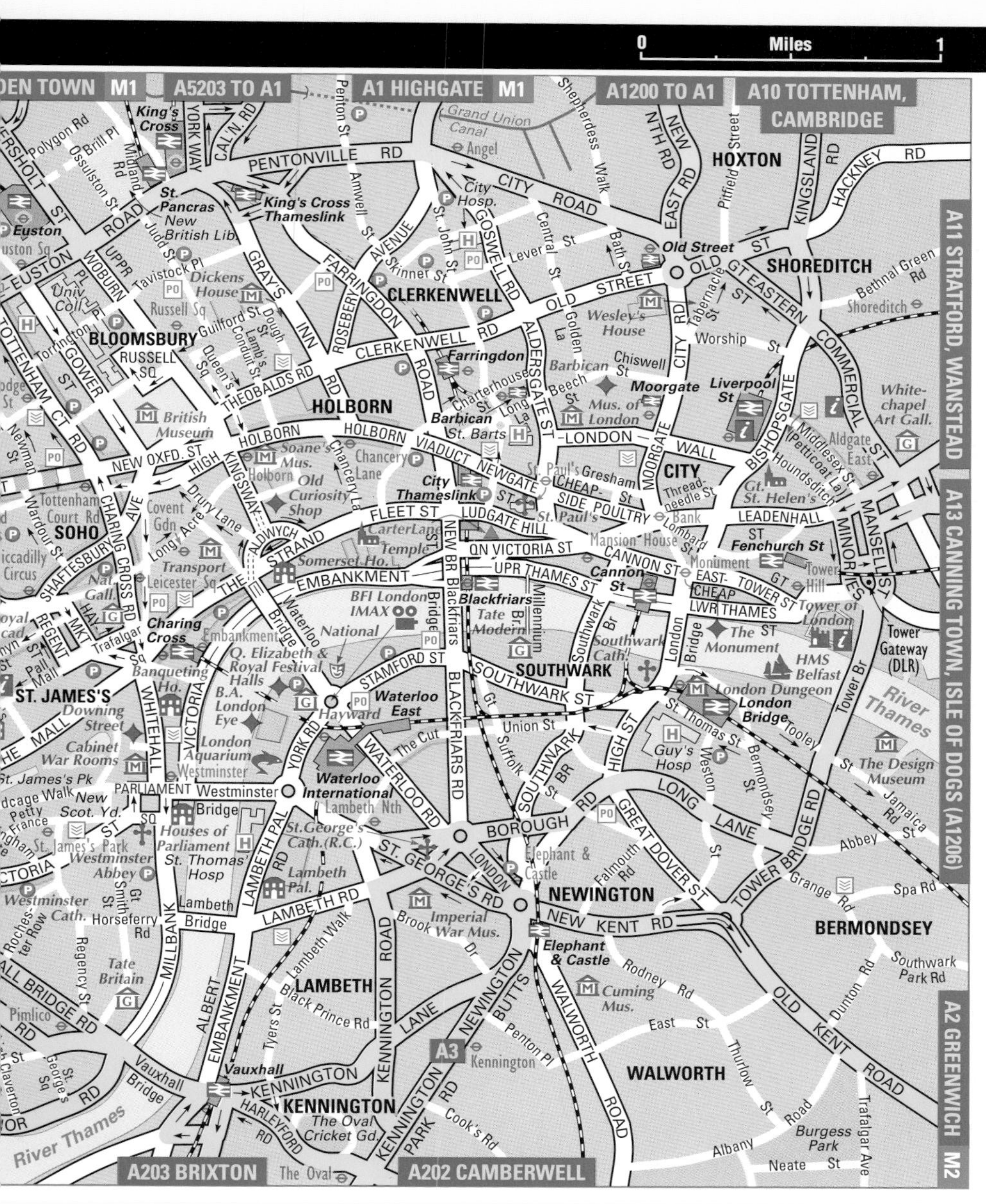
0 Miles 1
DEN TOWN M1
A5203 TO A1
A1 HIGHGATE M1
A1200 TO A1
A10 TOTTENHAM, CAMBRIDGE
A11 STRATFORD, WANSTEAD
A13 CANNING TOWN, ISLE OF DOGS (A1206)
A2 GREENWICH M2
A203 BRIXTON
A202 CAMBERWELL
A3
King's Cross
St. Pancras
New British Lib
King's Cross Thameslink
Euston
Euston Sq
PENTONVILLE RD
Grand Union Canal
Angel
CITY ROAD
City Hosp.
HOXTON
SHOREDITCH
Old Street
OLD STREET
CLERKENWELL
CLERKENWELL RD
Farringdon
BLOOMSBURY
RUSSELL SQ
Dickens House
Univ. Coll
British Museum
HOLBORN
THEOBALDS RD
Barbican
St. Barts
Mus. of London
Moorgate
Liverpool St
Wesley's House
LONDON WALL
CITY
Whitechapel Art Gall.
Aldgate East
NEW OXFD. ST
HIGH HOLBORN
KINGSWAY
Soane's Mus.
Old Curiosity Shop
Chancery Lane
City Thameslink
St. Paul's
CHEAPSIDE
POULTRY
Bank
Mansion House
LEADENHALL ST
Fenchurch St
Gt. St. Helen's
Tottenham Court Rd
SOHO
Covent Gdn
Piccadilly Circus
Transport Museum
Leicester Sq
ALDWYCH
STRAND
FLEET ST
LUDGATE HILL
QN VICTORIA ST
CANNON ST
Cannon St
Monument
Tower Hill
Tower Gateway (DLR)
Somerset Ho.
Temple
EMBANKMENT
UPR THAMES ST
LWR THAMES ST
EAST-CHEAP
Tower of London
Nat. Gall.
Charing Cross
Trafalgar Sq
Embankment
BFI London IMAX
Blackfriars
Tate Modern
Millennium Br
Southwark Cath.
The Monument
HMS Belfast
London Dungeon
London Bridge
River Thames
Tower Br
ST. JAMES'S
THE MALL
Banqueting Ho.
Downing Street
Cabinet War Rooms
Q. Elizabeth & Royal Festival Halls
National
B.A. London Eye
London Aquarium
Hayward
Waterloo East
Waterloo International
SOUTHWARK
SOUTHWARK ST
Union St
The Cut
Guy's Hosp
St Thomas St
Tooley St
The Design Museum
Westminster
PARLIAMENT SQ
New Scot. Yd.
Houses of Parliament
St. Thomas' Hosp
Westminster Abbey
Westminster Cath.
St. James's Park
St. James's Pk
Lambeth Nth
St.George's Cath.(R.C.)
Lambeth Pal.
BOROUGH RD
ST. GEORGE'S RD
Elephant & Castle
NEWINGTON
NEW KENT RD
LONG LANE
GREAT DOVER ST
TOWER BRIDGE RD
BERMONDSEY
Lambeth Bridge
LAMBETH RD
Imperial War Mus.
Cuming Mus.
Tate Britain
LAMBETH
Black Prince Rd
Pimlico
Vauxhall
Vauxhall Bridge
KENNINGTON RD
KENNINGTON
The Oval Cricket Gd.
Kennington
WALWORTH
WALWORTH ROAD
OLD KENT ROAD
Burgess Park
Albany Road
Neate St
Trafalgar Ave
River Thames
The Oval

Aberdeen

0 Miles ¼

Blackpool

0 Miles ¼

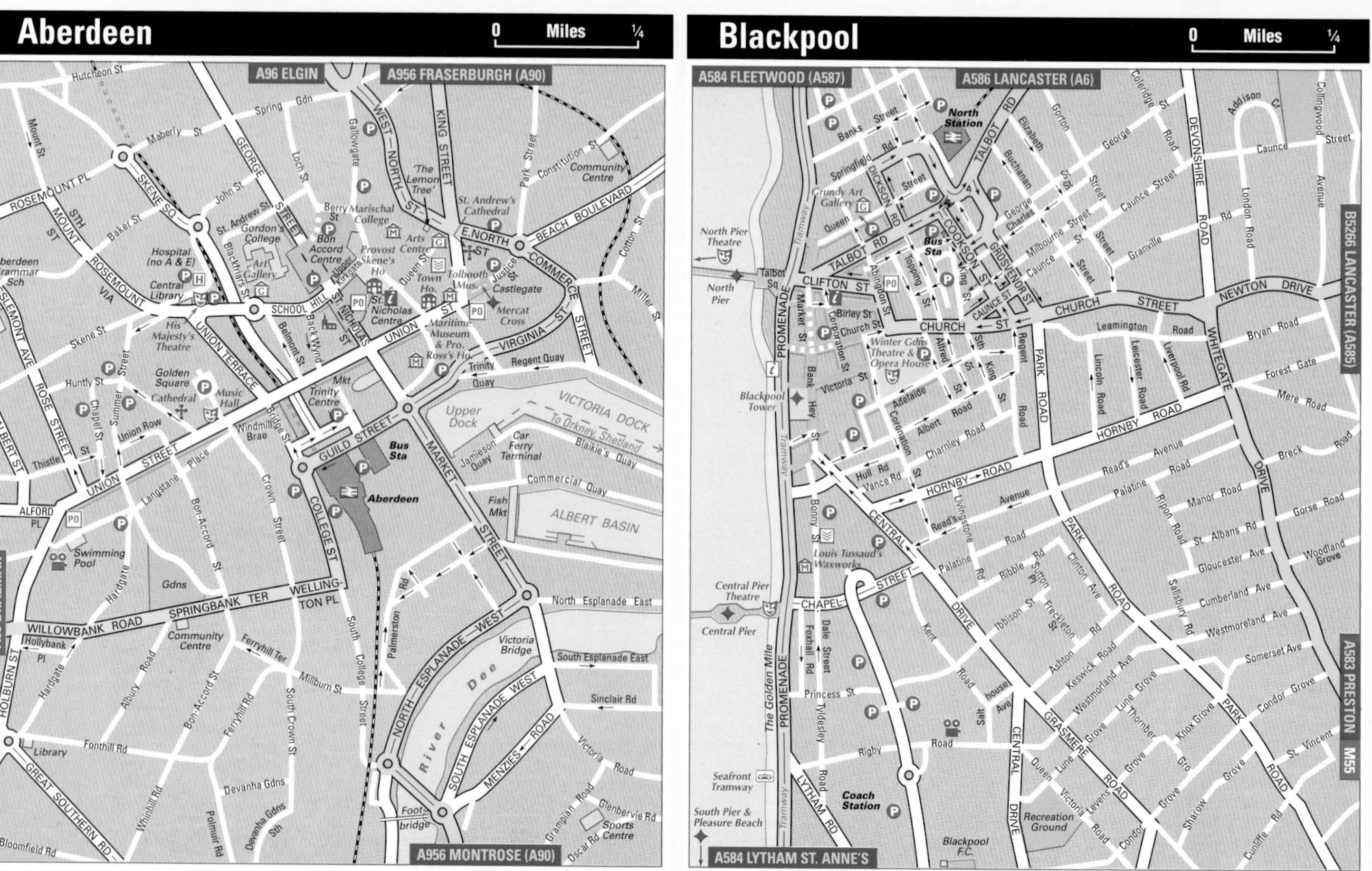
A96 ELGIN
A956 FRASERBURGH (A90)
A93 BRAEMAR
A956 MONTROSE (A90)
Aberdeen Grammar Sch
Hospital (no A & E)
Central Library
His Majesty's Theatre
Golden Square
Cathedral
Music Hall
Gordon's College
Art Gallery
Bon Accord Centre
Berry St
Marischal College
Provost Skene's Ho
Arts Centre
'The Lemon Tree'
St. Andrew's Cathedral
Town Ho.
Tolbooth Mus.
Castlegate
Mercat Cross
St. Nicholas Centre
Maritime Museum & Pro. Ross's Ho.
Trinity Centre
Bus Sta
Aberdeen
Upper Dock
VICTORIA DOCK
To Orkney, Shetland
Car Ferry Terminal
Fish Mkt
ALBERT BASIN
Victoria Bridge
River Dee
Swimming Pool
Gdns
Community Centre
Library
Sports Centre
Footbridge
Community Centre
UNION STREET
GEORGE STREET
KING STREET
WEST NORTH ST
BEACH BOULEVARD
COMMERCE STREET
VIRGINIA ST
MARKET STREET
GUILD STREET
COLLEGE ST
SCHOOL HILL
ROSEMOUNT VIA
ROSEMOUNT PL
SKENE SQ
UNION TERRACE
ROSE STREET
ALBERT ST
ESSLEMONT AVE
WILLOWBANK ROAD
SPRINGBANK TER
WELLINGTON PL
HOLBURN ST
GREAT SOUTHERN RD
NORTH ESPLANADE WEST
SOUTH ESPLANADE WEST
MENZIES ROAD
North Esplanade East
South Esplanade East
A584 FLEETWOOD (A587)
A586 LANCASTER (A6)
B5266 LANCASTER (A585)
A583 PRESTON
M55
A584 LYTHAM ST. ANNE'S
North Station
Bus Sta
Grundy Art Gallery
North Pier Theatre
North Pier
Talbot Sq
Winter Gdns Theatre & Opera House
Blackpool Tower
Louis Tussaud's Waxworks
Central Pier Theatre
Central Pier
The Golden Mile
Seafront Tramway
South Pier & Pleasure Beach
Coach Station
Blackpool F.C.
Recreation Ground
PROMENADE
Tramway
TALBOT RD
DICKSON RD
CLIFTON ST
CHURCH STREET
NEWTON DRIVE
WHITEGATE DRIVE
DEVONSHIRE ROAD
PARK ROAD
HORNBY ROAD
CENTRAL DRIVE
CHAPEL STREET
LYTHAM RD
GRASMERE ROAD
COOKSON ST
GROSVENOR ST
CAUNCE ST

Belfast

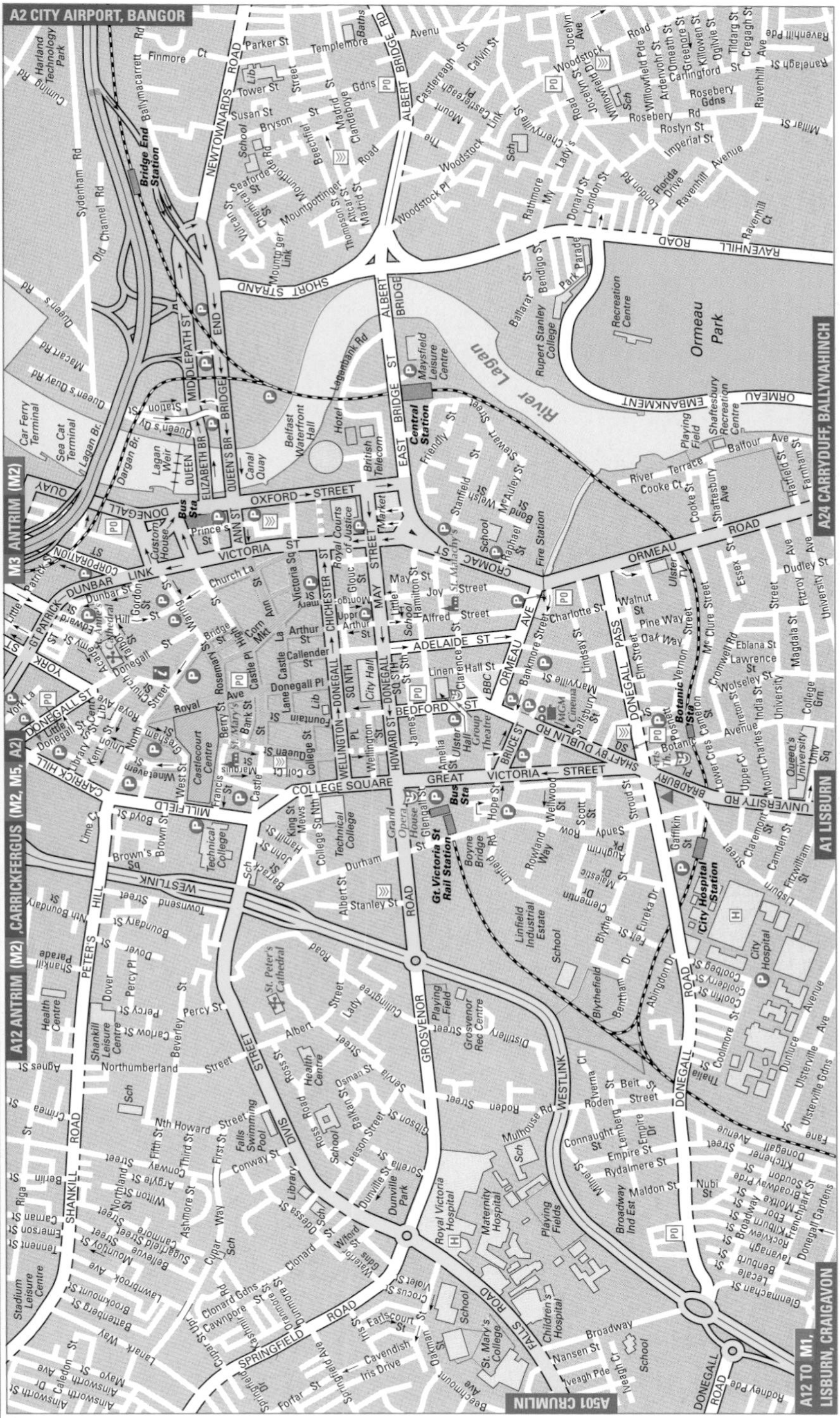
0 Miles 1/4
A2 CITY AIRPORT, BANGOR
A24 CARRYDUFF, BALLYNAHINCH
A1 LISBURN
A12 TO M1, LISBURN, CRAIGAVON
A501 CRUMLIN
A12 ANTRIM (M2), CARRICKFERGUS (M2, M5, A2)
M3 ANTRIM (M2)
Harland Technology Park
Bridge End Station
Central Station
Botanic Sta
City Hospital Station
Gt. Victoria St Rail Station
Bus Sta
River Lagan
Ormeau Park
Recreation Centre
Rupert Stanley College
Mayfield Leisure Centre
Belfast Waterfront Hall
Hotel
British Telecom
Lagan Weir
Car Ferry Terminal
Sea Cat Terminal
Custom House
Royal Courts of Justice
Market
City Hall
Castlecourt Centre
Technical College
Grand Opera House
Ulster Hall
Group Theatre
BBC
MGM Cinema
Queen's University
Ulster TV
Shaftesbury Recreation Centre
Playing Field
Fire Station
Linfield Industrial Estate
City Hospital
St. Peter's Cathedral
St. Anne's Cathedral
Grosvenor Rec Centre
Health Centre
Shankill Leisure Centre
Falls Swimming Pool
Library
Royal Victoria Hospital
Maternity Hospital
Children's Hospital
Playing Fields
St. Mary's College
Stadium Leisure Centre
Broadway Ind Est
Dunville Park
NEWTOWNARDS ROAD
ALBERT BRIDGE RD
SHORT STRAND
RAVENHILL ROAD
ORMEAU EMBANKMENT
EAST BRIDGE ST
QUEEN'S BR
QUEEN ELIZABETH BR
MIDDLEPATH ST
BRIDGE END
DONEGALL QUAY
OXFORD STREET
VICTORIA ST
CORPORATION ST
DUNBAR LINK
YORK ST
ORMEAU ROAD
ORMEAU AVE
CROMAC ST
ADELAIDE ST
BEDFORD ST
GREAT VICTORIA STREET
DUBLIN RD
SHAFTESBURY SQ
BRADBURY PL
UNIVERSITY RD
DONEGALL PASS
DONEGALL ROAD
COLLEGE SQUARE
MILLFIELD
CARRICK HILL
WESTLINK
PETER'S HILL
SHANKILL ROAD
DIVIS STREET
FALLS ROAD
SPRINGFIELD ROAD
GROSVENOR ROAD
LISBURN ROAD
Broadway
Donegall Pl
Chichester St
May Street
Royal Ave
Castle St
Wellington Pl
Howard St
Botanic Ave
Lisburn Rd

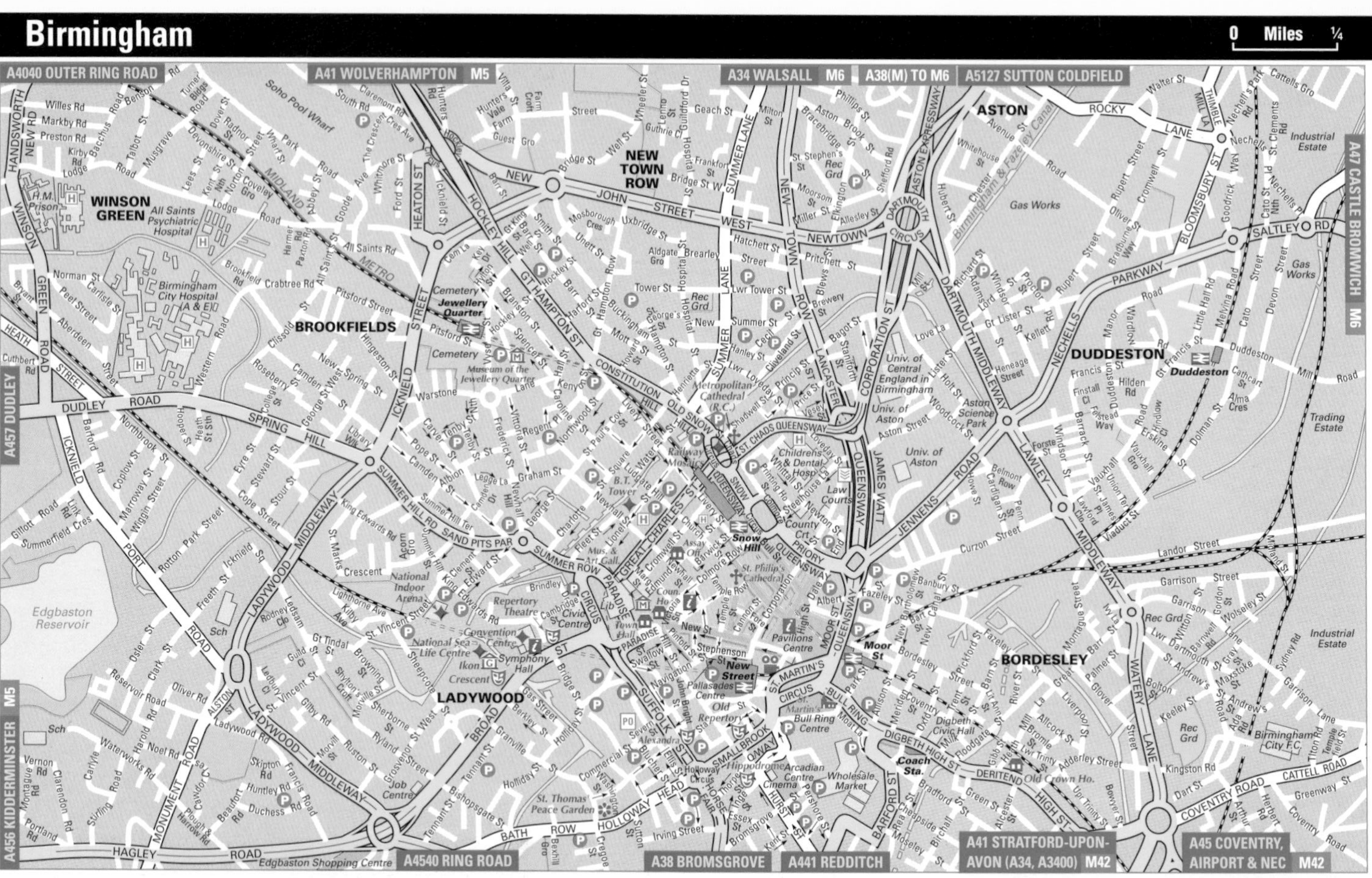
Birmingham
0 Miles ¼
A4040 OUTER RING ROAD
A41 WOLVERHAMPTON M5
A34 WALSALL M6
A38(M) TO M6
A5127 SUTTON COLDFIELD
A47 CASTLE BROMWICH M6
A45 COVENTRY, AIRPORT & NEC M42
A41 STRATFORD-UPON-AVON (A34, A3400) M42
A441 REDDITCH
A38 BROMSGROVE
A4540 RING ROAD
A456 KIDDERMINSTER M5
A457 DUDLEY
ASTON
NEW TOWN ROW
WINSON GREEN
BROOKFIELDS
DUDDESTON
BORDESLEY
LADYWOOD
H.M. Prison
All Saints Psychiatric Hospital
Birmingham City Hospital (A & E)
Jewellery Quarter
Museum of the Jewellery Quarter
Metropolitan Cathedral (R.C.)
Univ. of Central England in Birmingham
Univ. of Aston
Aston Science Park
Gas Works
Trading Estate
Industrial Estate
Snow Hill
St. Philip's Cathedral
New Street
Moor St
Pallasades Centre
Pavilions Centre
Bull Ring Centre
Coach Sta.
Wholesale Market
Arcadian Centre
Hippodrome
National Indoor Arena
National Sea Life Centre
Convention Centre
Symphony Hall
Repertory Theatre
Civic Centre
Mus. & Art Gall.
B.T. Tower
Ikon Crescent
St. Thomas' Peace Garden
Edgbaston Reservoir
Birmingham City F.C.
Edgbaston Shopping Centre
Soho Pool Wharf
Birmingham & Fazeley Canal
CORPORATION ST
JAMES WATT QUEENSWAY
DARTMOUTH MIDDLEWAY
LAWLEY MIDDLEWAY
LADYWOOD MIDDLEWAY
HAGLEY ROAD
BROAD ST
SUMMER ROW
DIGBETH HIGH ST
COVENTRY ROAD
DUDLEY ROAD
SPRING HILL
NEWTOWN ROW
GREAT HAMPTON ST
HOCKLEY HILL

Bristol

0 Miles ¼

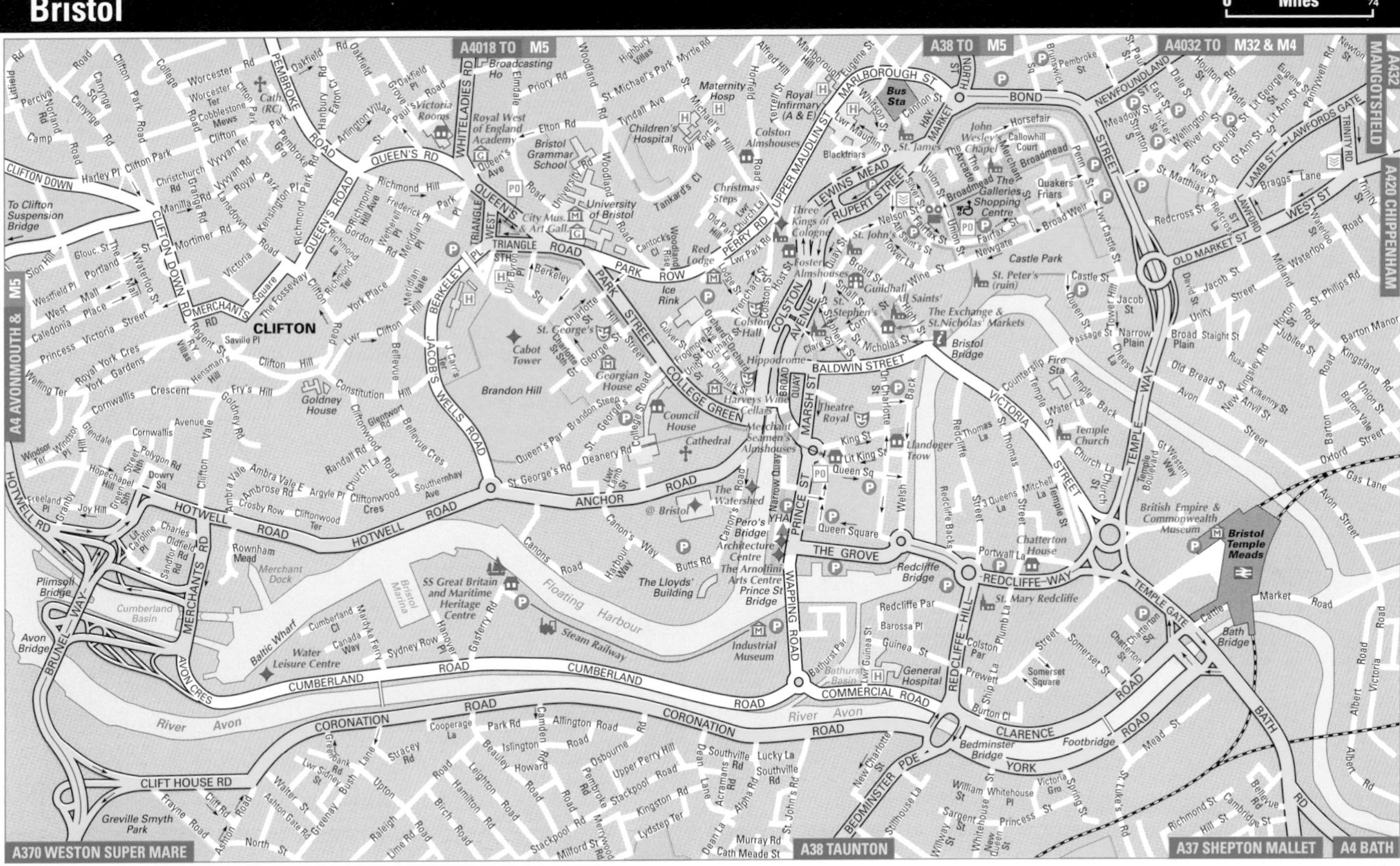

A4018 TO M5
A38 TO M5
A4032 TO M32 & M4
A432 MANGOTSFIELD
A420 CHIPPENHAM
A4 AVONMOUTH & M5
A370 WESTON SUPER MARE
A38 TAUNTON
A37 SHEPTON MALLET
A4 BATH
To Clifton Suspension Bridge
CLIFTON DOWN
CLIFTON DOWN RD
CLIFTON
PEMBROKE ROAD
QUEEN'S RD
QUEEN'S ROAD
WHITELADIES RD
Victoria Rooms
Royal West of England Academy
Bristol Grammar School
University of Bristol
City Mus. & Art Gall.
Children's Hospital
Maternity Hosp
Royal Infirmary (A & E)
Colston Almshouses
Christmas Steps
Bus Sta
MARLBOROUGH ST
UPPER MAUDLIN ST
BOND STREET
NEWFOUNDLAND ST
John Wesley's Chapel
The Arcade
Broadmead
The Galleries Shopping Centre
Castle Park
St. Peter's (ruin)
OLD MARKET ST
WEST ST
LAWFORD ST
LAMB ST
LAWFORDS GATE
TRINITY RD
PARK ROW
PARK STREET
Ice Rink
Red Lodge
Three Kings of Cologne
Foster Almshouses
Guildhall
All Saints'
The Exchange & St.Nicholas' Markets
Bristol Bridge
COLSTON AVENUE
Colston Hall
Hippodrome
BALDWIN STREET
BROAD QUAY
MARSH ST
Theatre Royal
Llandoger Trow
Harveys Wine Cellars
Merchant Seamen's Almshouses
COLLEGE GREEN
Council House
Cathedral
Georgian House
Cabot Tower
Brandon Hill
JACOB'S WELLS ROAD
BERKELEY PL
Goldney House
HOTWELL ROAD
ANCHOR ROAD
The Watershed
@ Bristol
Pero's Bridge
Architecture Centre
The Arnolfini Arts Centre
Prince St Bridge
Queen Square
PRINCE ST
THE GROVE
WAPPING ROAD
The Lloyds' Building
Floating Harbour
Steam Railway
Industrial Museum
SS Great Britain and Maritime Heritage Centre
Bristol Marina
Merchant Dock
Water Leisure Centre
Baltic Wharf
Cumberland Basin
Plimsoll Bridge
Avon Bridge
BRUNEL WAY
MERCHANTS RD
AVON CRES
CUMBERLAND ROAD
River Avon
CORONATION ROAD
CLIFT HOUSE RD
Greville Smyth Park
VICTORIA STREET
Temple Church
TEMPLE WAY
British Empire & Commonwealth Museum
Bristol Temple Meads
TEMPLE GATE
Bath Bridge
BATH RD
REDCLIFFE WAY
REDCLIFFE HILL
St. Mary Redcliffe
Chatterton House
Redcliffe Bridge
General Hospital
COMMERCIAL ROAD
CLARENCE ROAD
YORK ROAD
Bedminster Bridge
BEDMINSTER PDE
Footbridge

Bournemouth

0 Miles ¼

Bradford

0 Miles ¼

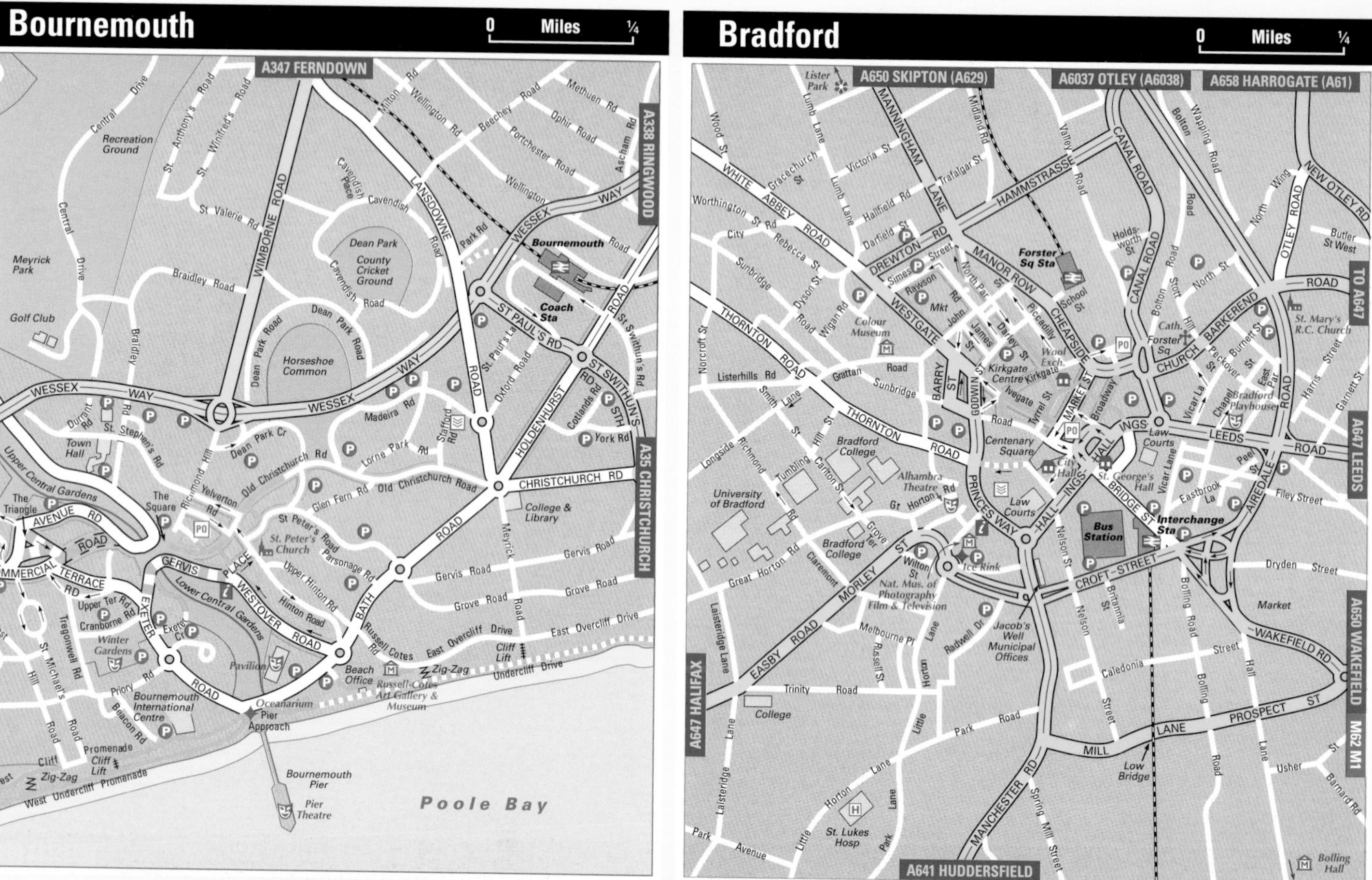
A347 FERNDOWN
A338 RINGWOOD
A35 CHRISTCHURCH
A35 POOLE
Recreation Ground
Meyrick Park
Golf Club
Dean Park County Cricket Ground
Horseshoe Common
Bournemouth
Coach Sta
WESSEX WAY
WIMBORNE ROAD
LANSDOWNE ROAD
ST PAUL'S RD
ST SWITHUN'S RD STH
HOLDENHURST RD
CHRISTCHURCH RD
Old Christchurch Road
BATH ROAD
WESTOVER ROAD
GERVIS PLACE
EXETER ROAD
COMMERCIAL RD
AVENUE RD
TERRACE RD
Town Hall
The Triangle
The Square
Upper Central Gardens
Lower Central Gardens
St. Peter's Church
College & Library
Pavilion
Winter Gardens
Bournemouth International Centre
Beach Office
Russell-Cotes Art Gallery & Museum
Oceanarium
Pier Approach
Bournemouth Pier
Pier Theatre
East Overcliff Drive
Undercliff Drive
West Undercliff Promenade
Cliff Lift
Zig-Zag
Poole Bay
A650 SKIPTON (A629)
A6037 OTLEY (A6038)
A658 HARROGATE (A61)
TO A647
A647 LEEDS
A650 WAKEFIELD
M62 M1
A641 HUDDERSFIELD
A647 HALIFAX
Lister Park
MANNINGHAM LANE
WHITE ABBEY ROAD
THORNTON ROAD
WESTGATE
MANOR ROW
CHEAPSIDE
HAMMSTRASSE
CANAL ROAD
OTLEY ROAD
BARKEREND ROAD
CHURCH BANK
LEEDS ROAD
AIREDALE
WAKEFIELD RD
PROSPECT ST
MILL LANE
MANCHESTER RD
CROFT STREET
BRIDGE ST
HALL INGS
PRINCES WAY
MORLEY ST
EASBY ROAD
Forster Sq Sta
Interchange Sta
Bus Station
Colour Museum
Kirkgate Centre
Wool Exch.
Cath.
Forster Sq
St. Mary's R.C. Church
Bradford Playhouse
Law Courts
City Hall
Centenary Square
St. George's Hall
Alhambra Theatre
Ice Rink
Nat. Mus. of Photography Film & Television
Jacob's Well Municipal Offices
Bradford College
University of Bradford
College
St. Lukes Hosp
Low Bridge
Bolling Hall

Brighton

0 Miles ¼

Cambridge

0 Miles ¼

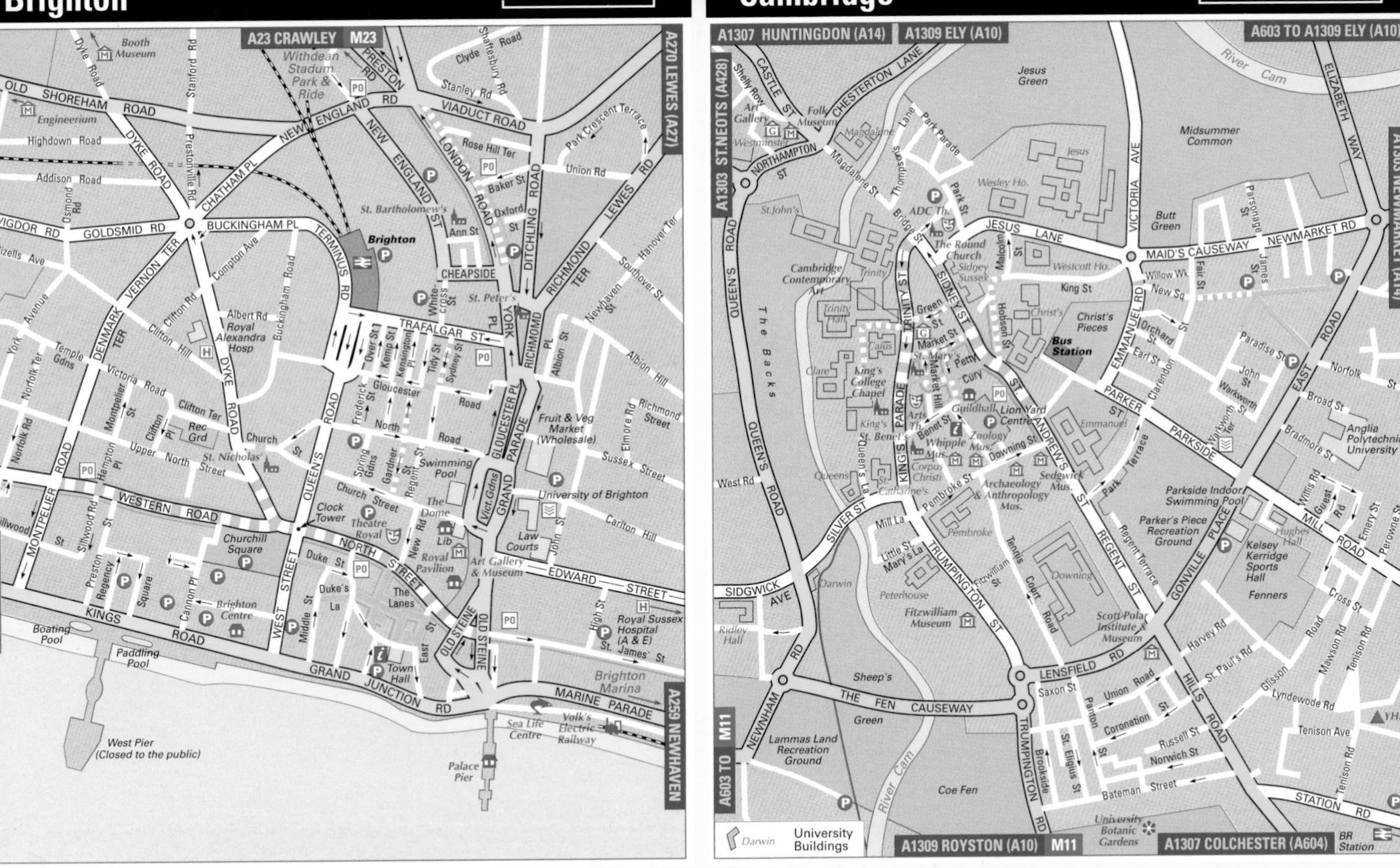
A23 CRAWLEY M23
A270 LEWES (A27)
A270 WORTHING (A27)
A259 WORTHING
A259 NEWHAVEN
Booth Museum
Engineerium
Withdean Stadum Park & Ride
OLD SHOREHAM ROAD
DYKE ROAD
NEW ENGLAND RD
VIADUCT ROAD
PRESTON RD
LONDON ROAD
DITCHLING ROAD
LEWES RD
RICHMOND TER
BUCKINGHAM PL
TERMINUS RD
CHATHAM PL
GOLDSMID RD
DAVIGDOR RD
VERNON TER
DENMARK TER
Brighton
St. Bartholomew's
CHEAPSIDE
St. Peter's
TRAFALGAR ST
YORK PL
GLOUCESTER PL
GRAND PARADE
Fruit & Veg Market (Wholesale)
University of Brighton
Royal Alexandra Hosp
QUEEN'S ROAD
WESTERN ROAD
MONTPELIER ROAD
Clock Tower
Theatre Royal
NORTH STREET
The Dome
Royal Pavilion
Art Gallery & Museum
EDWARD STREET
Law Courts
Royal Sussex Hospital (A & E)
Churchill Square
Brighton Centre
The Lanes
Town Hall
OLD STEINE
KINGS ROAD
GRAND JUNCTION RD
MARINE PARADE
Brighton Marina
Sea Life Centre
Volk's Electric Railway
Palace Pier
West Pier (Closed to the public)
Boating Pool
Paddling Pool
A1307 HUNTINGDON (A14)
A1309 ELY (A10)
A603 TO A1309 ELY (A10)
A1303 ST.NEOTS (A428)
A1303 NEWMARKET (A14)
A603 TO M11
A1309 ROYSTON (A10) M11
A1307 COLCHESTER (A604)
BR Station
Jesus Green
Midsummer Common
River Cam
Butt Green
CHESTERTON LANE
CASTLE ST
NORTHAMPTON ST
Magdalene St
JESUS LANE
MAID'S CAUSEWAY
NEWMARKET RD
VICTORIA AVE
ELIZABETH WAY
EMMANUEL RD
EAST ROAD
PARKER ST
PARKSIDE
MILL ROAD
Christ's Pieces
Bus Station
The Round Church
Trinity
King's College Chapel
Cambridge Contemporary Art
The Backs
QUEEN'S ROAD
TRINITY ST
SIDNEY ST
KING'S PARADE
ST ANDREW'S ST
REGENT ST
Guildhall
Lion Yard Centre
Archaeology & Anthropology Mus.
Sedgwick Mus.
Zoology Mus.
Whipple Mus.
Parkside Indoor Swimming Pool
Parker's Piece Recreation Ground
GONVILLE PLACE
Kelsey Kerridge Sports Hall
Fenners
Anglia Polytechnic University
Downing
Pembroke
Peterhouse
Fitzwilliam Museum
TRUMPINGTON ST
SILVER ST
SIDGWICK AVE
Scott Polar Institute & Museum
LENSFIELD RD
HILLS ROAD
STATION RD
Sheep's Green
THE FEN CAUSEWAY
NEWNHAM RD
Lammas Land Recreation Ground
Coe Fen
TRUMPINGTON RD
University Botanic Gardens
YHA
Darwin University Buildings

Cardiff

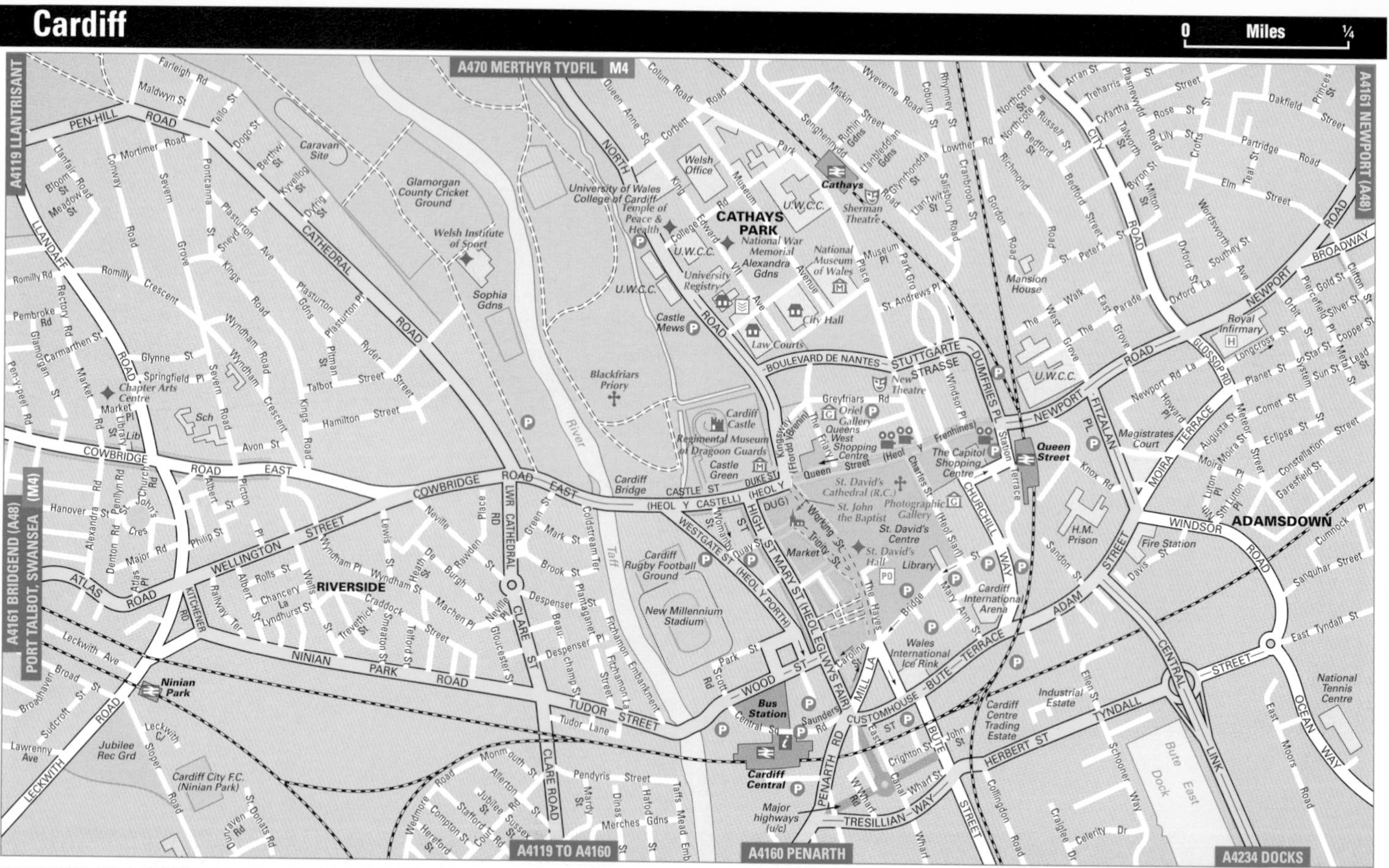
0 Miles 1/4
A470 MERTHYR TYDFIL M4
A4161 NEWPORT (A48)
A4119 LLANTRISANT
A4161 BRIDGEND (A48)
PORT TALBOT, SWANSEA (M4)
A4119 TO A4160
A4160 PENARTH
A4234 DOCKS
ADAMSDOWN
CATHAYS PARK
RIVERSIDE
Cathays
Queen Street
Cardiff Central
Ninian Park
Bus Station
Royal Infirmary
H.M. Prison
Magistrates Court
Fire Station
National Tennis Centre
Bute East Dock
Industrial Estate
Cardiff Centre Trading Estate
Cardiff International Arena
Wales International Ice Rink
St. David's Centre
St. David's Hall
Library
Market
The Capitol Shopping Centre
Photographic Gallery
St. David's Cathedral (R.C.)
St. John the Baptist
Queens West Shopping Centre
Oriel Gallery
New Theatre
Sherman Theatre
National Museum of Wales
City Hall
Law Courts
National War Memorial
Alexandra Gdns
University Registry
U.W.C.C.
Welsh Office
Temple of Peace & Health
University of Wales College of Cardiff
Castle Mews
Cardiff Castle
Regimental Museum of Dragoon Guards
Castle Green
Blackfriars Priory
Cardiff Bridge
Cardiff Rugby Football Ground
New Millennium Stadium
River Taff
Sophia Gdns
Welsh Institute of Sport
Glamorgan County Cricket Ground
Caravan Site
Mansion House
Chapter Arts Centre
Sch
Cardiff City F.C. (Ninian Park)
Jubilee Rec Grd
Major highways (u/c)
PEN-HILL ROAD
LLANDAFF ROAD
CATHEDRAL ROAD
NORTH ROAD
CITY ROAD
NEWPORT ROAD
BROADWAY
GLOSSOP RD
MOIRA TERRACE
FITZALAN PL
WINDSOR ROAD
ADAM STREET
CENTRAL LINK
OCEAN WAY
TYNDALL STREET
HERBERT ST
BUTE TERRACE
BUTE STREET
CUSTOMHOUSE ST
MILL LA
TRESILLIAN WAY
PENARTH RD
WOOD ST
ST MARY ST (HEOL EGLWYS FAIR)
WESTGATE ST (HEOL Y PORTH)
CASTLE ST (HEOL Y CASTELL)
HIGH ST (HEOL Y DUG)
DUKE ST
BOULEVARD DE NANTES
STUTTGARTER STRASSE
DUMFRIES PL
CHURCHILL WAY
COWBRIDGE ROAD EAST
LWR CATHEDRAL RD
CLARE ST
CLARE ROAD
WELLINGTON STREET
NINIAN PARK ROAD
TUDOR STREET
KITCHENER RD
ATLAS ROAD
LECKWITH ROAD

Coventry

0 Miles ¼

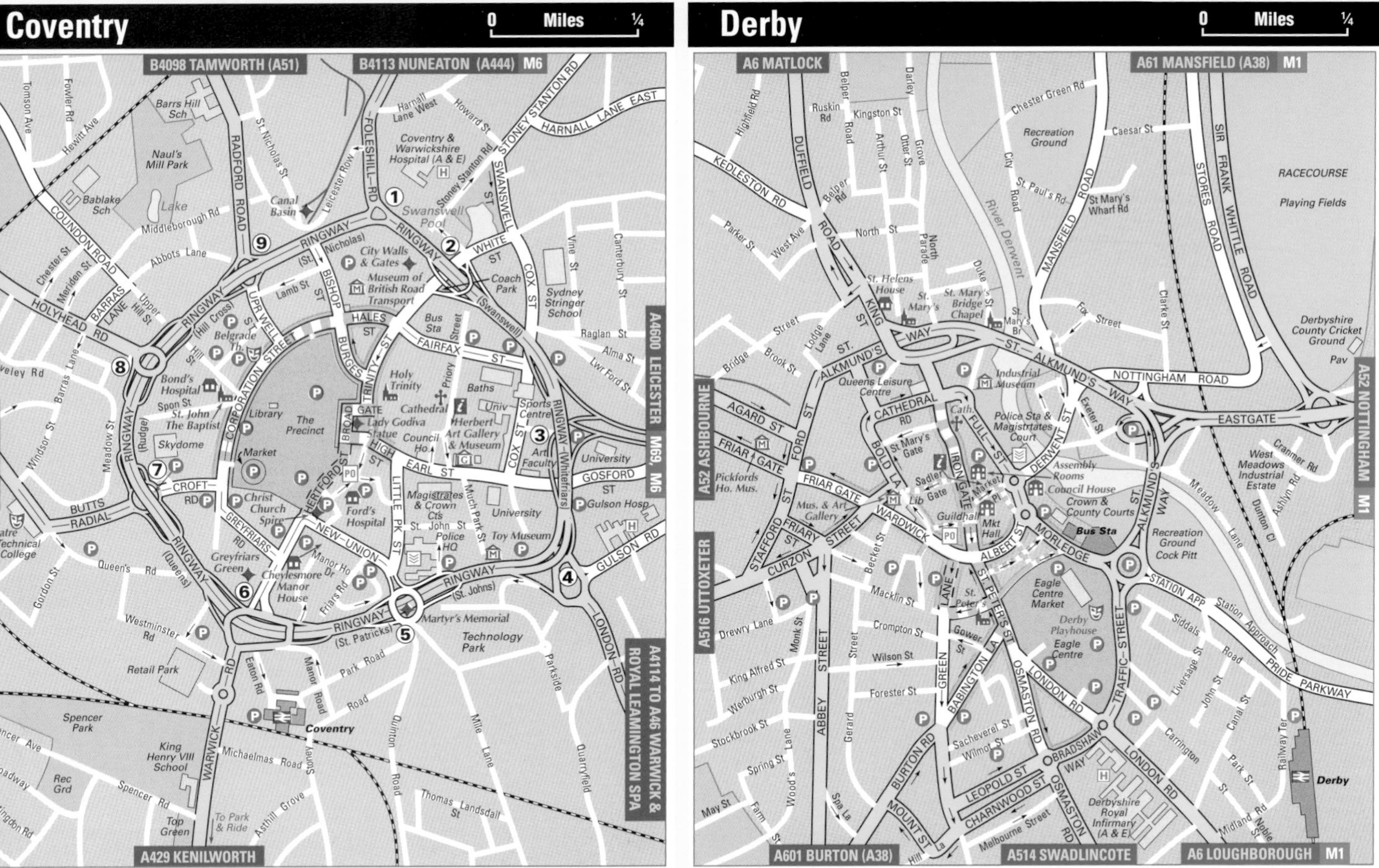
B4098 TAMWORTH (A51)
B4113 NUNEATON (A444) M6
A4600 LEICESTER M69, M6
A4114 TO A46 WARWICK & ROYAL LEAMINGTON SPA
A429 KENILWORTH
B4101 KNOWLE
A4114 BIRMINGHAM (A45) M42
RINGWAY
(St. Nicholas)
(Swanswell)
(Whitefriars)
(St. Johns)
(St. Patricks)
(Queens)
(Rudge)
(Hill Cross)
Coventry & Warwickshire Hospital (A & E)
Swanswell Pool
Canal Basin
City Walls & Gates
Museum of British Road Transport
Coach Park
Sydney Stringer School
Bus Sta
Holy Trinity
Cathedral
Herbert Art Gallery & Museum
Lady Godiva Statue
Council Ho
The Precinct
Library
Market
Belgrade Th.
Bond's Hospital
St. John The Baptist
Skydome
Christ Church Spire
Ford's Hospital
Magistrates & Crown Cts
Police HQ
University
Toy Museum
Sports Centre
Art Faculty
Gulson Hosp
Greyfriars Green
Cheylesmore Manor House
Martyr's Memorial
Technology Park
Retail Park
Coventry
Spencer Park
King Henry VIII School
Rec Grd
Theatre Technical College
Naul's Mill Park
Barrs Hill Sch
Bablake Sch
To Park & Ride
1
2
3
4
5
6
7
8
9

Derby

0 Miles ¼

A6 MATLOCK
A61 MANSFIELD (A38) M1
A52 NOTTINGHAM M1
A6 LOUGHBOROUGH M1
A514 SWADLINCOTE
A601 BURTON (A38)
A516 UTTOXETER
A52 ASHBOURNE
RACECOURSE
Playing Fields
Derbyshire County Cricket Ground
Pav
SIR FRANK WHITTLE ROAD
STORES ROAD
NOTTINGHAM ROAD
EASTGATE
ST. ALKMUND'S WAY
River Derwent
Recreation Ground
West Meadows Industrial Estate
St. Helens House
St. Mary's
St. Mary's Bridge Chapel
Industrial Museum
Queens Leisure Centre
Cath.
Police Sta & Magistrates Court
Assembly Rooms
Council House
Crown & County Courts
Bus Sta
Guildhall
Mkt Hall
Pickfords Ho. Mus.
Mus. & Art Gallery
Recreation Ground Cock Pitt
Eagle Centre Market
Derby Playhouse
Eagle Centre
St. Peter's
Derbyshire Royal Infirmary (A & E)
Derby

Dublin

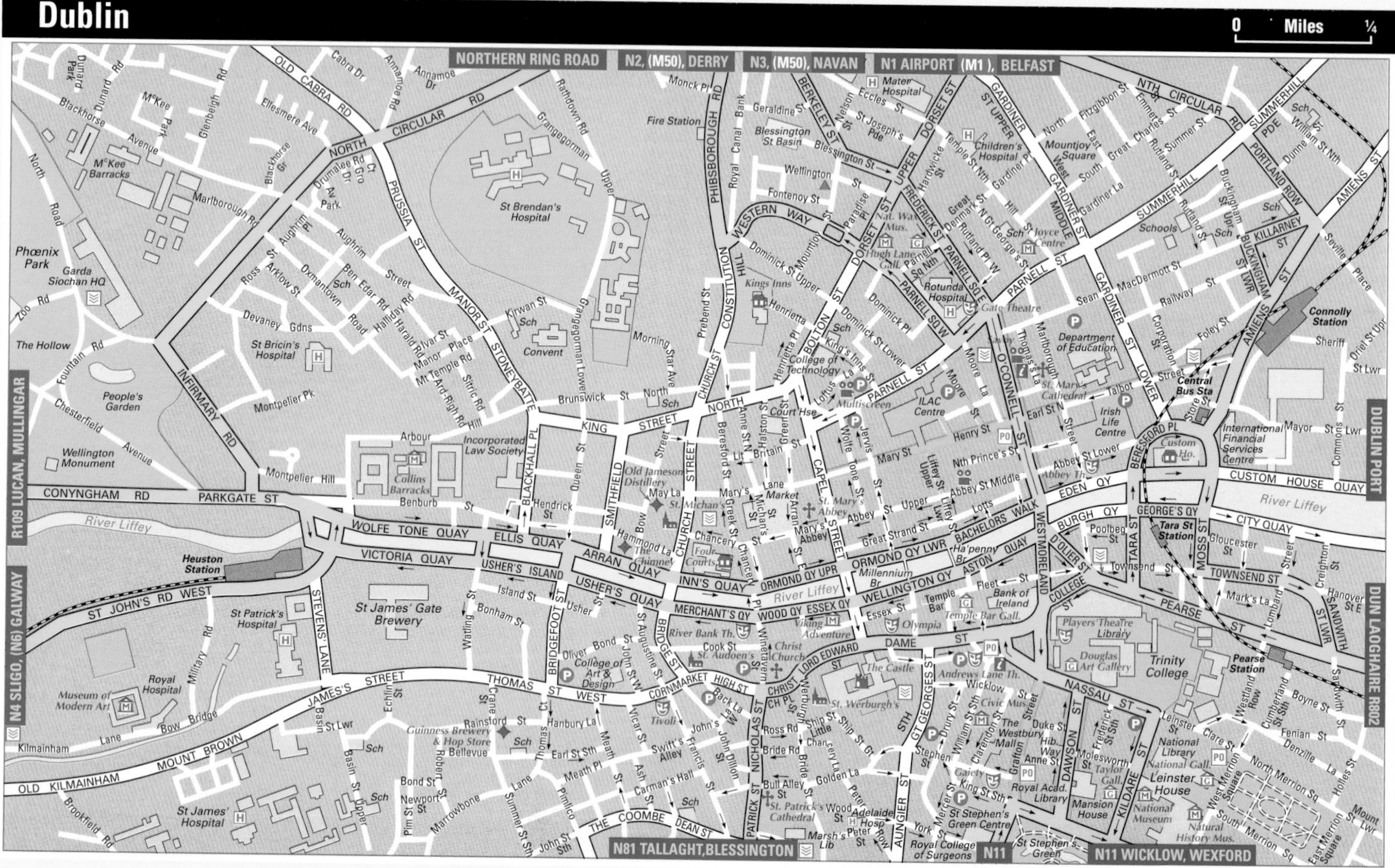

0 Miles ¼
NORTHERN RING ROAD
N2, (M50), DERRY
N3, (M50), NAVAN
N1 AIRPORT (M1), BELFAST
DUBLIN PORT
DUN LAOGHAIRE R802
N11 WICKLOW, WEXFORD
N11
N81 TALLAGHT,BLESSINGTON
N4 SLIGO, (N6) GALWAY
R109 LUCAN, MULLINGAR
River Liffey
Connolly Station
Tara St Station
Pearse Station
Heuston Station
Central Bus Sta
Custom Ho.
International Financial Services Centre
Trinity College
Players' Theatre Library
Douglas Art Gallery
Leinster House
National Gall.
National Library
National Museum
Natural History Mus.
Mansion House
Royal Acad. Library
St Stephen's Green
St Stephen's Green Centre
Royal College of Surgeons
The Castle
Christ Church
St. Werburgh's
St. Patrick's Cathedral
Marsh's Lib
Four Courts
Old Jameson Distillery
St James' Gate Brewery
Guinness Brewery & Hop Store
Royal Hospital
Museum of Modern Art
St James' Hospital
St Patrick's Hospital
St Bricin's Hospital
St Brendan's Hospital
Collins Barracks
McKee Barracks
Phœnix Park
Garda Siochan HQ
Wellington Monument
People's Garden
Mater Hospital
Rotunda Hospital
Children's Hospital
Gate Theatre
ILAC Centre
Irish Life Centre
Department of Education
Kings Inns
College of Technology
Incorporated Law Society
College of Art & Design
Bank of Ireland
Temple Bar Gall.
Olympia
O'CONNELL ST
WESTMORELAND
DAME ST
PARNELL ST
GARDINER ST
DORSET ST
CAPEL STREET
CHURCH STREET
THOMAS ST WEST
JAMES'S STREET
CONSTITUTION HILL
PHIBSBOROUGH RD
NTH CIRCULAR RD
CONYNGHAM RD
PARKGATE ST
INFIRMARY RD
ST JOHN'S RD WEST
MOUNT BROWN
OLD KILMAINHAM
WOLFE TONE QUAY
VICTORIA QUAY
CUSTOM HOUSE QUAY
CITY QUAY
PEARSE ST
NASSAU ST
KILDARE ST
DAWSON ST
AUNGIER ST
PATRICK ST
THE COOMBE

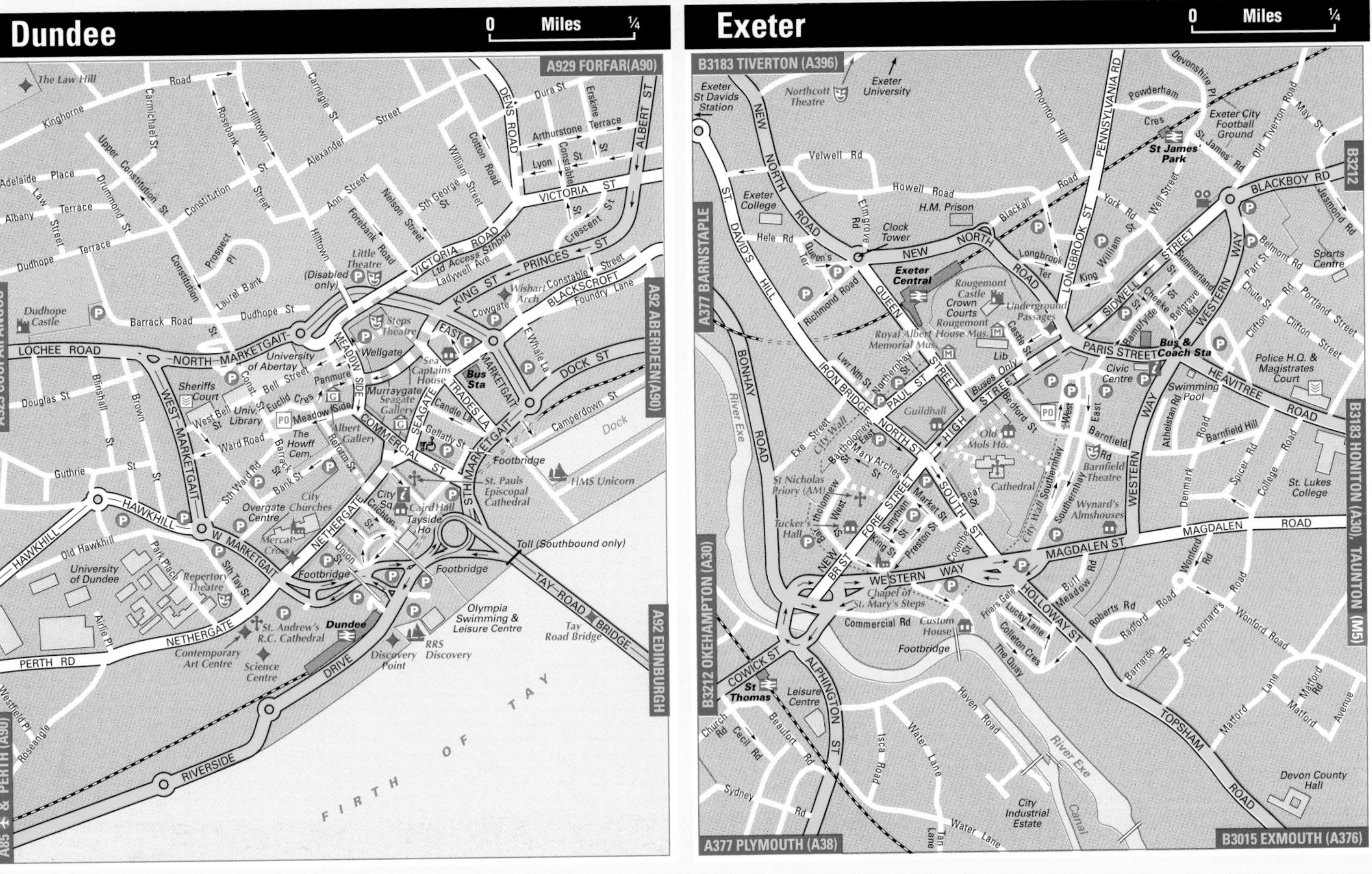

Dundee
0 Miles ¼
A929 FORFAR(A90)
A92 ABERDEEN(A90)
A92 EDINBURGH
A85 & PERTH (A90)
A923 COUPAR ANGUS
The Law Hill
Dudhope Castle
LOCHEE ROAD
NORTH MARKETGAIT
WEST MARKETGAIT
VICTORIA ROAD
PRINCES ST
KING ST
DOCK ST
HAWKHILL
PERTH RD
NETHERGATE
RIVERSIDE DRIVE
TAY ROAD BRIDGE
Toll (Southbound only)
University of Abertay
Sheriffs Court
Univ. Library
Little Theatre
Steps Theatre
Wellgate
Sea Captains House
Bus Sta
Murraygate Seagate Gallery
The Howff Cem.
Albert Gallery
Overgate Centre
City Churches
Mercat Cross
City Sq
Caird Hall
Tayside Ho
St. Pauls Episcopal Cathedral
HMS Unicorn
Dock
Olympia Swimming & Leisure Centre
RRS Discovery
Discovery Point
Dundee
St. Andrew's R.C. Cathedral
Science Centre
Contemporary Art Centre
Repertory Theatre
University of Dundee
Wishart Arch
FIRTH OF TAY
Exeter
0 Miles ¼
B3183 TIVERTON (A396)
B3212
B3183 HONITON (A30), TAUNTON (M5)
B3015 EXMOUTH (A376)
A377 PLYMOUTH (A38)
B3212 OKEHAMPTON (A30)
A377 BARNSTAPLE
Exeter St Davids Station
Exeter University
Northcott Theatre
Exeter College
H.M. Prison
Clock Tower
Exeter Central
Rougemont Castle
Crown Courts
Rougemont House Mus.
Royal Albert Memorial Mus.
Underground Passages
Lib
Guildhall
Old Mols Ho.
Cathedral
St Nicholas Priory (AM)
Tucker's Hall
Chapel of St. Mary's Steps
Custom House
Footbridge
St Thomas
Leisure Centre
City Industrial Estate
River Exe
Canal
Civic Centre
Bus & Coach Sta
Swimming Pool
Barnfield Theatre
Wynard's Almshouses
Police H.Q. & Magistrates Court
St. Lukes College
Sports Centre
Exeter City Football Ground
St James' Park
Devon County Hall
NEW NORTH ROAD
QUEEN ST
HIGH STREET
FORE STREET
SOUTH ST
PARIS STREET
SIDWELL STREET
WESTERN WAY
HEAVITREE ROAD
MAGDALEN ROAD
MAGDALEN ST
HOLLOWAY ST
TOPSHAM ROAD
ALPHINGTON ST
COWICK ST
BONHAY ROAD
ST. DAVID'S HILL
IRON BRIDGE
BLACKBOY RD
LONGBROOK ST
PENNSYLVANIA RD

Edinburgh

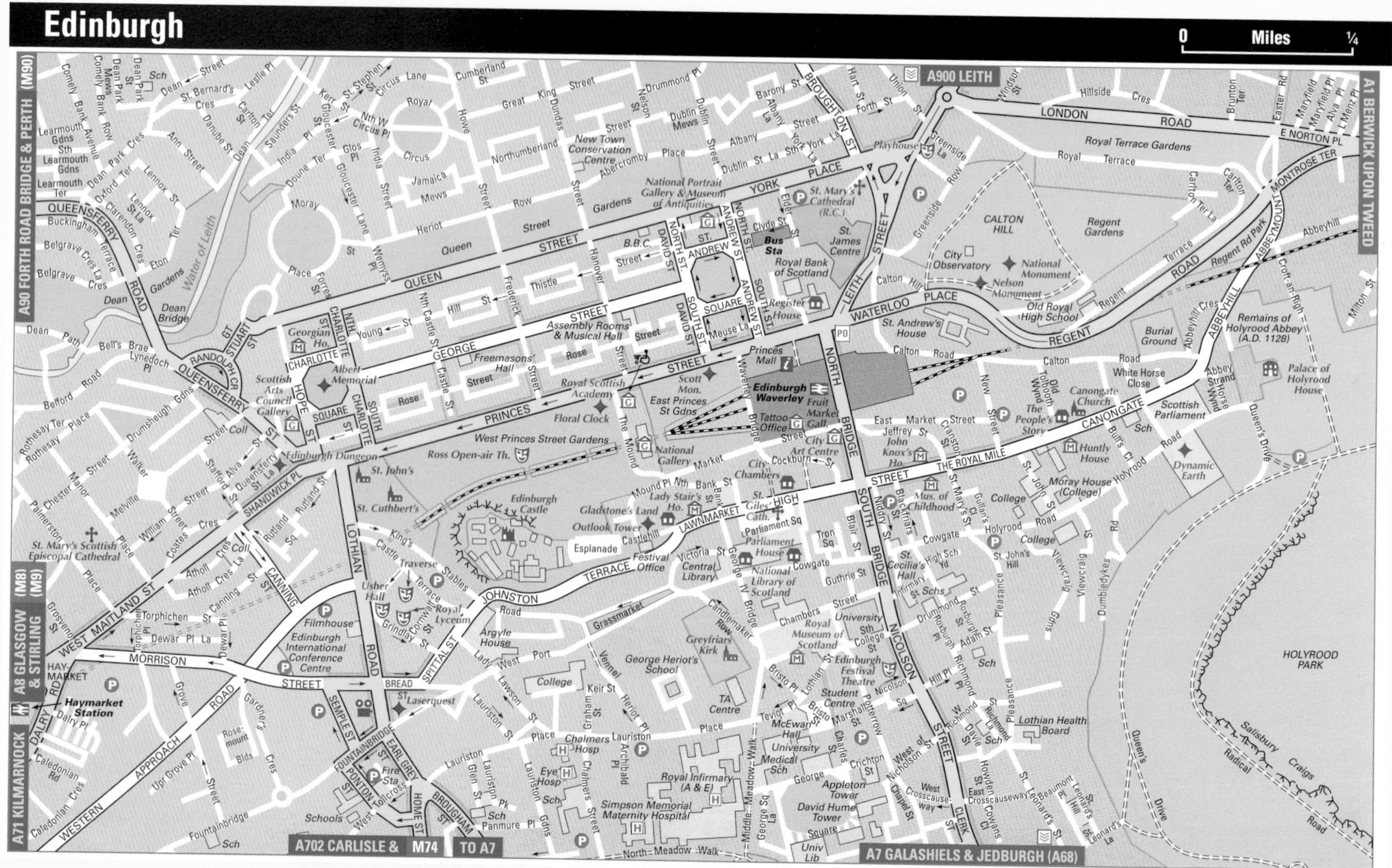
0 Miles ¼
A900 LEITH
A1 BERWICK UPON TWEED
A90 FORTH ROAD BRIDGE & PERTH (M90)
A8 GLASGOW & STIRLING (M8) (M9)
A71 KILMARNOCK
A702 CARLISLE & M74
TO A7
A7 GALASHIELS & JEDBURGH (A68)
CALTON HILL
Regent Gardens
Royal Terrace Gardens
City Observatory
National Monument
Nelson Monument
Old Royal High School
St. Andrew's House
St. Mary's Cathedral (R.C.)
St. James Centre
Bus Sta
Royal Bank of Scotland
Register House
National Portrait Gallery & Museum of Antiquities
New Town Conservation Centre
Playhouse
Edinburgh Waverley
Princes Mall
Fruit Market Gall.
Tattoo Office
City Art Centre
Scott Mon.
East Princes St Gdns
Royal Scottish Academy
Floral Clock
National Gallery
West Princes Street Gardens
Ross Open-air Th.
Assembly Rooms & Musical Hall
Freemasons' Hall
B.B.C.
Georgian Ho.
Albert Memorial
Scottish Arts Council Gallery
Edinburgh Dungeon
St. John's
St. Cuthbert's
Edinburgh Castle
Esplanade
Gladstone's Land
Outlook Tower
Lady Stair's Ho.
St. Giles' Cath.
City Chambers
Parliament House
National Library of Scotland
Central Library
Festival Office
Greyfriars Kirk
George Heriot's School
Royal Museum of Scotland
Edinburgh Festival Theatre
Student Centre
McEwan Hall
University Medical Sch
Royal Infirmary (A & E)
Simpson Memorial Maternity Hospital
Appleton Tower
David Hume Tower
Univ Lib
John Knox's Ho.
Mus. of Childhood
Moray House (College)
Huntly House
The People's Story
Canongate Church
Scottish Parliament
Dynamic Earth
Burial Ground
Remains of Holyrood Abbey (A.D. 1128)
Palace of Holyrood House
HOLYROOD PARK
Salisbury Craigs
Lothian Health Board
Usher Hall
Royal Lyceum
Traverse
Filmhouse
Edinburgh International Conference Centre
Laserquest
Haymarket Station
St. Mary's Scottish Episcopal Cathedral
PRINCES STREET
GEORGE STREET
QUEEN STREET
THE ROYAL MILE
NORTH BRIDGE
SOUTH BRIDGE
LOTHIAN ROAD
CANONGATE
QUEENSFERRY ROAD
LONDON ROAD
WESTERN APPROACH ROAD

Glasgow

0 Miles ¼

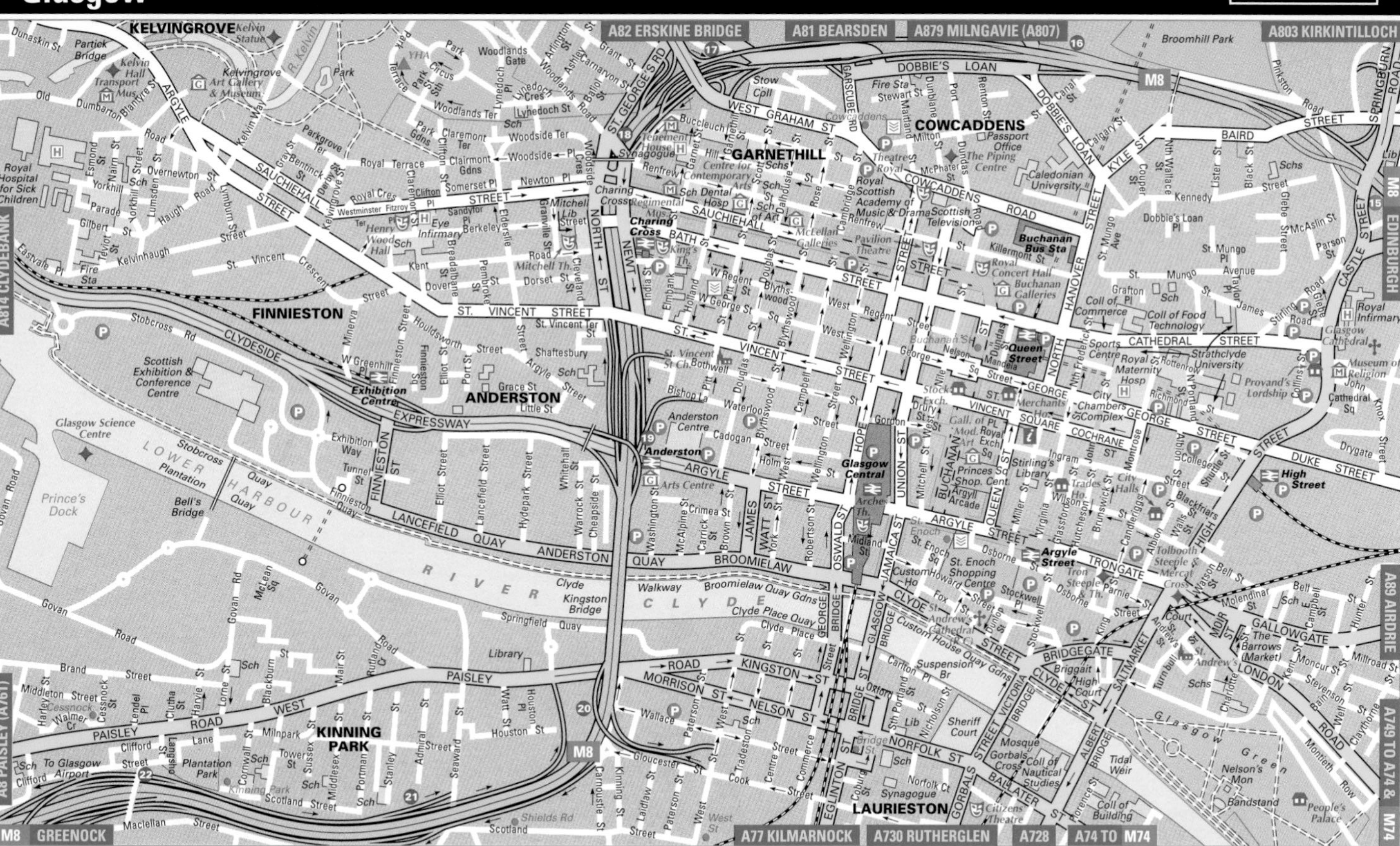
KELVINGROVE
GARNETHILL
COWCADDENS
FINNIESTON
ANDERSTON
KINNING PARK
LAURIESTON
A82 ERSKINE BRIDGE
A81 BEARSDEN
A879 MILNGAVIE (A807)
A803 KIRKINTILLOCH
M8 EDINBURGH
A89 AIRDRIE
A749 TO A74 & M74
A74 TO M74
A728
A730 RUTHERGLEN
A77 KILMARNOCK
M8 GREENOCK
A8 PAISLEY (A761)
A814 CLYDEBANK
RIVER CLYDE
LOWER HARBOUR
Glasgow Central
Queen Street
High Street
Argyle Street
Anderston
Exhibition Centre
Charing Cross
Buchanan Bus Sta
SAUCHIEHALL STREET
ARGYLE STREET
ST. VINCENT STREET
GEORGE STREET
CATHEDRAL STREET
BUCHANAN ST
HOPE ST
UNION ST
CLYDESIDE EXPRESSWAY
BROOMIELAW
PAISLEY ROAD WEST
GALLOWGATE
TRONGATE
Scottish Exhibition & Conference Centre
Glasgow Science Centre
Prince's Dock
Royal Hospital for Sick Children
Kelvingrove Art Gallery & Museum
Kelvin Hall Transport Mus.
Royal Infirmary
Glasgow Cathedral
Strathclyde University
Caledonian University
Royal Concert Hall
Buchanan Galleries
St. Enoch Shopping Centre
Sheriff Court
Glasgow Green
People's Palace
Broomhill Park

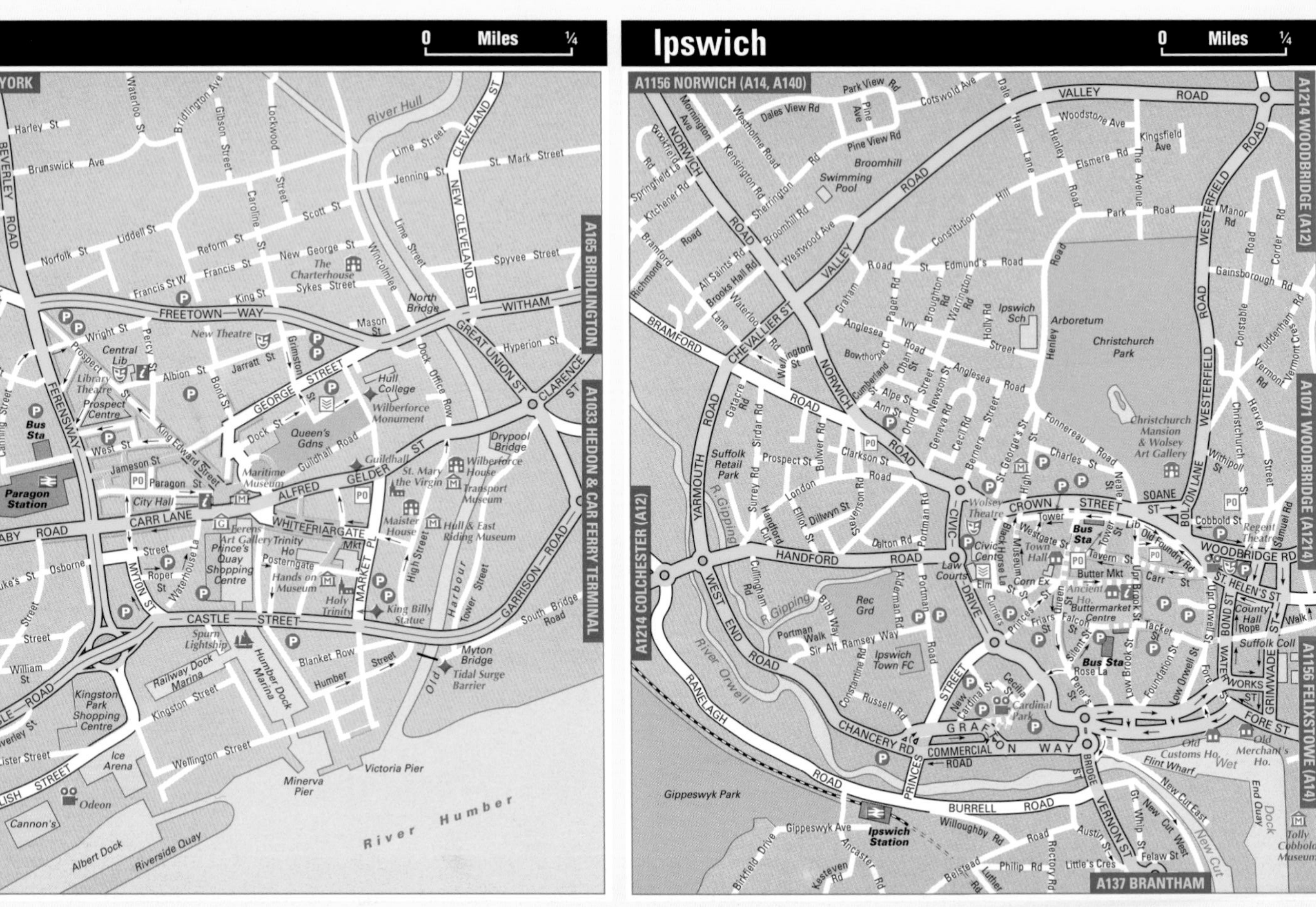
Hull
0 Miles ¼
A1079 YORK
A165 BRIDLINGTON
A1033 HEDON & CAR FERRY TERMINAL
A1105 HUMBER BRIDGE & SELBY (A63) M62
A63 SELBY M62 & AIRPORT (A15)
BEVERLEY ROAD
SPRING BANK
FREETOWN WAY
FERENSWAY
GEORGE STREET
GREAT UNION ST
CLARENCE ST
NEW CLEVELAND ST
CLEVELAND ST
WITHAM
ALFRED GELDER ST
CARR LANE
ANLABY ROAD
WHITEFRIARGATE
MARKET PL
CASTLE STREET
MYTON ST
HESSLE ROAD
ENGLISH STREET
GARRISON ROAD
River Hull
River Humber
Paragon Station
Bus Sta
Hull Truck Theatre
New Theatre
Central Lib
Library Theatre
Prospect Centre
The Charterhouse
North Bridge
Hull College
Wilberforce Monument
Queen's Gdns
Maritime Museum
Guildhall
City Hall
St. Mary the Virgin
Wilberforce House
Transport Museum
Maister House
Hull & East Riding Museum
Drypool Bridge
Berens Art Gallery
Prince's Quay Shopping Centre
Trinity Ho
Hands on Museum
Holy Trinity
King Billy Statue
Spurn Lightship
Humber Dock Marina
Railway Dock Marina
Kingston Park Shopping Centre
Ice Arena
Odeon
Cannon's
Myton Bridge
Tidal Surge Barrier
Victoria Pier
Minerva Pier
Albert Dock
Riverside Quay
Ipswich
0 Miles ¼
A1156 NORWICH (A14, A140)
A1214 WOODBRIDGE (A12)
A1071 WOODBRIDGE (A1214)
A1156 FELIXSTOWE (A14)
A137 BRANTHAM
A1214 COLCHESTER (A12)
NORWICH ROAD
VALLEY ROAD
WESTERFIELD ROAD
BRAMFORD ROAD
CHEVALLIER ST
YARMOUTH ROAD
HANDFORD ROAD
WEST END ROAD
CIVIC DRIVE
CROWN STREET
SOANE ST
BOLTON LANE
WOODBRIDGE RD
ST. HELEN'S ST
GRIMWADE ST
FORE ST
STAR LANE
GRAFTON WAY
COMMERCIAL ROAD
PRINCES ST
CHANCERY RD
RANELAGH ROAD
BURRELL ROAD
VERNON ST
BRIDGE ST
Christchurch Park
Arboretum
Christchurch Mansion & Wolsey Art Gallery
Ipswich Sch
Swimming Pool
Broomhill
Suffolk Retail Park
Wolsey Theatre
Civic Centre
Law Courts
Town Hall
Corn Ex
Bus Sta
Butter Mkt
Ancient Ho.
Buttermarket Centre
Regent Theatre
County Hall
Suffolk Coll
Cardinal Park
Rec Grd
Ipswich Town FC
Old Customs Ho.
Flint Wharf
Old Merchant's Ho.
Wet Dock
End Quay
Tolly Cobbold Museum
New Cut
River Orwell
R. Gipping
Gippeswyk Park
Ipswich Station

Leeds

0 Miles ¼

A660 SKIPTON (A65)
A61 HARROGATE
A58 WETHERBY
A64 YORK
A65 SKIPTON
A647 BRADFORD
A62 HUDDERSFIELD & M62
A643 DEWSBURY (A653) & M621
A653 DEWSBURY & (M621, M1, M62)
A61 CASTLEFORD (A639) & M1
LITTLE WOODHOUSE
MABGATE
QUARRY HILL
RICHMOND HILL
STEANDER
WAREHOUSE HILL
CROWN POINT
CAVALIER HILL
GRANARY WHARF
CAMP FIELD
NEW WORTLEY
Leeds University
Leeds Metropolitan University
Leeds Met University
Leeds General Infirmary (A & E)
St. James' Hospital
Yorkshire Television Studios
TV Studios
Merrion Centre
St. Johns Centre
Headrow Shopping Centre
Leeds Shopping Plaza
Victoria Quarter
Kirkgate Market
Bus & Coach Sta
Leeds Station
City Square
Town Hall
Civic Hall
City Art Lib.
Grand Theatre
City Palace of Varieties
West Yorkshire Playhouse
Quarry House (NHS/DSS Headquarters)
Royal Armouries Museum
Crown Point Retail Park
International Swimming Pool
Holy Trinity
Corn Exch
Leeds & Liverpool Canal
River Aire
A58(M)
A64(M)
KIRKSTALL ROAD
BURLEY ROAD
PARK LANE
WESTGATE
THE HEADROW
EASTGATE
WELLINGTON ST
WELLINGTON RD
WHITEHALL ROAD
BOAR LANE
NEW YORK ST
NORTH STREET
REGENT ST
BURMANTOFS STREET
YORK ROAD
EAST STREET
HUNSLET LANE
MEADOW LANE
NEVILLE ST
VICTORIA RD
WATER LANE
HOLBECK LANE
INGRAM ROAD
CANAL STREET

Liverpool

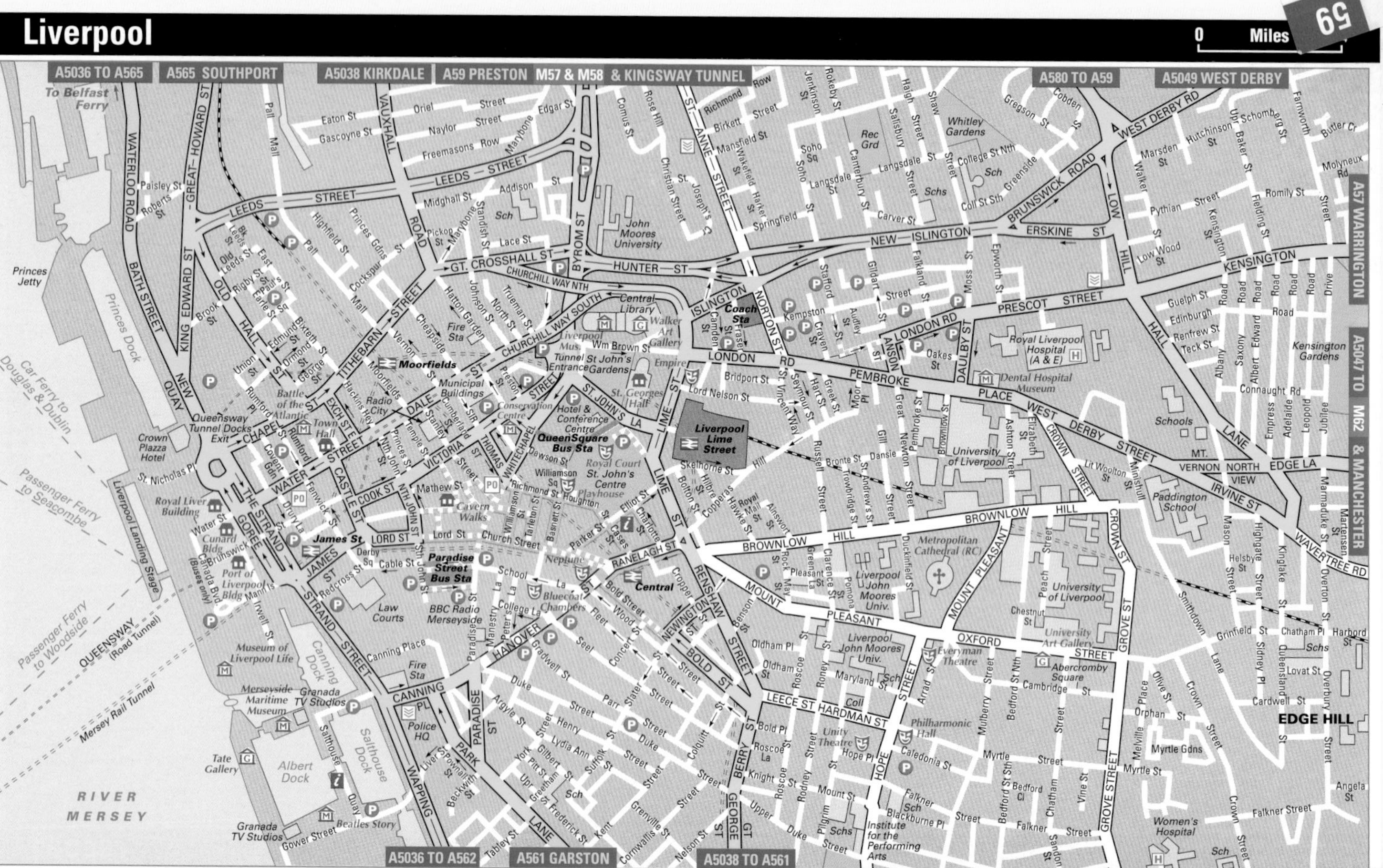
0 Miles
A5036 TO A565
A565 SOUTHPORT
A5038 KIRKDALE
A59 PRESTON
M57 & M58 & KINGSWAY TUNNEL
A580 TO A59
A5049 WEST DERBY
A57 WARRINGTON
A5047 TO M62 & MANCHESTER
A5036 TO A562
A561 GARSTON
A5038 TO A561
To Belfast Ferry
Princes Jetty
Princes Dock
Car Ferry to Douglas & Dublin
Passenger Ferry to Seacombe
Passenger Ferry to Woodside
QUEENSWAY (Road Tunnel)
Mersey Rail Tunnel
RIVER MERSEY
Liverpool Landing Stage
Crown Plaza Hotel
Royal Liver Building
Cunard Bldg
Port of Liverpool Bldg
Canada Bvd. (Buses only)
Museum of Liverpool Life
Canning Dock
Merseyside Maritime Museum
Granada TV Studios
Salthouse Dock
Albert Dock
Tate Gallery
Beatles Story
Queensway Tunnel Docks Exit
Battle of the Atlantic
Town Hall
Moorfields
Radio City
Municipal Buildings
Conservation Centre
Central Library
Walker Art Gallery
Liverpool Mus.
Tunnel Entrance
St John's Gardens
Empire
St. Georges Hall
Hotel & Conference Centre
QueenSquare Bus Sta
Royal Court
St. John's Centre
Playhouse
Cavern Walks
Paradise Street Bus Sta
BBC Radio Merseyside
Law Courts
Fire Sta
Police HQ
Neptune
Bluecoat Chambers
Central
Liverpool Lime Street
Coach Sta
John Moores University
Royal Liverpool Hospital (A & E)
Dental Hospital Museum
University of Liverpool
Schools
Paddington School
Metropolitan Cathedral (RC)
Liverpool John Moores Univ.
Everyman Theatre
University Art Gallery
Abercromby Square
Unity Theatre
Philharmonic Hall
Institute for the Performing Arts
Women's Hospital
EDGE HILL
Whitley Gardens
Rec Grd
Kensington Gardens
WATERLOO ROAD
BATH STREET
NEW QUAY
GREAT HOWARD ST
KING EDWARD ST
LEEDS STREET
VAUXHALL ROAD
OLD HALL ST
TITHEBARN STREET
GT. CROSSHALL ST
BYROM ST
HUNTER ST
CHURCHILL WAY NTH
CHURCHILL WAY SOUTH
DALE ST
VICTORIA ST
WATER ST
CASTLE ST
THE STRAND
STRAND STREET
JAMES ST
LORD ST
Church Street
HANOVER ST
PARADISE ST
CANNING PL
WAPPING
PARK LANE
ST. JOHN'S LA
LIME ST
LONDON RD
ISLINGTON
NORTON ST
ST. ANNE STREET
NEW ISLINGTON
ERSKINE ST
BRUNSWICK ROAD
WEST DERBY RD
LOW HILL
KENSINGTON
PRESCOT STREET
PEMBROKE PLACE
WEST DERBY STREET
MT. VERNON
EDGE LA
IRVINE ST
WAVERTREE RD
BROWNLOW HILL
MOUNT PLEASANT
RENSHAW STREET
BERRY ST
OXFORD STREET
HOPE STREET
LEECE ST
HARDMAN ST
GROVE STREET
CROWN ST
BOLD ST
RANELAGH ST
Smithdown Lane
Crown Street
Falkner Street
Duke Street
Upper Duke Street

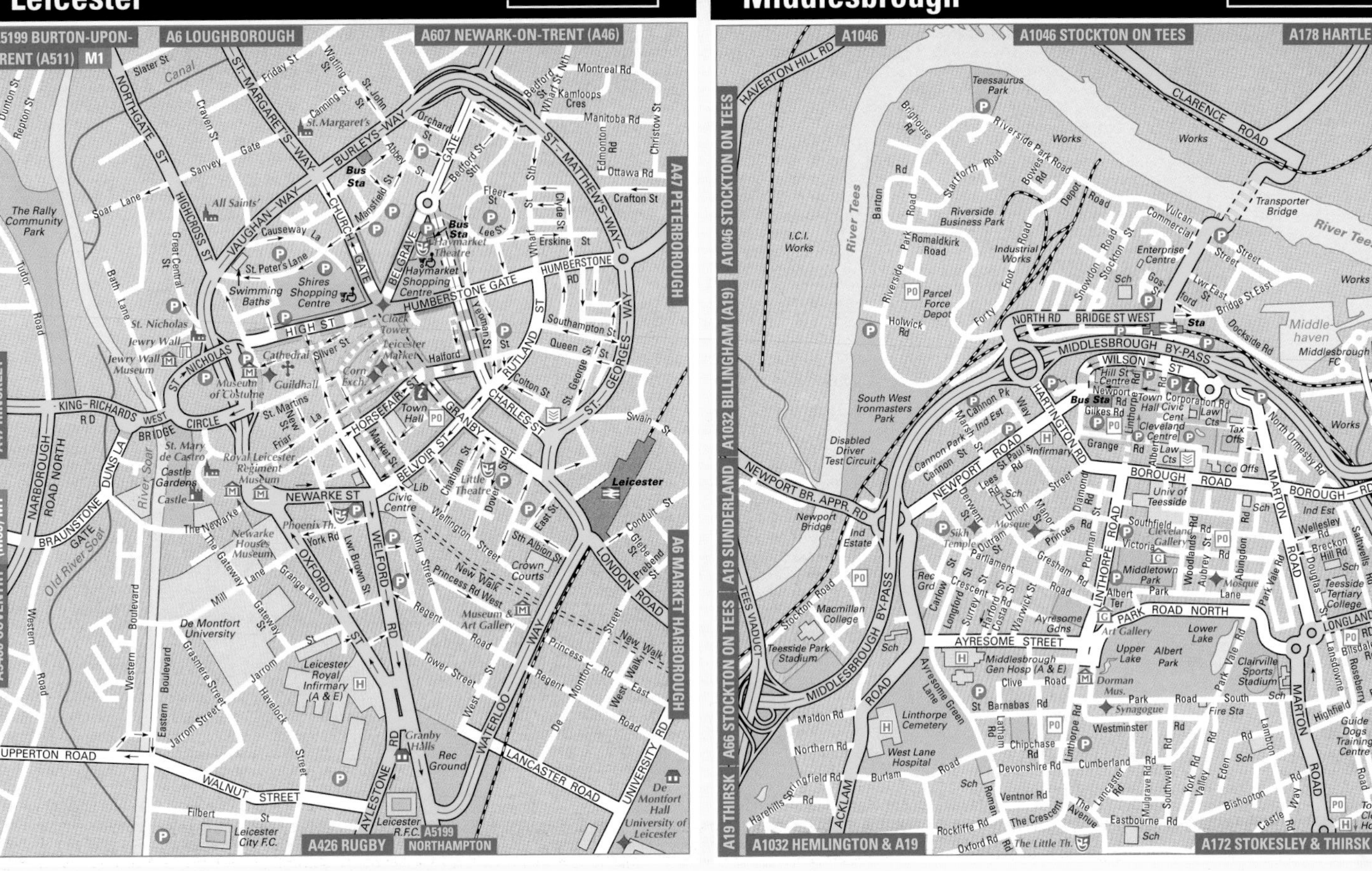
Leicester
0 Miles ¼
A5199 BURTON-UPON-TRENT (A511)
M1
A6 LOUGHBOROUGH
A607 NEWARK-ON-TRENT (A46)
A47 PETERBOROUGH
A6 MARKET HARBOROUGH
A426 RUGBY
A5199 NORTHAMPTON
A5460 COVENTRY (M69) M1
A47 HINCKLEY
Clock Tower
Leicester Market
Haymarket Shopping Centre
Shires Shopping Centre
Cathedral
Guildhall
Town Hall
Leicester
De Montfort University
Leicester Royal Infirmary (A & E)
Leicester City F.C.
University of Leicester
Middlesbrough
0 Miles ½
A1046
A1046 STOCKTON ON TEES
A178 HARTLEPOOL
A66 REDCAR (A1085)
A1085 REDCAR
A172 STOKESLEY & THIRSK (A19)
A1032 HEMLINGTON & A19
A19 THIRSK
A66 STOCKTON ON TEES
A19 SUNDERLAND
A1032 BILLINGHAM (A19)
River Tees
Transporter Bridge
Middlesbrough F.C.
Univ of Teesside
Middlesbrough Gen Hosp (A & E)
Albert Park
Teesside Park Stadium
TEES VIADUCT

For LONDON see pages 42-45

Manchester

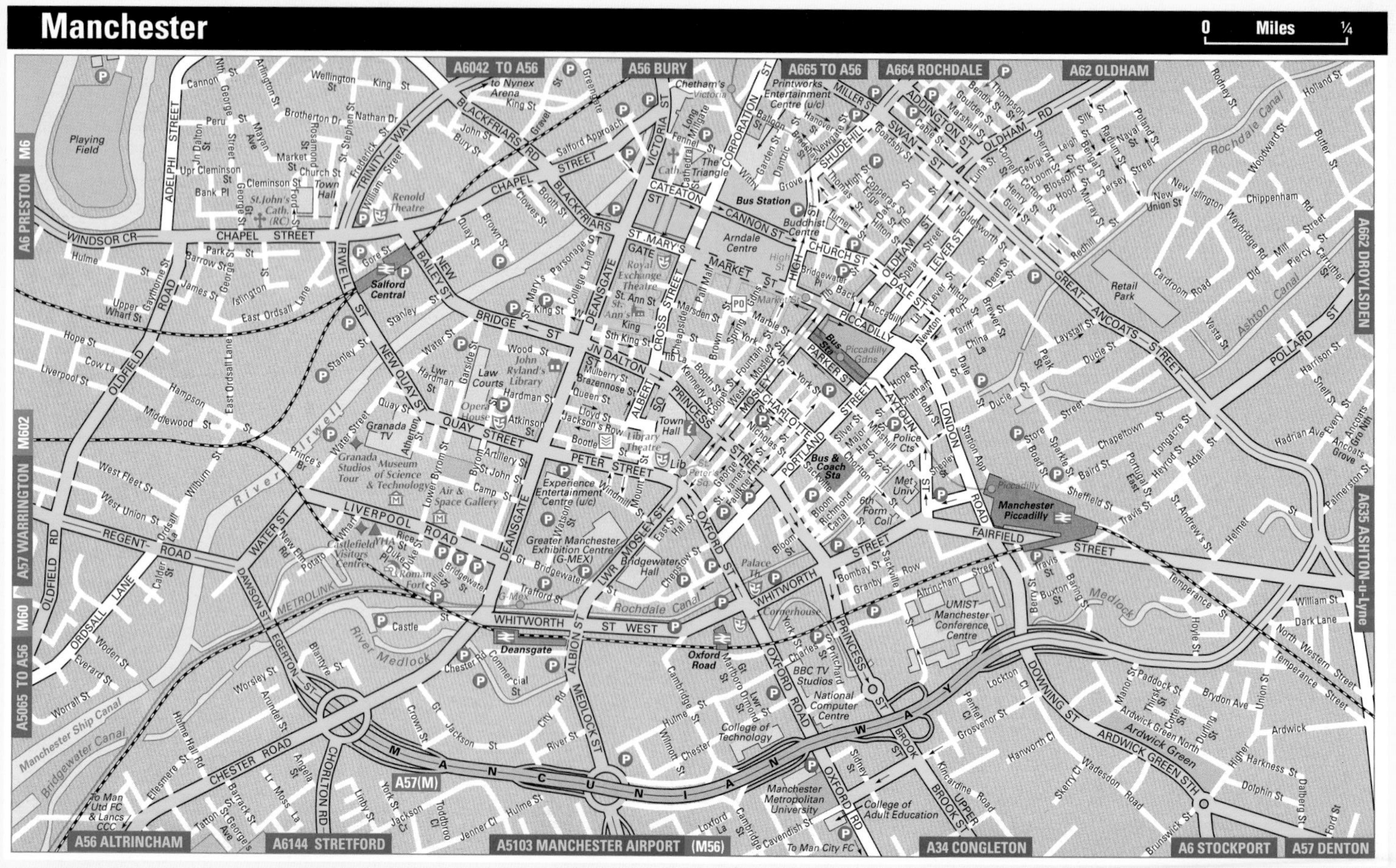

0 Miles 1/4
A6042 TO A56
to Nynex Arena
A56 BURY
A665 TO A56
A664 ROCHDALE
A62 OLDHAM
A662 DROYLSDEN
A635 ASHTON-u-Lyne
A57 DENTON
A6 STOCKPORT
A34 CONGLETON
A5103 MANCHESTER AIRPORT (M56)
To Man City FC
A6144 STRETFORD
A56 ALTRINCHAM
To Man Utd FC & Lancs CCC
A5065 TO A56
M60
A57 WARRINGTON
M602
A6 PRESTON
M6
Playing Field
Manchester Piccadilly
Piccadilly
Oxford Road
Deansgate
Salford Central
Bus Station
Bus & Coach Sta
Bus Sta
Piccadilly Gdns
Arndale Centre
Town Hall
Retail Park
UMIST Manchester Conference Centre
Manchester Metropolitan University
College of Technology
College of Adult Education
National Computer Centre
BBC TV Studios
Cornerhouse
Greater Manchester Exhibition Centre (G-MEX)
Experience Entertainment Centre (u/c)
Granada Studios Tour
Granada TV
Museum of Science & Technology
Air & Space Gallery
Castlefield Visitors Centre
Roman Fort
Royal Exchange Theatre
Printworks Entertainment Centre (u/c)
Buddhist Centre
Chetham's
The Triangle
Renold Theatre
Palace Th.
Bridgewater Hall
Law Courts
Opera House
John Rylands Library
Library Theatre
Police Cts
Met Univ
6th Form Coll
St. John's Cath. (RC)
MANCUNIAN WAY
A57(M)
METROLINK
Rochdale Canal
Bridgewater Canal
Manchester Ship Canal
Ashton Canal
River Irwell
River Medlock
GREAT ANCOATS STREET
PICCADILLY
LONDON ROAD
FAIRFIELD STREET
PORTLAND STREET
OXFORD ROAD
PRINCESS STREET
DEANSGATE
CHESTER ROAD
REGENT ROAD
TRINITY WAY
CHAPEL STREET
ADELPHI STREET
ORDSALL LANE
WATER ST
LIVERPOOL ROAD
QUAY STREET
PETER STREET
CROSS STREET
CORPORATION ST
WHITWORTH ST WEST
DOWNING ST
ARDWICK GREEN STH

Milton Keynes

0 Miles 1/2

Northampton

0 Miles 1/4

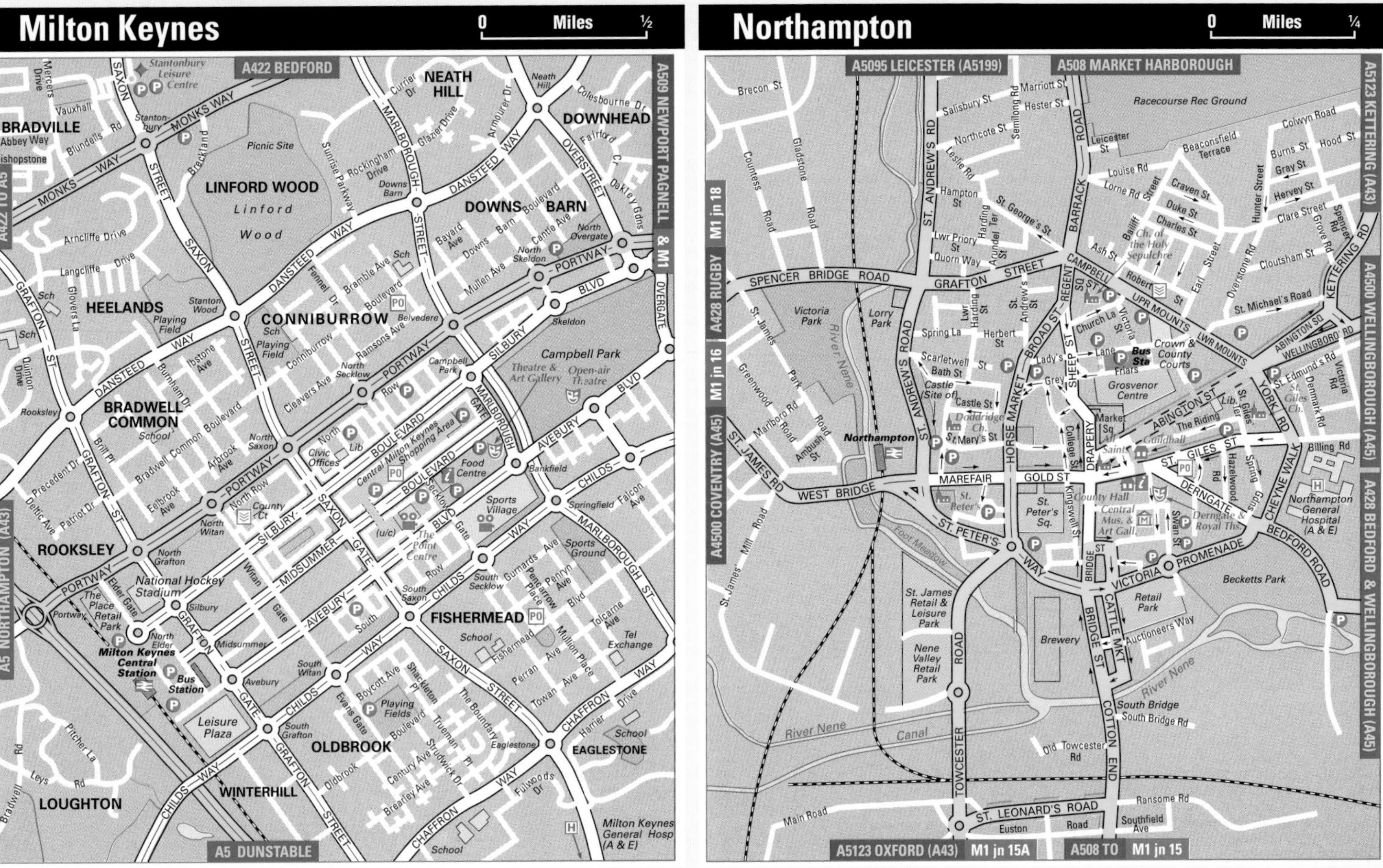
A422 BEDFORD
A509 NEWPORT PAGNELL & M1
A422 TO A5
A5 NORTHAMPTON (A43)
A5 DUNSTABLE
OVERGATE
NEATH HILL
DOWNHEAD
DOWNS BARN
BRADVILLE
LINFORD WOOD
Linford Wood
HEELANDS
CONNIBURROW
BRADWELL COMMON
ROOKSLEY
FISHERMEAD
OLDBROOK
EAGLESTONE
WINTERHILL
LOUGHTON
Stantonbury Leisure Centre
Picnic Site
Campbell Park
Theatre & Art Gallery
Open-air Theatre
Central Milton Keynes Shopping Area
Civic Offices
Food Centre
Sports Village
The Point Centre
Sports Ground
National Hockey Stadium
The Place Retail Park
Milton Keynes Central Station
Bus Station
Leisure Plaza
Playing Fields
Tel Exchange
Milton Keynes General Hosp (A & E)
MONKS WAY
SAXON STREET
DANSTEED WAY
MARLBOROUGH STREET
GRAFTON STREET
PORTWAY
SILBURY BLVD
AVEBURY BLVD
MIDSUMMER BLVD
CHILDS WAY
CHAFFRON WAY
OVERSTREET
Sunrise Parkway
A5095 LEICESTER (A5199)
A508 MARKET HARBOROUGH
A5123 KETTERING (A43)
A4500 WELLINGBOROUGH (A45)
A428 BEDFORD & WELLINGBOROUGH (A45)
M1 jn 18
A428 RUGBY
M1 jn 16
A4500 COVENTRY (A45)
A5123 OXFORD (A43)
M1 jn 15A
A508 TO
M1 jn 15
Racecourse Rec Ground
Victoria Park
Lorry Park
River Nene
Northampton
Grosvenor Centre
Bus Sta
County Hall
Central Mus. & Art Gall.
Derngate & Royal Ths.
St. Peter's Sq.
Becketts Park
Retail Park
Brewery
St. James Retail & Leisure Park
Nene Valley Retail Park
Canal
Northampton General Hospital (A & E)
SPENCER BRIDGE ROAD
GRAFTON STREET
ST. ANDREW'S RD
ST. ANDREW'S ROAD
BARRACK ROAD
HORSE MARKET
MAREFAIR
GOLD ST
DRAPERY
WEST BRIDGE
ST. PETER'S WAY
ST. JAMES RD
TOWCESTER ROAD
ST. LEONARD'S ROAD
BRIDGE ST
CATTLE MKT
COTTON END
VICTORIA PROMENADE
BEDFORD ROAD
CHEYNE WALK
DERNGATE
ST. GILES ST
ABINGTON ST
YORK RD
KETTERING RD
UPR MOUNTS
LWR MOUNTS
South Bridge
Main Road

Newcastle

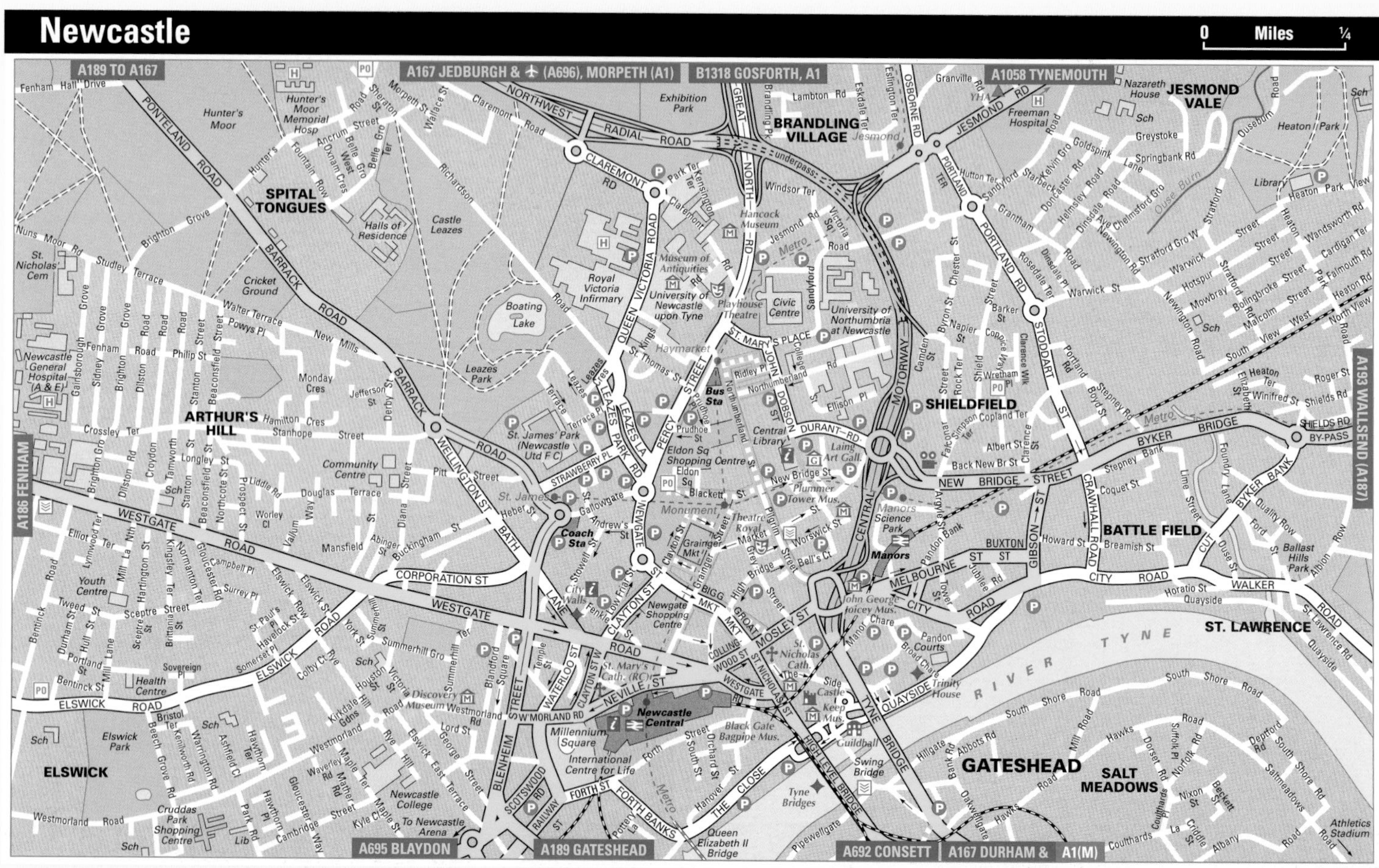

0 Miles ¼
A189 TO A167
A167 JEDBURGH & (A696), MORPETH (A1)
B1318 GOSFORTH, A1
A1058 TYNEMOUTH
A193 WALLSEND (A187)
A186 FENHAM
A695 BLAYDON
A189 GATESHEAD
A692 CONSETT
A167 DURHAM & A1(M)
JESMOND VALE
BRANDLING VILLAGE
SPITAL TONGUES
ARTHUR'S HILL
SHIELDFIELD
BATTLE FIELD
ST. LAWRENCE
GATESHEAD
SALT MEADOWS
ELSWICK
RIVER TYNE
Hunter's Moor
Hunter's Moor Memorial Hosp
Exhibition Park
Castle Leazes
Halls of Residence
Cricket Ground
Boating Lake
Leazes Park
Royal Victoria Infirmary
Museum of Antiquities
University of Newcastle upon Tyne
Hancock Museum
Playhouse Theatre
Civic Centre
University of Northumbria at Newcastle
Haymarket
Bus Sta
Central Library
Laing Art Gall.
Eldon Sq Shopping Centre
Plummer Tower Mus.
Monument
Theatre Royal
Grainger Mkt
Manors Science Park
Manors
John George Joicey Mus.
St. James' Park (Newcastle Utd F C)
Coach Sta
City Walls
Newgate Shopping Centre
St. Mary's Cath. (RC)
St. Nicholas Cath.
Castle Keep Mus.
Guildhall
Newcastle Central
Black Gate Bagpipe Mus.
Millennium Square
International Centre for Life
Swing Bridge
Tyne Bridges
Queen Elizabeth II Bridge
Trinity House
Pandon Courts
Discovery Museum
Newcastle College
To Newcastle Arena
Cruddas Park Shopping Centre
Elswick Park
Health Centre
Youth Centre
Community Centre
Newcastle General Hospital (A & E)
St. Nicholas' Cem
Freeman Hospital
Nazareth House
Heaton Park
Library
Athletics Stadium
PONTELAND ROAD
BARRACK ROAD
NORTHWEST RADIAL ROAD
CLAREMONT RD
QUEEN VICTORIA ROAD
GREAT NORTH RD
OSBORNE RD
JESMOND RD
PORTLAND RD
STODDART ST
CENTRAL MOTORWAY
BYKER BRIDGE
SHIELDS RD BY-PASS
NEW BRIDGE STREET
CITY ROAD
WALKER ROAD
QUAYSIDE
TYNE BRIDGE
HIGH LEVEL BRIDGE
WESTGATE ROAD
ELSWICK ROAD
CORPORATION ST
WELLINGTON ST
BLENHEIM STREET
SCOTSWOOD RD
FORTH BANKS
THE CLOSE
PERCY STREET
NEWGATE ST
JOHN DOBSON ST
ST. MARY'S PLACE
DURANT RD
MOSLEY ST
CLAYTON ST
NEVILLE ST

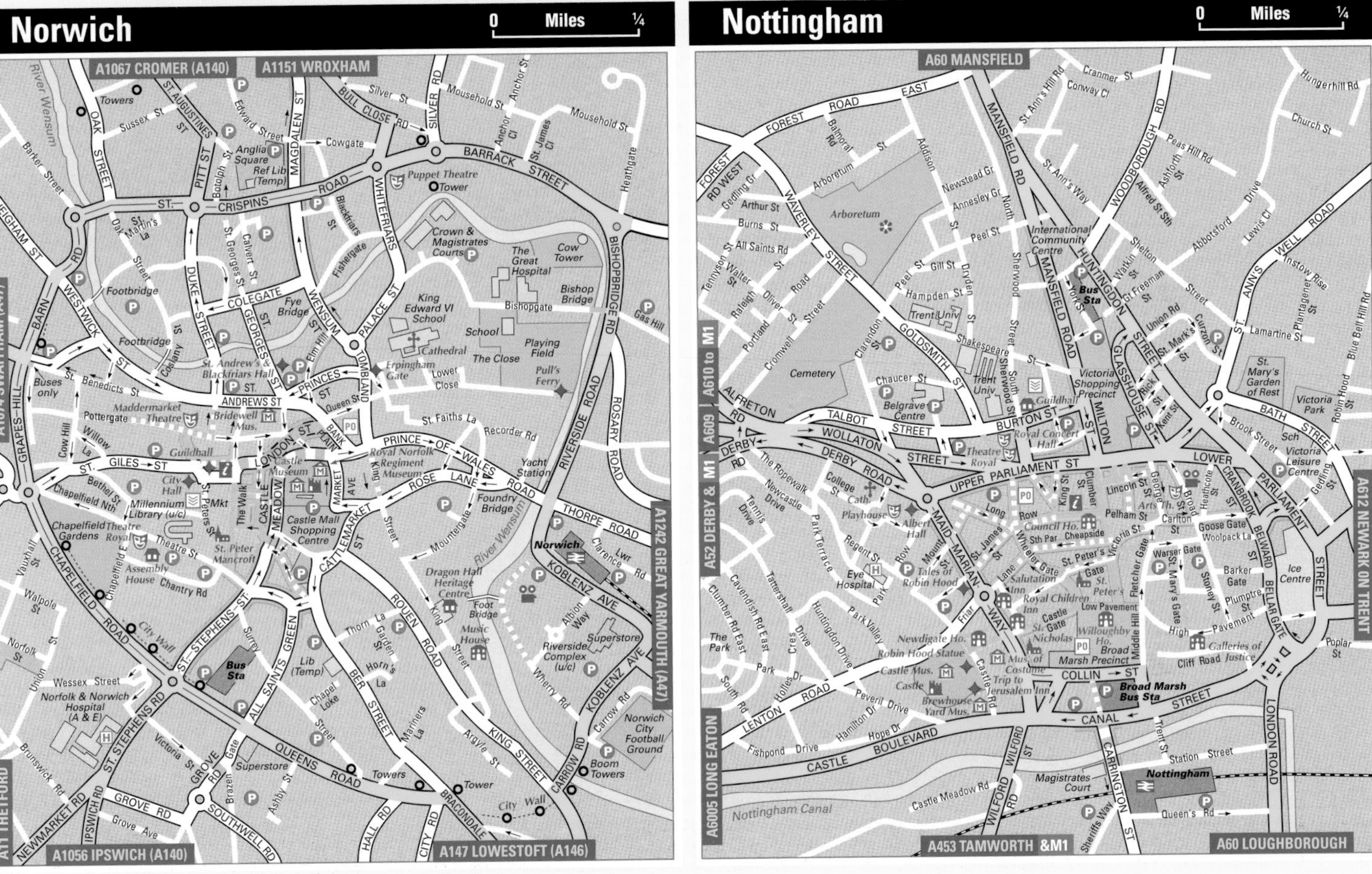
Norwich
0 Miles ¼
A1067 CROMER (A140)
A1151 WROXHAM
A1242 GREAT YARMOUTH (A47)
A147 LOWESTOFT (A146)
A1056 IPSWICH (A140)
A11 THETFORD
A1074 SWAFFHAM (A47)
Nottingham
0 Miles ¼
A60 MANSFIELD
A612 NEWARK ON TRENT
A60 LOUGHBOROUGH
A453 TAMWORTH &M1
A6005 LONG EATON
A52 DERBY & M1
A609
A610 to M1

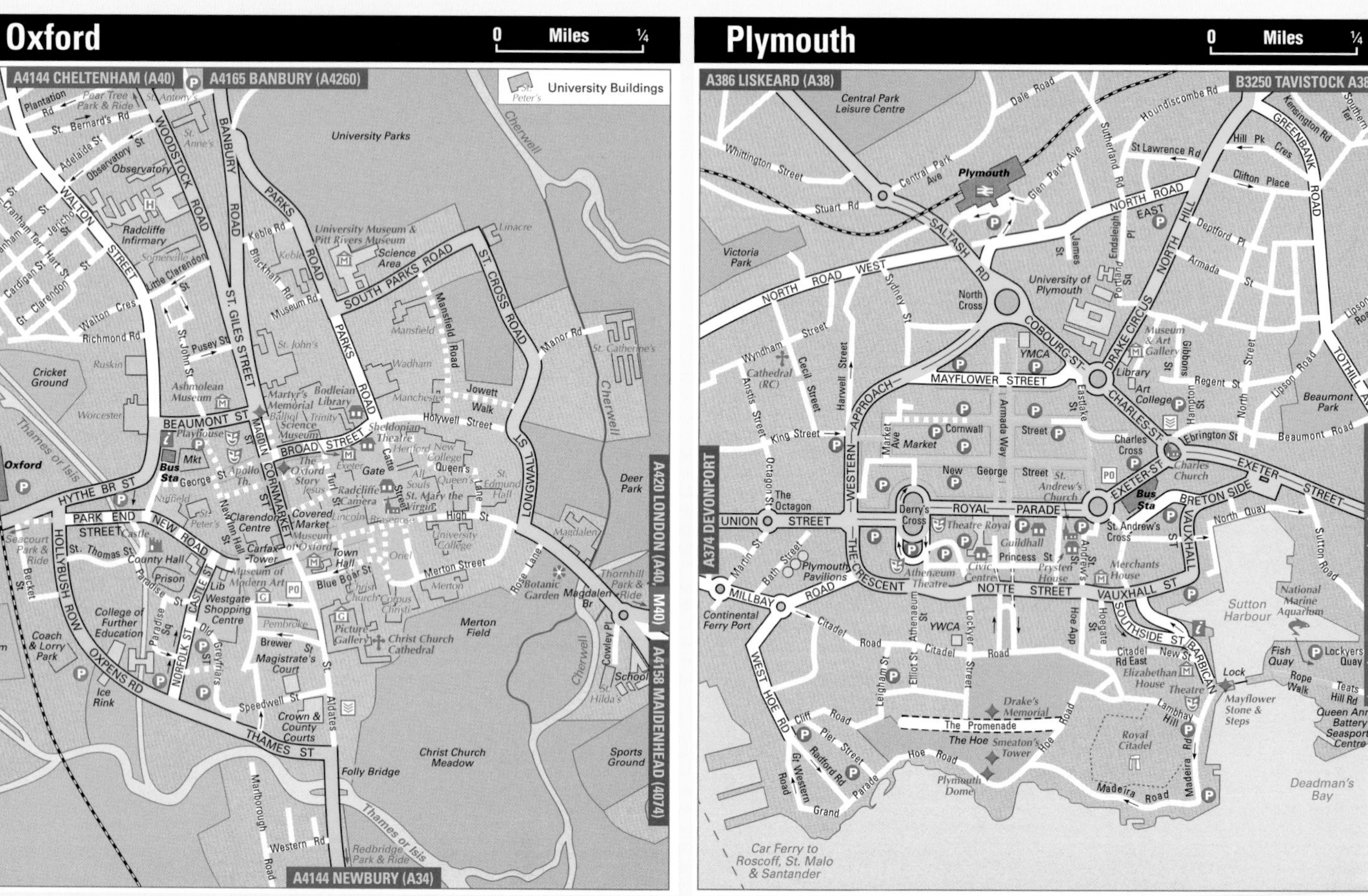
Oxford
0 Miles ¼
A4144 CHELTENHAM (A40)
A4165 BANBURY (A4260)
University Buildings
A420 LONDON (A40, M40)
A4158 MAIDENHEAD (4074)
A420 SWINDON
A4144 NEWBURY (A34)
University Parks
WOODSTOCK ROAD
BANBURY ROAD
PARKS ROAD
SOUTH PARKS ROAD
ST. CROSS ROAD
ST. GILES STREET
WALTON STREET
BEAUMONT ST
BROAD STREET
CORNMARKET ST
MAGDLN ST
HYTHE BR ST
PARK END STREET
NEW ROAD
HOLLYBUSH ROW
OXPENS RD
THAMES ST
CASTLE ST
NORFOLK ST
LONGWALL ST
High St
Holywell Street
Mansfield Road
Jowett Walk
Manor Rd
Merton Street
Blue Boar St
St. Aldates
Speedwell St
Rose Lane
Cowley Pl
Magdalen Br
Botanic Garden
Merton Field
Christ Church Meadow
Christ Church Cathedral
Folly Bridge
Cricket Ground
Deer Park
Sports Ground
Thames or Isis
Cherwell
Radcliffe Infirmary
Ashmolean Museum
Martyr's Memorial
Bodleian Library
Sheldonian Theatre
Radcliffe Camera
Carfax Tower
Covered Market
Westgate Shopping Centre
College of Further Education
Ice Rink
Coach & Lorry Park
Oxford
Plymouth
0 Miles ¼
A386 LISKEARD (A38)
B3250 TAVISTOCK A386
A374 EXETER (A38) & KINGSBRIDGE (A379)
A374 DEVONPORT
Central Park Leisure Centre
Victoria Park
NORTH ROAD WEST
SALTASH RD
NORTH ROAD EAST
NORTH HILL
GREENBANK ROAD
TOTHILL AVE
COBOURG ST
DRAKE CIRCUS
CHARLES ST
EXETER STREET
EXETER ST
MAYFLOWER STREET
WESTERN APPROACH
ROYAL PARADE
UNION STREET
THE CRESCENT
NOTTE STREET
VAUXHALL ST
BRETON SIDE
SOUTHSIDE ST
BARBICAN
MILLBAY ROAD
WEST HOE RD
Armada Way
Cornwall Street
New George Street
Citadel Road
Lockyer Street
Hoe Road
Madeira Road
The Promenade
The Hoe
Drake's Memorial
Smeaton's Tower
Plymouth Dome
Royal Citadel
Sutton Harbour
National Marine Aquarium
Mayflower Stone & Steps
Continental Ferry Port
Car Ferry to Roscoff, St. Malo & Santander
Deadman's Bay
Plymouth Pavilions
University of Plymouth
Theatre Royal
Guildhall
Civic Centre
Charles Church

Portsmouth

Reading

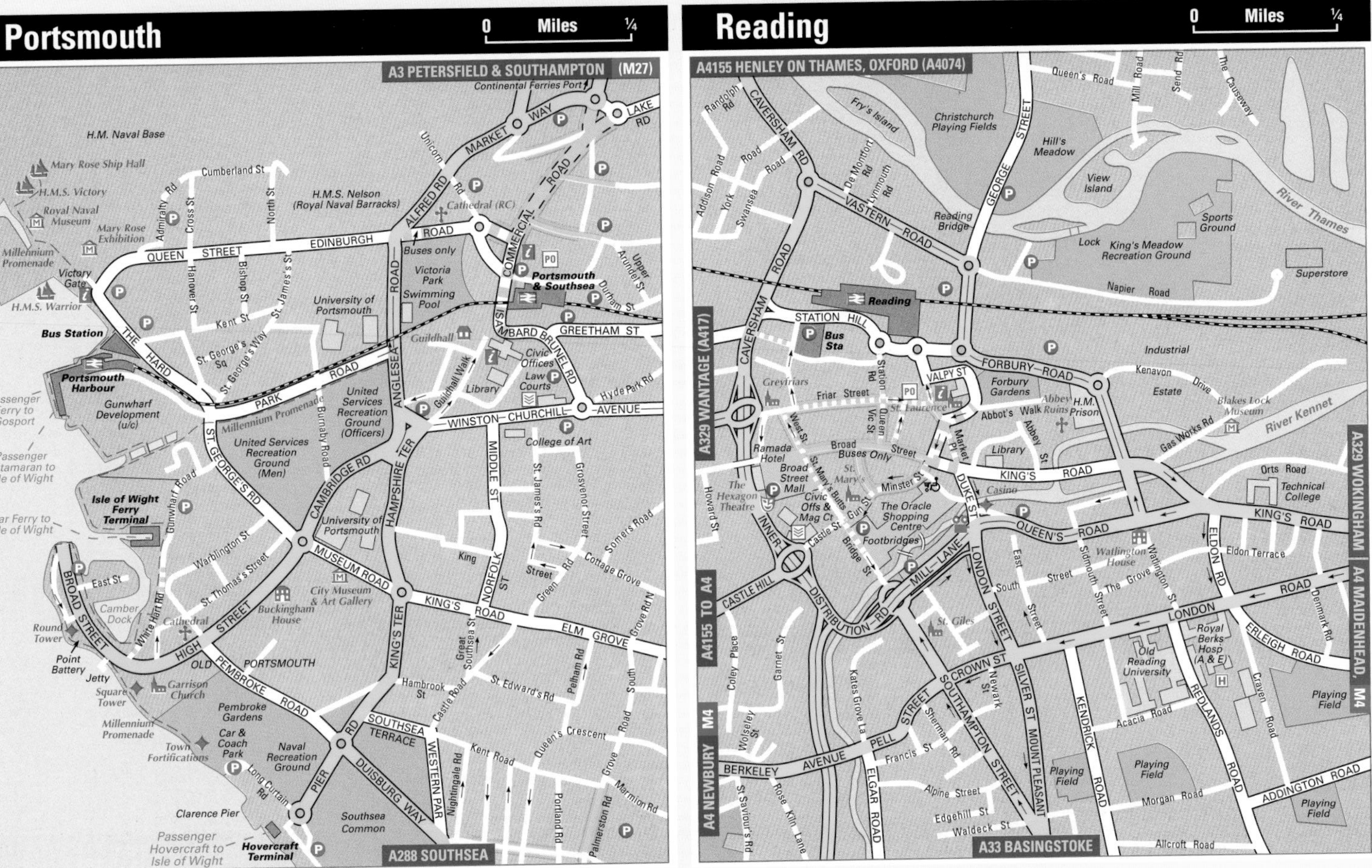

Portsmouth
0 Miles ¼
A3 PETERSFIELD & SOUTHAMPTON (M27)
Continental Ferries Port
H.M. Naval Base
Mary Rose Ship Hall
H.M.S. Victory
Royal Naval Museum
Mary Rose Exhibition
Millennium Promenade
Victory Gate
H.M.S. Warrior
Bus Station
Portsmouth Harbour
Gunwharf Development (u/c)
Passenger Ferry to Gosport
Passenger Catamaran to Isle of Wight
Isle of Wight Ferry Terminal
Car Ferry to Isle of Wight
Camber Dock
Round Tower
Point Battery
Jetty
Square Tower
Garrison Church
Millennium Promenade
Town Fortifications
Pembroke Gardens
Car & Coach Park
Naval Recreation Ground
Clarence Pier
Passenger Hovercraft to Isle of Wight
Hovercraft Terminal
Southsea Common
A288 SOUTHSEA
QUEEN STREET
EDINBURGH ROAD
H.M.S. Nelson (Royal Naval Barracks)
Cumberland St
Admiralty Rd
Cross St
North St
Hanover St
Bishop St
St. James's St
Kent St
St. George's Sq
St. George's Way
THE HARD
PARK ROAD
Millennium Promenade
University of Portsmouth
United Services Recreation Ground (Men)
United Services Recreation Ground (Officers)
Burnaby Road
ST. GEORGE'S RD
Gunwharf Road
Warblington St
St. Thomas's Street
Cathedral
White Hart Rd
East St
BROAD STREET
HIGH STREET
OLD PORTSMOUTH
PEMBROKE ROAD
PIER RD
Long Curtain Rd
DUISBURG WAY
Buckingham House
City Museum & Art Gallery
MUSEUM ROAD
CAMBRIDGE RD
University of Portsmouth
KING'S TER
KING'S ROAD
ELM GROVE
HAMPSHIRE TER
ANGLESEA ROAD
Victoria Park
Swimming Pool
Buses only
ALFRED RD
Unicorn Rd
MARKET WAY
Cathedral (RC)
COMMERCIAL ROAD
LAKE RD
PO
Portsmouth & Southsea
Upper Arundel St
Durham St
ISAMBARD BRUNEL RD
GREETHAM ST
Guildhall
Guildhall Walk
Civic Offices
Law Courts
Library
Hyde Park Rd
WINSTON CHURCHILL AVENUE
College of Art
MIDDLE ST
NORFOLK ST
King Street
St. James's Rd
Grosvenor Street
Green Rd
Cottage Grove
Somers Road
Grove Rd N
Great Southsea St
Hambrook St
Castle Road
St. Edward's Rd
Pelham Rd
South Road
Queen's Crescent
Grove Road
SOUTHSEA TERRACE
WESTERN PAR
Nightingale Rd
Kent Road
Portland Rd
Palmerston Rd
Marmion Rd
Reading
0 Miles ¼
A4155 HENLEY ON THAMES, OXFORD (A4074)
Randolph Rd
Addison Road
York Road
Swansea Road
CAVERSHAM RD
Fry's Island
De Montfort Rd
Lynmouth Rd
VASTERN ROAD
Christchurch Playing Fields
Reading Bridge
GEORGE STREET
Hill's Meadow
View Island
Lock
King's Meadow Recreation Ground
Sports Ground
River Thames
Superstore
Napier Road
Queen's Road
Mill Road
Send Rd
The Causeway
Reading
STATION HILL
Bus Sta
A329 WANTAGE (A417)
CAVERSHAM ROAD
Greyfriars
Friar Street
Station Rd
Queen Vic St
PO
VALPY ST
St. Laurence
Forbury Gardens
FORBURY ROAD
Industrial Estate
Kenavon Drive
Blakes Lock Museum
River Kennet
Gas Works Rd
Abbey Ruins
H.M. Prison
Abbot's Walk
Abbey St
Library
West St
Broad Street
Buses Only
Market Pl
Ramada Hotel
Broad Street Mall
The Hexagon Theatre
Howard St
St. Mary's Butts
St. Mary's
Civic Offs & Mag Ct
Castle St
Gun St
Minster St
The Oracle Shopping Centre
Footbridges
Bridge St
DUKE ST
Casino
KING'S ROAD
QUEEN'S ROAD
INNER DISTRIBUTION RD
CASTLE HILL
MILL LANE
A4155 TO A4
Coley Place
Garnet St
Kates Grove La
St. Giles
LONDON STREET
East Street
South Street
Sidmouth Street
Wallington House
The Grove
Watlington St
Orts Road
Technical College
ELDON RD
Eldon Terrace
KING'S ROAD
A329 WOKINGHAM
A4 MAIDENHEAD, M4
LONDON ROAD
ERLEIGH ROAD
Denmark Rd
Royal Berks Hosp (A & E)
Old Reading University
Craven Road
Playing Field
CROWN ST
Newark St
SILVER ST
MOUNT PLEASANT
SOUTHAMPTON STREET
Sherman Rd
KENDRICK ROAD
REDLANDS ROAD
Acacia Road
Playing Field
Playing Field
Morgan Road
ADDINGTON ROAD
Playing Field
Allcroft Road
A33 BASINGSTOKE
PELL STREET
Francis St
Alpine Street
Edgehill St
Waldeck St
ELGAR ROAD
BERKELEY AVENUE
Rose Kiln Lane
St Saviour's Rd
Wolseley St
A4 NEWBURY M4

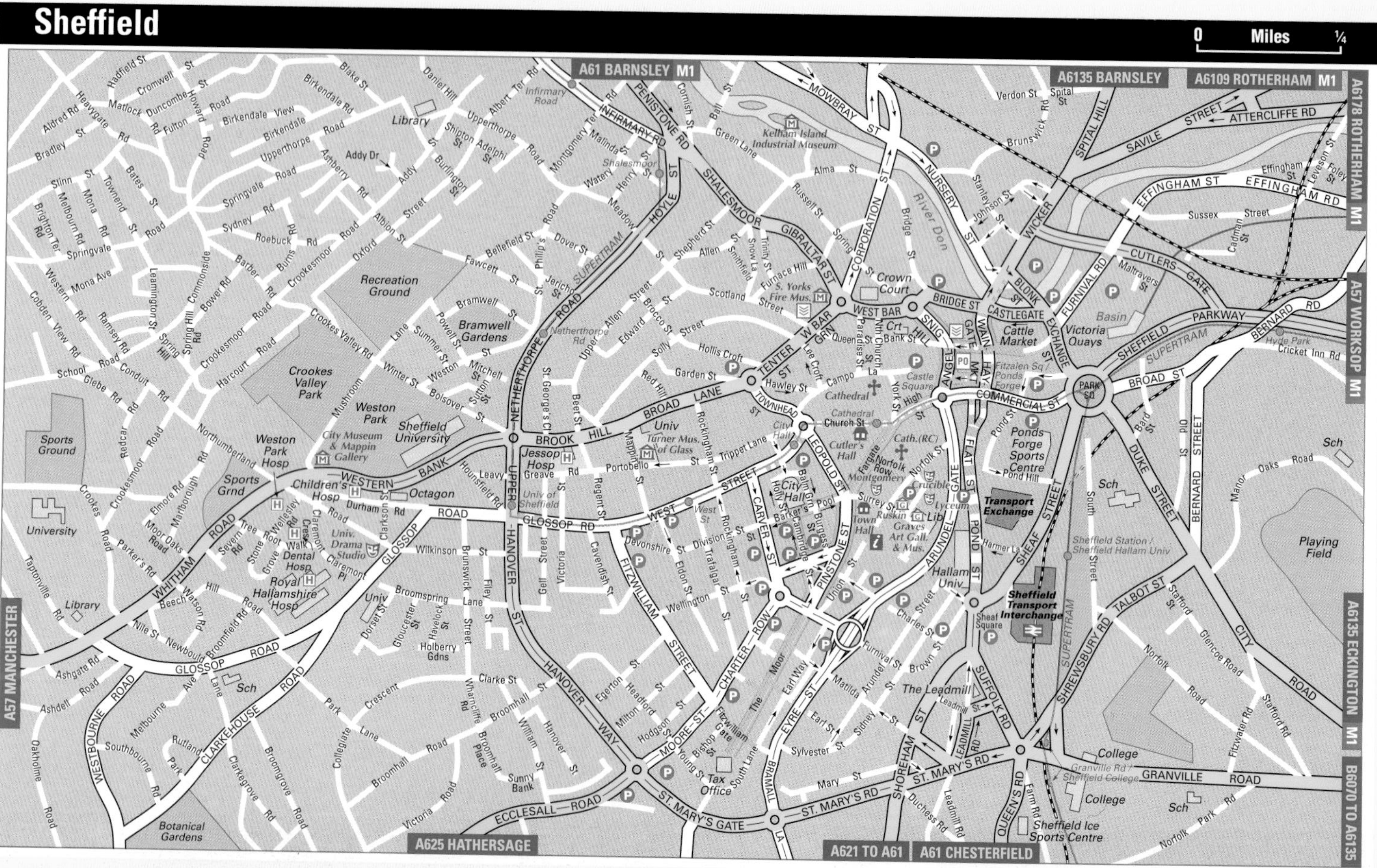
Sheffield
0 Miles 1/4
A61 BARNSLEY M1
A6135 BARNSLEY
A6109 ROTHERHAM M1
A6178 ROTHERHAM M1
A57 WORKSOP M1
A6135 ECKINGTON M1
B6070 TO A6135
A57 MANCHESTER
A625 HATHERSAGE
A621 TO A61
A61 CHESTERFIELD
ATTERCLIFFE RD
SAVILE STREET
SPITAL HILL
EFFINGHAM ST
EFFINGHAM RD
WICKER
NURSERY ST
MOWBRAY ST
CORPORATION ST
River Don
Kelham Island Industrial Museum
SHALESMOOR
PENISTONE RD
INFIRMARY RD
HOYLE ST
NETHERTHORPE ROAD
SUPERTRAM
GIBRALTAR ST
WEST BAR
WEST BAR GRN
TENTER ST
TOWNHEAD ST
BROAD LANE
BROOK HILL
WESTERN BANK
UPPER HANOVER ST
HANOVER WAY
GLOSSOP RD
WEST STREET
CARVER ST
LEOPOLD ST
PINSTONE ST
ARUNDEL GATE
CHARTER ROW
FITZWILLIAM STREET
MOORE ST
ECCLESALL ROAD
ST. MARY'S GATE
ST. MARY'S RD
BRAMALL LA
EYRE ST
SHOREHAM ST
SUFFOLK RD
QUEEN'S RD
SHREWSBURY RD
GRANVILLE ROAD
CITY ROAD
DUKE STREET
SHEAF STREET
PARK SQ
BERNARD STREET
PARKWAY
SHEFFIELD PARKWAY
CUTLERS GATE
FURNIVAL RD
EXCHANGE ST
BLONK ST
CASTLEGATE
WAINGATE
HAYMKT
SNIG HILL
BRIDGE ST
ANGEL ST
FLAT ST
POND ST
COMMERCIAL ST
Victoria Quays
Basin
Cattle Market
Ponds Forge Sports Centre
Transport Exchange
Sheffield Transport Interchange
Sheffield Station / Sheffield Hallam Univ
Hallam Univ
Cathedral
Cath.(RC)
Cutler's Hall
City Hall
Town Hall
Lyceum
Crucible
Graves Art Gall. & Mus.
Crown Court
S. Yorks Fire Mus.
Univ
Turner Mus. of Glass
Jessop Hosp
Univ of Sheffield
Octagon
Sheffield University
Weston Park
City Museum & Mappin Gallery
Crookes Valley Park
Recreation Ground
Bramwell Gardens
Children's Hosp
Weston Park Hosp
Royal Hallamshire Hosp
Dental Hosp
Univ. Drama Studio
Sports Grnd
Sports Ground
University
Library
Botanical Gardens
The Leadmill
Tax Office
Sheffield Ice Sports Centre
College
Playing Field
The Moor
WHITHAM ROAD
CLARKEHOUSE ROAD
WESTBOURNE ROAD
GLOSSOP ROAD

Southampton
0 Miles ¼
A33 WINCHESTER M3
A3024 FAREHAM M27
A3025 PORTSMOUTH M27
A3024 SALISBURY (A36) M27
Hospital (no A & E)
Avenue Hall & Nuffield Theatre
St. Mary's Leisure Centre
Titanic Memorial
Buses and cycles only southwards (peak hours)
West Park
East Park
Art Gallery
Civic Cent
Guild Hall
The Mayflower Theatre
The Polygon
Millan Gallery
Inst of Higher Education
Southampton
Coach Station
West Quay Retail Park
Leisure World
Marland Centre
Palmerston Park
The Bargate Monument
Hanover Buildings
Bargate Centre
Hoglands Park
City College
St. Mary's
Arundel Tower
Catchcold Tower
The Quays Swimming and Diving Complex
Tudor House
St. Michael's
West Gate
Medieval Merchant's Ho.
Maritime Museum
God's House Tower
God's House
Mayflower Park
Mayflower Memorial
Dock Gate
Dock Gate 4
Queen's Park
Level crossing
Chapel Level crossing
Hall of Aviation
Virgin Cinema
Canute's Pavilion
Ocean Village Marina
S.S. Shieldhall
Town Quay
Hythe Ferry (Passenger)
Car Ferry and Passenger Catamaran to Isle of Wight
River Test
River Itchen
Commercial Rd
Cumberland Pl
Brunswick Pl
London Rd
Havelock Rd
Civic Centre Rd
New Road
East Park Ter
St. Andrew's Rd
Kingsway — St. Mary's Place
Palmerston Road
Portland Terrace
Western Esplanade
West Quay Road
Town Quay
Castle Way
Bernard St
Queen's Way
Queen's Ter
Platform Rd
Marsh La
Central Bridge
Terminus Ter
Canute Road
Albert Rd Nth
Albert Rd Sth
Marine Parade
Britannia Rd
Northam Rd
Melbourne St
Anderson's Road
Endle St
Floating Bridge Rd
Channel Rd
Ocean Way
European Way
Brazil Road
Central Road
Atlantic Way
West Road
Trafalgar Road
Herbert Walker Ave
West Quay Road
Morris Rd
Devonshire Rd
Blechynden Ter
West Pk Road
W Marlands Rd
Abovebar Street
Ogle Rd
Pound Tree Rd
South Front
Houndwell Pl
East Street
High St
Bugle St
Orchard Lane
Oxford St
Briton St
St. Mary Street
James St
Golden Grove
Graham Road
Oxford Avenue
Argyle Road
Brinton's Road
St. Mary's Road
Nichols Rd
Derby Road
Hartington Rd
Radcliffe Rd
Rochester St
Belvidere Rd
Southend
0 Miles ¼
A127 BASILDON & SOUTHEND AIRPORT
A13 TILBURY
A13 SHOEBURYNESS
Southend United F.C.
South East Essex College
Civic Centre
Magistrates Court
Library
Victoria Station
Victoria Plaza Shopping Centre
Southend Central
Swimming Pool
County Court
Bus Station
The Royals Shopping Centre
Art Gallery
Cliffs Pavilion
Band Stand
Cliff Lift
Never Never Land
Peter Pan's Playground
Adventure Island
Southend Pier
Thames Estuary
West Street
East Street
West Road
Victoria Avenue
Queensway
London Road
Southchurch Rd
Sutton Road
Western Esplanade
Marine Parade
Gainsborough Drive
Shakespeare Drive
Tudor Rd
North Rd
Salisbury Avenue
Balmoral Rd
Hamlet Ct Rd
Chelmsford Ave
Harcourt Ave
Colchester Rd
Boston Avenue
Baxter Avenue
Sweyne Ave
North Road
Carnarvon Rd
Tunbridge Road
Tickfield Ave
Crowborough Road
Kenway
Glenhurst Rd
Bircham Rd
Vale Ave
Browning Ave
Ruskin Ave
Sycamore Gro
Tennyson Ave
Byron Ave
Dryden Ave
Bournemouth Park Rd
Redstock Rd
Stanfield Rd
Stadium Rd
Greyhound Way
Grainger Rd
Short St
Milton St
Maldon Road
St. Ann's Road
Guildford Road
Swanage Rd
Wimborne Rd
Boscombe Rd
North Ave
Central Ave
South Ave
Lancaster Gdns
Tyrrel Dr
St. John's Rd
St. Helen's Rd
Milton Rd
Canewdon Rd
St. Vincent's Rd
Avenue Ter
Avenue Road
Park Ter
Park Road
Queens Road
Princes Street
Hamlet Road
Ashburnham Road
Gordon Rd
Napier Ave
College Way
London Road
Elmer Ave
Elmer App
High St
Chichester Rd
Warrior Sq
Whitegate Road
Tylers Ave
Baltic Ave
York Rd
Heygate Ave
Church Rd
Clifftown Road
Scratton Rd
Weston Rd
Clarence Rd
Clarence St
Cambridge Road
Alexandra Road
Alexandra St
Royal Ter
Clifftown Parade
Westcliff Parade
Pier Hill
Kilworth Ave
Hastings Rd
Cromer Rd
St. Leonard's Rd
Albert Rd
Wesley Rd
Stanley Rd
Hartington Rd
Pleasant Rd
Lucy Rd

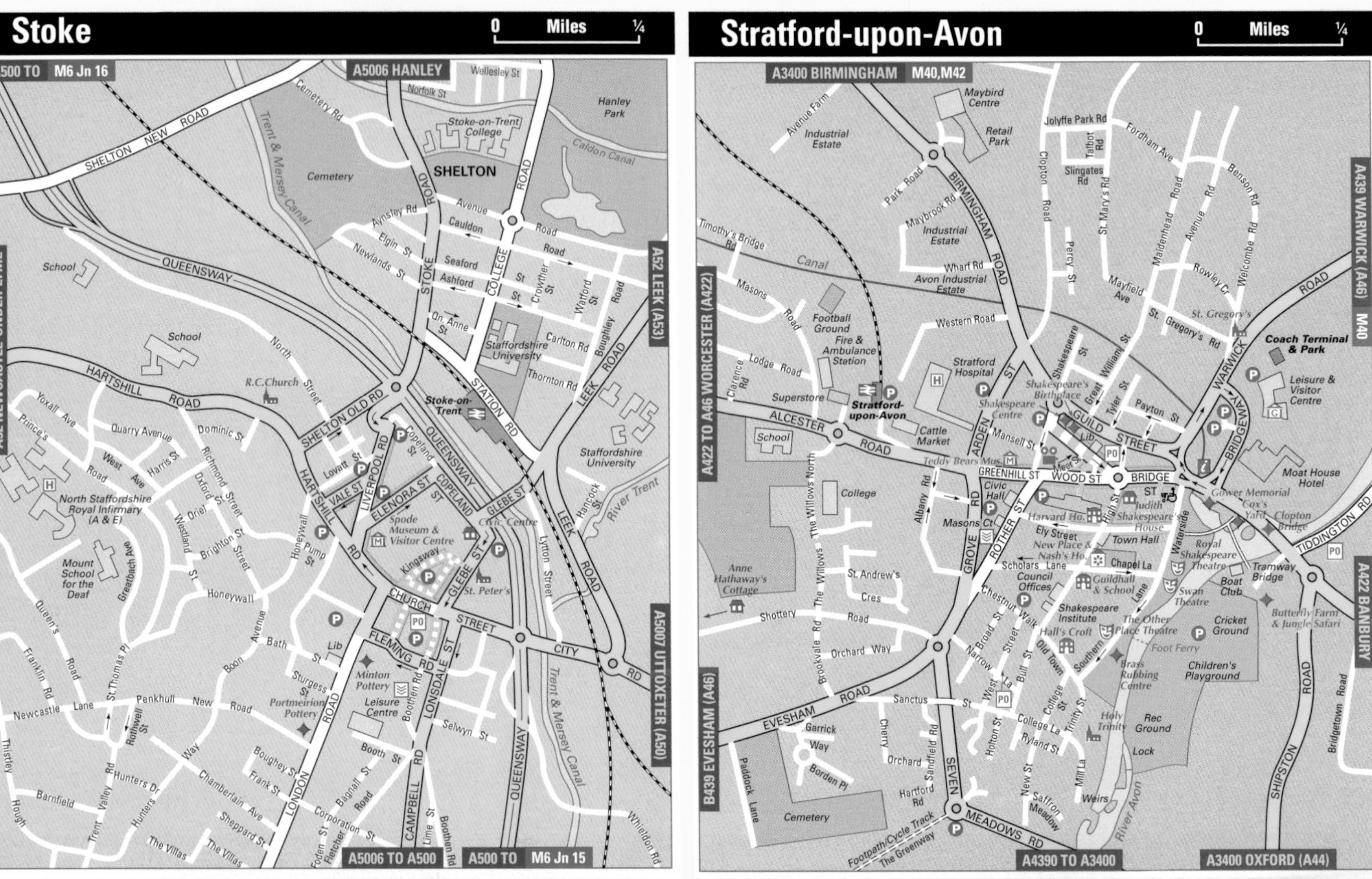
Stoke
0 Miles ¼
A500 TO M6 Jn 16
A5006 HANLEY
A52 LEEK (A53)
A5007 UTTOXETER (A50)
A500 TO M6 Jn 15
A5006 TO A500
A52 NEWCASTLE-UNDER-LYME
SHELTON
Stoke-on-Trent College
Hanley Park
Caldon Canal
Cemetery
Trent & Mersey Canal
SHELTON NEW ROAD
QUEENSWAY
STOKE ROAD
COLLEGE ROAD
Stoke-on-Trent
STATION RD
Staffordshire University
LEEK ROAD
River Trent
HARTSHILL ROAD
SHELTON OLD RD
LIVERPOOL RD
GLEBE ST
CHURCH STREET
CITY RD
LONDON ROAD
CAMPBELL RD
LONSDALE ST
Spode Museum & Visitor Centre
Minton Pottery
Portmeirion Pottery
Leisure Centre
North Staffordshire Royal Infirmary (A & E)
Mount School for the Deaf
School
R.C.Church
Civic Centre
St. Peter's
Stratford-upon-Avon
0 Miles ¼
A3400 BIRMINGHAM M40,M42
A439 WARWICK (A46) M40
A422 BANBURY
A3400 OXFORD (A44)
A4390 TO A3400
B439 EVESHAM (A46)
A422 TO A46 WORCESTER (A422)
Maybird Centre
Retail Park
Industrial Estate
BIRMINGHAM ROAD
Coach Terminal & Park
Leisure & Visitor Centre
Moat House Hotel
Stratford-upon-Avon
Stratford Hospital
Shakespeare's Birthplace
Shakespeare Centre
Football Ground
Fire & Ambulance Station
Cattle Market
ALCESTER ROAD
GREENHILL ST
WOOD ST
BRIDGE ST
Harvard Ho.
Judith Shakespeare's House
Town Hall
Royal Shakespeare Theatre
Swan Theatre
Gower Memorial
Clopton Bridge
Tramway Bridge
Boat Club
Butterfly Farm & Jungle Safari
Cricket Ground
Children's Playground
The Other Place Theatre
Brass Rubbing Centre
Holy Trinity
Rec Ground
River Avon
Hall's Croft
Shakespeare Institute
Guildhall & School
Council Offices
College
Anne Hathaway's Cottage
EVESHAM ROAD
SEVEN MEADOWS RD
Cemetery
Footpath/Cycle Track
The Greenway
SHIPSTON ROAD
TIDDINGTON RD

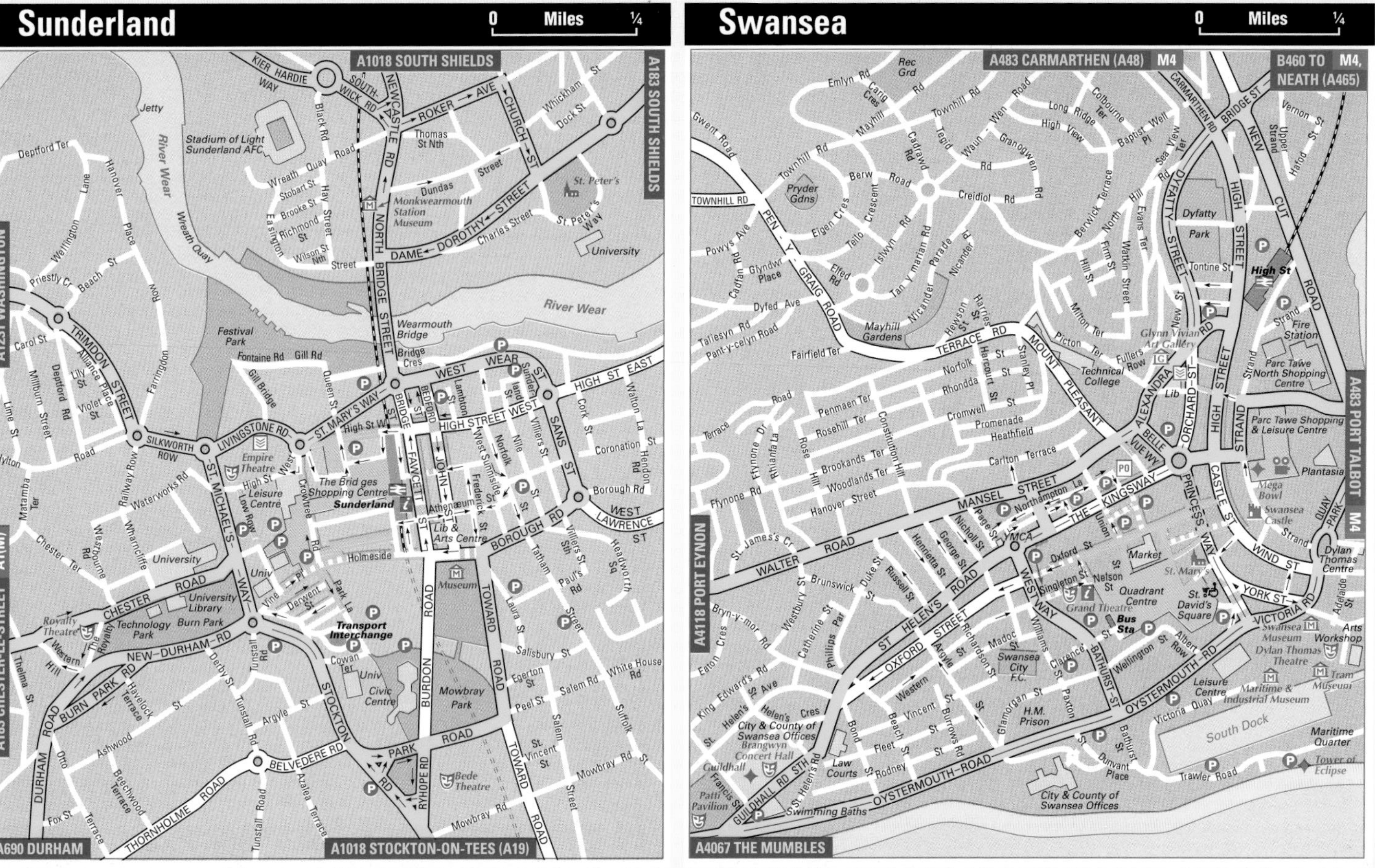
Sunderland
0 Miles ¼
A1018 SOUTH SHIELDS
A183 SOUTH SHIELDS
A1231 WASHINGTON
A1(M)
A183 CHESTER-LE-STREET
A690 DURHAM
A1018 STOCKTON-ON-TEES (A19)
River Wear
Jetty
Stadium of Light Sunderland AFC
Wreath Quay
Monkwearmouth Station Museum
St. Peter's
University
Festival Park
Wearmouth Bridge
NORTH BRIDGE STREET
NEWCASTLE RD
ROKER AVE
CHURCH ST
DAME DOROTHY STREET
HIGH ST EAST
HIGH STREET WEST
WEST WEAR ST
SANS ST
BOROUGH RD
WEST LAWRENCE ST
FAWCETT ST
JOHN ST
ST. MARY'S WAY
LIVINGSTONE RD
SILKWORTH ROW
ST. MICHAEL'S WAY
TRIMDON STREET
CHESTER ROAD
NEW DURHAM RD
BURN PARK RD
STOCKTON RD
BURDON ROAD
TOWARD ROAD
PARK RD
RYHOPE RD
BELVEDERE RD
THORNHOLME ROAD
DURHAM ROAD
Empire Theatre
Leisure Centre
The Bridges Shopping Centre
Sunderland
Athenaeum St
Lib & Arts Centre
Museum
Mowbray Park
Transport Interchange
Civic Centre
Univ
University Library
Burn Park
Technology Park
Royalty Theatre
Bede Theatre
Swansea
0 Miles ¼
A483 CARMARTHEN (A48) M4
B460 TO M4, NEATH (A465)
A483 PORT TALBOT M4
A4118 PORT EYNON
A4067 THE MUMBLES
TOWNHILL RD
PEN - Y - GRAIG ROAD
Pryder Gdns
Mayhill Gardens
TERRACE RD
MOUNT PLEASANT
Technical College
Glynn Vivian Art Gallery
ALEXANDRA RD
ORCHARD ST
HIGH STREET
STRAND
NEW CUT ROAD
High St
Fire Station
Parc Tawe North Shopping Centre
Parc Tawe Shopping & Leisure Centre
Plantasia
Mega Bowl
Swansea Castle
Dylan Thomas Centre
DYFATTY STREET
Dyfatty Park
MANSEL STREET
WALTER ROAD
THE KINGSWAY
PRINCESS WAY
CASTLE ST
WIND ST
YORK ST
VICTORIA RD
ST HELEN'S ROAD
OXFORD STREET
WEST WAY
BATHURST ST
OYSTERMOUTH ROAD
Market
St. Mary's
Quadrant Centre
Grand Theatre
Bus Sta
St. David's Square
Swansea City F.C.
H.M. Prison
Law Courts
City & County of Swansea Offices
Brangwyn Concert Hall
Guildhall
Patti Pavilion
Swimming Baths
Leisure Centre
Maritime & Industrial Museum
Swansea Museum
Dylan Thomas Theatre
Tram Museum
Arts Workshop
South Dock
Maritime Quarter
Tower of Eclipse

Windsor

York

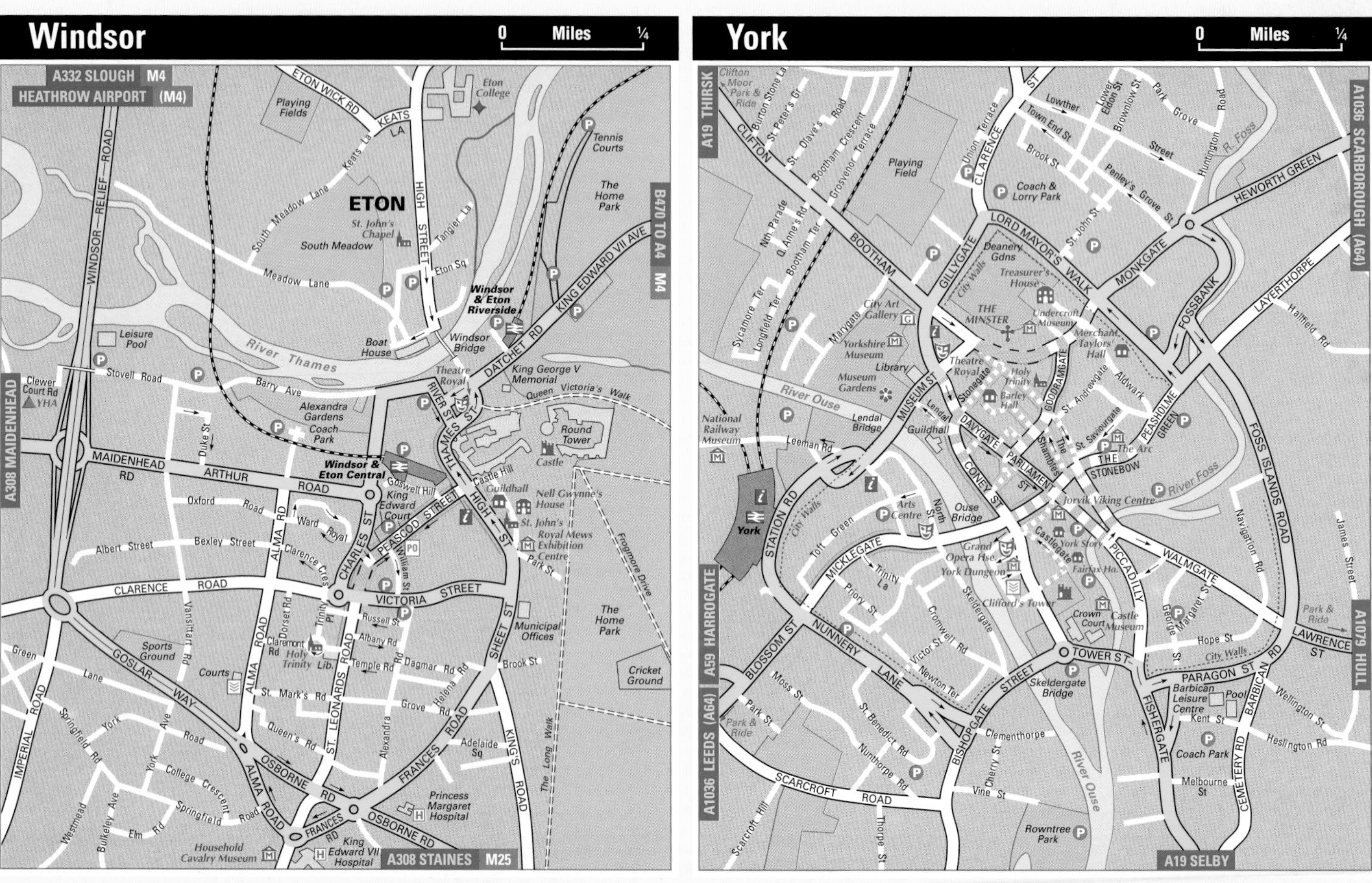
Windsor
0 Miles ¼
A332 SLOUGH M4
HEATHROW AIRPORT (M4)
B470 TO A4 M4
A308 MAIDENHEAD
A308 STAINES M25
ETON
Eton College
Playing Fields
ETON WICK RD
KEATS LA
Keats La
South Meadow Lane
St. John's Chapel
South Meadow
HIGH STREET
Tangier La
Eton Sq
Meadow Lane
Windsor & Eton Riverside
Boat House
Windsor Bridge
River Thames
Leisure Pool
Clewer Court Rd
YHA
Stovell Road
Barry Ave
Theatre Royal
DATCHET RD
KING EDWARD VII AVE
Tennis Courts
The Home Park
King George V Memorial
Queen Victoria's Walk
Alexandra Gardens
Coach Park
RIVER ST
THAMES ST
Round Tower
Castle
Castle Hill
WINDSOR RELIEF ROAD
Duke St
MAIDENHEAD RD
ARTHUR ROAD
Windsor & Eton Central
Goswell Hill
King Edward Court
Guildhall
Nell Gwynne's House
St. John's
Royal Mews Exhibition Centre
Park St
Frogmore Drive
Oxford Road
Ward
Royal
ALMA RD
Albert Street
Bexley Street
Clarence Cres
CHARLES ST
PEASCOD STREET
William St
HIGH ST
CLARENCE ROAD
VICTORIA STREET
SHEET ST
Municipal Offices
The Home Park
Vansittart Rd
Dorset Rd
Trinity Pl
Russell St
Albany Rd
Claremont Rd
Holy Trinity
Lib.
Temple Rd
Dagmar Rd
Brook St
Cricket Ground
Sports Ground
Courts
ALMA ROAD
ST. LEONARDS ROAD
St. Mark's Rd
Grove Rd
Helena Rd
Green Lane
GOSLAR WAY
IMPERIAL ROAD
Springfield Rd
York Ave
Road
Queen's Rd
Alexandra
FRANCES ROAD
Adelaide Sq
KING'S ROAD
The Long Walk
York
College Crescent
Springfield Road
OSBORNE RD
ALMA ROAD
Princess Margaret Hospital
Westmead
Bulkeley Ave
Elm Rd
Household Cavalry Museum
FRANCES RD
King Edward VII Hospital
OSBORNE RD
York
0 Miles ¼
A19 THIRSK
A1036 SCARBOROUGH (A64)
A59 HARROGATE
A1036 LEEDS (A64)
A1079 HULL
A19 SELBY
Clifton Moor Park & Ride
Burton Stone La
St. Peter's Gr
St. Olave's Road
Bootham Crescent
Grosvenor Terrace
CLIFTON
Playing Field
Union Terrace
CLARENCE ST
Lowther
Lower Eldon St
Brownlow St
Park Grove
Road
Town End St
Street
Huntington
R. Foss
Brook St
Penley's Grove St
HEWORTH GREEN
Coach & Lorry Park
Nth. Parade
Q. Anne's Rd
Bootham Ter
BOOTHAM
GILLYGATE
Deanery Gdns
LORD MAYOR'S WALK
St. John St
MONKGATE
Sycamore Ter
Longfield Ter
Marygate
City Art Gallery
City Walls
Treasurer's House
THE MINSTER
Undercroft Museum
Merchant Taylors' Hall
FOSSBANK
LAYERTHORPE
Hallfield Rd
Yorkshire Museum
Library
Museum Gardens
Theatre Royal
Holy Trinity
Barley Hall
Stonegate
GOODRAMGATE
St. Andrewgate
Aldwark
River Ouse
MUSEUM ST
Lendal
Lendal Bridge
Guildhall
DAVYGATE
PEASHOLME GREEN
National Railway Museum
Leeman Rd
CONEY ST
PARLIAMENT ST
Shambles
The
St. Saviourgate
The Arc
THE STONEBOW
River Foss
FOSS ISLANDS ROAD
York
STATION RD
City Walls
Toft Green
Arts Centre
North St
Ouse Bridge
Jorvik Viking Centre
Navigation Rd
James Street
MICKLEGATE
Trinity La
Grand Opera Hse.
York Dungeon
Castlegate
York Story
Fairfax Ho.
PICCADILLY
WALMGATE
Priory St
Cromwell Rd
Skeldergate
Clifford's Tower
Crown Court
Castle Museum
George St
Margaret St
Hope St
City Walls
Park & Ride
LAWRENCE ST
BLOSSOM ST
NUNNERY LANE
Victor St
Newton Ter
TOWER ST
PARAGON ST
BARBICAN RD
Moss St
Park St
Park & Ride
St. Benedict Rd
Nunthorpe Rd
BISHOPGATE STREET
Skeldergate Bridge
Clementhorpe
Cherry St
FISHERGATE
Barbican Leisure Centre
Pool
Kent St
Wellington St
Heslington Rd
Coach Park
CEMETERY RD
SCARCROFT ROAD
Vine St
Melbourne St
Scarcroft Hill
Thorpe St
Rowntree Park

ABBREVIATIONS

erd C	*Aberdeen City*
erds	*Aberdeenshire*
ngl	*Anglesey*
g/Bute	*Argyll & Bute*
ath/NE Som'set	*Bath & North East Somerset*
eds	*Bedfordshire*
Gwent	*Blaenau Gwent*
ackb'n	*Blackburn with Darwen*
ackp'l	*Blackpool*
ournem'th	*Bournemouth*
ackn'l	*Bracknell Forest*
idg	*Bridgend*
righton/Hove	*Brighton and Hove*
ristol	*City & County of Bristol*
ucks	*Buckinghamshire*
aerph	*Caerphilly*
ambs	*Cambridgeshire*
ard	*Cardiff*
arms	*Carmarthenshire*
/Edinb	*City of Edinburgh*
eredig'n	*Ceredigion*
/Glasg	*City of Glasgow*
han Is	*Channel Islands*
hes	*Cheshire*
lack	*Clackmannanshire*
Cornw'l	*Cornwall*
Cumb	*Cumbria*
C/York	*City of York*
Denbs	*Denbighshire*
Derby	*Derbyshire*
Derby C	*Derby City*
D'lington	*Darlington*
Dumf/Gal	*Dumfries & Galloway*
Dundee C	*Dundee City*
E Ayrs	*East Ayrshire*
E Dunb	*East Dunbartonshire*
E Loth	*East Lothian*
E Renf	*East Renfrewshire*
ER Yorks	*East Riding of Yorkshire*
E Sussex	*East Sussex*
Falk	*Falkirk*
Flints	*Flintshire*
Glos	*Gloucestershire*
Gtr Lon	*Greater London*
Gtr Man	*Greater Manchester*
Gwyn	*Gwynedd*
Hants	*Hampshire*
Hartlep'l	*Hartlepool*
Heref'd	*Herefordshire*
Herts	*Hertfordshire*
H'land	*Highland*
I/Man	*Isle of Man*
Invercl	*Inverclyde*
I/Scilly	*Isles of Scilly*
I/Wight	*Isle of Wight*
Kingston/Hull	*Kingston upon Hull*
Lancs	*Lancashire*
Leics	*Leicestershire*
Leics C	*Leicester City*
Lincs	*Lincolnshire*
Mersey	*Merseyside*
Merth Tyd	*Merthyr Tydfil*
Middlesbro	*Middlesbrough*
Midloth	*Midlothian*
M/Keynes	*Milton Keynes*
Monmouths	*Monmouthshire*
N Ayrs	*North Ayrshire*
N Lanarks	*North Lanarkshire*
N Lincs	*North Lincolnshire*
N Som'set	*North Somerset*
N Yorks	*North Yorkshire*
NE Lincs	*North East Lincolnshire*
Neath P Talb	*Neath Port Talbot*
Newp	*Newport*
Northants	*Northamptonshire*
Northum	*Northumberland*
Nott'ham	*City of Nottingham*
Notts	*Nottinghamshire*
Oxon	*Oxfordshire*
Pembs	*Pembrokeshire*
Perth/Kinr	*Perth & Kinross*
Peterbro	*Peterborough*
Portsm'th	*Portsmouth*
Plym'th	*Plymouth*
Redcar/Clevel'd	*Redcar & Cleveland*
Renf	*Renfrewshire*
Rh Cyn Taff	*Rhondda Cynon Taff*
Rutl'd	*Rutland*
S Ayrs	*South Ayrshire*
S Glos	*South Gloucestershire*
S Lanarks	*South Lanarkshire*
S Yorks	*South Yorkshire*
Scot Borders	*Scottish Borders*
Shetl'd	*Shetland*
Shrops	*Shropshire*
Som'set	*Somerset*
Southend	*Southend-on-Sea*
Staffs	*Staffordshire*
S'thampton	*Southampton*
Stirl	*Stirling*
Stockton	*Stockton on Tees*
Stoke	*Stoke-on-Trent*
Swan	*Swansea*
Telford	*Telford and Wrekin*
Thurr'k	*Thurrock*
Torf	*Torfaen*
Tyne/Wear	*Tyne & Wear*
V/Glam	*Vale of Glamorgan*
W Berks	*West Berkshire*
W Dunb	*West Dunbartonshire*
W Isles	*Western Isles*
W Loth	*West Lothian*
W Midlands	*West Midlands*
W Sussex	*West Sussex*
W Yorks	*West Yorkshire*
Warwick	*Warwickshire*
Wilts	*Wiltshire*
Windsor	*Windsor and Maidenhead*
Worcs	*Worcestershire*
Wrex	*Wrexham*

A

Auchtermuchty *Fife* 25 K17
Auchtertyre *H'land* 27 H12
Aucloggeen *Galway* 35 R6
Audlem *Ches* 10 S18
Audley *Staffs* 10 R19
Augher *Tyrone* 32 P9
Aughnacloy *Tyrone* 33 P10
Aughrim *Clare* 35 R6
Aughrim *Galway* 35 R7
Aughrim *Wicklow* 40 S11
Auldearn *H'land* 28 G16
Aultbea *H'land* 27 G12
Austwick *N Yorks* 15 P19
Avebury *Wilts* 5 V20
Avening *Glos* 5 U19
Aveton Gifford *Devon* 3 X16
Aviemore *H'land* 24 H16
Avoca *Wicklow* 40 S11
Avoch *H'land* 28 G15
Avonmouth *Bristol* 4 U18
Axbridge *Som'set* 4 V18
Axminster *Devon* 4 W17
Axmouth *Devon* 4 W17
Aylesbury *Bucks* 6 U22
Aylesford *Kent* 7 V24
Aylesham *Kent* 7 V26
Aylsham *Norfolk* 13 S26
Aynho *Northants* 11 U21
Ayr *S Ayrs* 19 M14
Aysgarth *N Yorks* 15 P19
Ayton *N Yorks* 17 P23
Ayton *Scot Borders* 21 L19

B

Bac *W Isles* 26 F11
Backwell *N Som'set* 4 V18
Bacton *Norfolk* 13 S26
Bacup *Lancs* 15 Q19
Badenscoth *Aberds* 29 H19
Badenyon *Aberds* 25 H17
Badrallach *H'land* 27 G13
Bagh a Chaisteil *W Isles* 22 J8
Bagillt *Flints* 15 R17
Bagshot *Surrey* 6 V22
Baildon *W Yorks* 15 Q20
Baile Ailein *W Isles* 26 F10
Bailieborough *Cavan* 37 Q10
Bainbridge *N Yorks* 15 P19
Bainton *ER Yorks* 17 Q22
Bakewell *Derby* 11 R20
Bala *Gwyn* 8 S16
Balbeggie *Perth/Kinr* 24 K17
Balblair *H'land* 28 G15
Balbriggan *Dublin* 37 Q11
Balcombe *W Sussex* 6 V23
Balderton *Notts* 11 R22
Baldock *Herts* 12 U23
Baldoyle *Dublin* 37 R11
Balfron *Stirl* 24 K15
Balintore *H'land* 28 G16
Balla *Mayo* 35 Q5
Ballachulish *H'land* 23 J13
Ballagh *Galway* 35 R5
Ballagh *Limerick* 38 T5
Ballagh *Tipperary* 39 S8
Ballaghaderreen *Roscommon* 35 Q6
Ballantrae *S Ayrs* 18 M14
Ballasalla *I/Man* 14 P14
Ballater *Aberds* 25 H17
Ballaugh *I/Man* 14 P14
Ballickmoyler *Laois* 40 S9
Ballin Cloher *Kerry* 38 T4
Ballina *Mayo* 35 P5
Ballina *Tipperary* 39 S7
Ballinadee *Cork* 39 U6
Ballinafad *Sligo* 35 P7
Ballinagar *Offaly* 36 R9
Ballinakill *Laois* 40 S9
Ballinalack *Westmeath* 36 Q9
Ballinalea *Wicklow* 40 R11
Ballinalee *Longford* 36 Q8
Ballinamallard *Fermanagh* 32 P8
Ballinameen *Roscommon* 35 Q7
Ballinamore Bridge *Galway* 35 R7
Ballinamore *Leitrim* 36 P8
Ballinascarty *Cork* 39 U6
Ballinasloe *Galway* 35 R7
Ballincollig *Cork* 39 U6
Ballincurrig *Cork* 39 U7
Ballindaggan *Wexford* 40 S10
Ballinderreen *Galway* 35 R6
Ballinderry *Tipperary* 35 R7
Ballinderry Upr. *Antrim* 33 N11
Ballindine *Mayo* 35 Q6
Ballindooly *Galway* 35 R5
Ballineen *Cork* 39 U6
Ballingarry *Limerick* 39 T6
Ballingarry *Tipperary* 36 R7
Ballingarry *Tipperary* 39 S8
Ballingeary *Cork* 38 U5
Ballinhassig *Cork* 39 U6
Ballinlea *Antrim* 33 M11
Ballinlough *Roscommon* 35 Q6
Ballinluig *Perth/Kinr* 24 J16
Ballinrobe *Mayo* 35 Q5
Ballinskelligs *Kerry* 38 U3
Ballinspittle *Cork* 39 U6
Ballintober *Mayo* 34 Q5
Ballintober *Roscommon* 35 Q7
Ballintoy *Antrim* 33 M11
Ballintra *Donegal* 32 N7
Ballintroohan *Donegal* 33 M9
Ballinunty *Tipperary* 39 S8
Ballinure *Tipperary* 39 S8
Ballitore *Kildare* 40 R10
Ballivor *Meath* 37 Q10
Balloch *H'land* 28 H15
Balloch *W Dunb* 24 K14
Ballochan *Aberds* 25 H18
Ballon *Carlow* 40 S10
Ballure *Donegal* 32 N7
Ballyagran *Limerick* 39 T6
Ballybay *Monaghan* 37 P10
Ballybofey *Donegal* 32 N8
Ballyboghil *Dublin* 37 Q11
Ballybogy *Antrim* 33 M10
Ballybritt *Offaly* 36 R8
Ballybrittas *Laois* 36 R9
Ballybrophy *Laois* 39 S8
Ballybunion *Kerry* 38 S4
Ballycahill *Tipperary* 39 S8
Ballycanew *Wexford* 40 S11
Ballycarney *Wexford* 40 S10
Ballycarry *Antrim* 33 N12
Ballycastle *Mayo* 34 P5
Ballycastle *Antrim* 33 M11
Ballyclare *Antrim* 33 N12
Ballyclerahan *Tipperary* 39 T8
Ballyclogh *Cork* 39 T6
Ballycolla *Laois* 40 S9
Ballyconneely *Galway* 34 R3
Ballyconnell *Cavan* 36 P8
Ballyconnell *Sligo* 32 P6
Ballycotton *Cork* 39 U7
Ballycrossaun *Galway* 36 R7
Ballycroy *Mayo* 34 P4
Ballycumber *Offaly* 36 R8
Ballydangan *Roscommon* 36 R7
Ballydavid *Galway* 35 R7
Ballydavid *Kerry* 38 T3
Ballydavis *Laois* 40 R9
Ballydehob *Cork* 38 U5
Ballydonegan *Cork* 38 U3
Ballyduff *Kerry* 38 T4
Ballyduff *Waterford* 39 T7
Ballydugan *Down* 33 P12
Ballyfarnan *Roscommon* 35 P7
Ballyferriter *Kerry* 38 T3
Ballyfin *Laois* 40 R9
Ballyforan *Roscommon* 35 R7
Ballygar *Galway* 35 Q7
Ballygarrett *Wexford* 40 S11
Ballygawley *Sligo* 32 P7
Ballygawley *Tyrone* 33 P9
Ballyglass *Mayo* 35 Q5
Ballygorman *Donegal* 32 M9
Ballygowan *Down* 33 N12
Ballygrant *Arg/Bute* 18 L11
Ballyhaght *Limerick* 39 T6
Ballyhahill *Limerick* 38 S5
Ballyhaise *Cavan* 36 P9
Ballyhalbert *Down* 33 P13
Ballyhale *Galway* 35 R5
Ballyhaunis *Mayo* 35 Q6
Ballyhean *Mayo* 34 Q5
Ballyheige *Kerry* 38 T4
Ballyhooly *Cork* 39 T7
Ballyhornan *Down* 33 P12
Ballyjamesduff *Cavan* 36 Q9
Ballykelly *Londonderry* 33 M9
Ballykillin *Donegal* 32 M9
Ballylanders *Limerick* 39 T7
Ballylaneen *Waterford* 40 T9
Ballyliffin *Donegal* 32 M9
Ballylongford *Kerry* 38 S5
Ballylooby *Tipperary* 39 T8
Ballylynan *Laois* 40 S9
Ballymacarbry *Waterford* 39 T8
Ballymacoda *Cork* 39 U8
Ballymagorry *Tyrone* 32 N9
Ballymahon *Longford* 36 Q8
Ballymakenny *Louth* 37 Q11
Ballymartin *Down* 37 P12
Ballymena *Antrim* 33 N11
Ballymoe *Galway* 35 Q7
Ballymoney *Antrim* 33 M10
Ballymore Eustace *Kildare* 37 R10
Ballymore *Westmeath* 36 R8
Ballymote *Sligo* 35 P6
Ballymullakill *Roscommon* 36 R7
Ballymurphy *Carlow* 40 S10
Ballymurray *Roscommon* 36 Q7
Ballynabola *Wexford* 40 T10
Ballynacally *Clare* 38 S5
Ballynacarrigy *Westmeath* 36 Q8
Ballynacorra *Cork* 39 U7
Ballynagore *Westmeath* 36 R9
Ballynahinch *Down* 33 P12
Ballynahown *Westmeath* 36 R8
Ballynamona *Cork* 39 T6
Ballynamult *Waterford* 39 T8
Ballyneety *Limerick* 39 S6
Ballynure *Antrim* 33 N12
Ballyporeen *Tipperary* 39 T7
Ballyragget *Kilkenny* 40 S9
Ballyroan *Laois* 40 S9
Ballyroe *Cork* 39 T7
Ballyronan *Londonderry* 33 N10
Ballyroney *Down* 33 P11
Ballysadare *Sligo* 32 P6
Ballyshannon *Donegal* 32 P7
Ballyshannon *Kildare* 37 R10
Ballyshrule *Galway* 35 R7
Ballysloe *Tipperary* 39 S8
Ballysteen *Limerick* 39 S6
Ballyvaghan *Clare* 35 R5
Ballyvourney *Cork* 38 U5
Ballyvoy *Antrim* 33 M11
Ballywalter *Down* 33 N13
Ballyward *Down* 33 P11
Ballywilliam *Wexford* 40 T10
Balmaclellan *Dumf/Gal* 19 M15
Balmedie *Aberds* 25 H19
Balnapaling *H'land* 28 G15
Balquhidder *Stirl* 24 K15
Balrath *Meath* 37 Q11
Balrothery *Dublin* 37 Q11
Balsall *W Midlands* 11 T20
Balsham *Cambs* 12 T24
Baltimore *Cork* 39 V5
Baltinglass *Wicklow* 40 S10
Baltracey *Kildare* 37 R10
Baltray *Louth* 37 Q11
Balvicar *Arg/Bute* 23 K12
Bamber Bridge *Lancs* 15 Q18
Bamburgh *Northum* 21 L20
Bamford *Derby* 16 R20
Bampton *Devon* 4 W17
Bampton *Oxon* 5 U20
Banagher *Offaly* 36 R8
Banbridge *Down* 33 P11
Banbury *Oxon* 11 T21
Banchory *Aberds* 25 H18
Bandon *Cork* 39 U6
Banff *Aberds* 29 G18
Bangor *Mayo* 34 P4
Bangor *Down* 33 N12
Bangor *Gwyn* 8 R15
Bangor-is-y-coed *Wrex* 10 S18
Banham *Norfolk* 13 T26
Bankend *Dumf/Gal* 20 M16
Bankfoot *Perth/Kinr* 24 J16
Bankhead *Aberd C* 25 H19
Banks *Lancs* 15 Q18
Bannockburn *Stirl* 24 K16
Bannow *Wexford* 40 T10
Banstead *Surrey* 6 V23
Banteer *Cork* 39 T6
Bantry *Cork* 38 U5
Banwell *N Som'set* 4 V18
Bar Hill *Cambs* 12 T24
Barabhas *W Isles* 26 F10
Baranailt *Londonderry* 33 N9
Barassie *S Ayrs* 19 L14
Barbon *Cumb* 15 P18
Bardney *Lincs* 17 R23
Barefield *Clare* 39 S6
Barford *Warwick* 11 T20
Bargoed *Caerph* 4 U17
Bargrennan *Dumf/Gal* 19 M14
Barham *Kent* 7 V26
Barkway *Herts* 12 U24
Barlborough *Derby* 16 R21
Barlby *N Yorks* 16 Q21
Barley *Herts* 12 T24
Barmby Moor *ER Yorks* 17 Q22
Barmoor Castle *Northum* 21 L19
Barmouth *Gwyn* 8 S15
Barna *Galway* 35 R5
Barnaderg *Galway* 35 R6
Barnard Castle *Durham* 21 N20
Barnesmore *Donegal* 32 N7
Barnet *Gtr Lon* 6 U23
Barnetby le Wold *N Lincs* 17 Q23
Barnham *Suffolk* 13 T25
Barnhill *Moray* 28 G17
Barnoldswick *Lancs* 15 Q19
Barnsley *S Yorks* 16 Q21
Barnstaple *Devon* 3 V15
Barnt Green *Worcs* 11 T20
Barr *S Ayrs* 19 M14
Barraduff *Kerry* 38 T5
Barran *Cavan* 32 P8
Barrhead *E Renf* 19 L15
Barrhill *S Ayrs* 18 M14
Barrow upon Humber *N Lincs* 17 Q23
Barrowford *Lancs* 15 Q19
Barrow-In-Furness *Cumb* 15 P17
Barry *Angus* 25 K18
Barry *V/Glam* 4 V17
Barton *N Yorks* 16 P20
Barton upon Humber *N Lincs* 17 Q23
Barton-le-Clay *Beds* 12 U23
Barwell *Leics* 11 S21
Baschurch *Shrops* 10 S18
Basildon *Essex* 7 U25
Basingstoke *Hants* 5 V21
Baslow *Derby* 16 R20
Baston *Lincs* 12 S23
Bath *Bath/NE Som'set* 5 V19
Bathford *Bath/NE Som'set* 5 V19
Bathgate *W Loth* 24 L16
Batley *W Yorks* 16 Q20
Batterstown *Meath* 37 R10
Battle *E Sussex* 7 W24
Bawdeswell *Norfolk* 13 S26
Bawdsey *Suffolk* 13 T26
Bawnboy *Cavan* 36 P8
Bawtry *S Yorks* 16 R21
Bayston Hill *Shrops* 10 S18
Beachley *Glos* 4 U18
Beaconsfield *Bucks* 6 U22
Beadnell *Northum* 21 L20
Bealin *Westmeath* 36 R8
Bealnablath *Cork* 39 U6
Beaminster *Dorset* 4 W18
Bearsden *E Dunb* 19 L15
Bearsted *Kent* 7 V25
Beattock *Dumf/Gal* 20 M17
Beaufort *Kerry* 38 T4
Beaufort *Bl Gwent* 4 U17
Beaulieu *Hants* 5 W21
Beauly *H'land* 28 H15
Beaumaris *Angl* 8 R15
Bebington *Mersey* 15 R17
Beccles *Suffolk* 13 T27
Beck Row *Suffolk* 12 T24
Beckermet *Cumb* 14 P1
Beckfoot *Cumb* 20 N1
Beckhampton *Wilts* 5 V2
Beckingham *Notts* 17 R2
Beckington *Som'set* 5 V1
Bedale *N Yorks* 16 P2
Beddgelert *Gwyn* 8 R1
Bedford *Beds* 12 T2
Bedlington *Northum* 21 M2
Bedwas *Caerph* 4 U1
Bedworth *Warwick* 11 T2
Beech Hill *Down* 33 P1
Beeford *ER Yorks* 17 Q2
Beelaha *Clare* 38 S
Beer *Devon* 4 W1
Beeston *Notts* 11 S2
Beeswing *Dumf/Gal* 19 M1
Begelly *Pembs* 9 U1
Beguildy *Powys* 10 T1
Beighton *S Yorks* 16 R2
Beith *N Ayrs* 19 L1
Belbroughton *Worcs* 10 T1
Belchford *Lincs* 17 R2
Belclare *Galway* 35 R
Belcoo *Fermanagh* 32 P
Belderg *Mayo* 34 P
Belfast *Antrim* 33 N1
Belford *Northum* 21 L2
Belgooly *Cork* 39 U
Bellacorick *Mayo* 34 P
Bellaghy *Londonderry* 33 N1
Bellahy *Sligo* 35 Q
Bellanagare *Roscommon* 35 Q
Bellanaleck *Fermanagh* 32 P
Bellanamore *Donegal* 32 N7
Bellananagh *Cavan* 36 Q
Bellavary *Mayo* 35 Q5
Belleek *Donegal* 32 P7
Belleek *Armagh* 33 P1
Belleville *Galway* 35 R
Bellinamuck *Longford* 36 Q
Bellingham *Northum* 21 M1
Bellsbank *E Ayrs* 19 M15
Bellshill *N Lanarks* 19 L15
Belmont *Blackb'n* 15 Q1
Belmullet *Mayo* 34 P
Belper *Derby* 11 R21
Belsay *Northum* 21 M2
Beltinge *Kent* 7 V2
Belton *N Lincs* 17 Q22
Belton *Norfolk* 13 S27
Beltra *Mayo* 34 Q5
Beltra *Sligo* 32 P
Belturbet *Cavan* 36 P
Bembridge *I/Wight* 5 W21
Benburb *Tyrone* 33 P1
Benington *Lincs* 12 R24
Benllech *Angl* 8 R15
Bennettsbridge *Kilkenny* 40 S9
Benson *Oxon* 5 U21
Bentley *Hants* 6 V22
Bentley *S Yorks* 16 Q21
Benwick *Cambs* 12 T23
Beragh *Tyrone* 32 N9
Bere Alston *Devon* 3 X15
Bere Regis *Dorset* 5 W19
Berkeley *Glos* 5 U19
Berkhamsted *Herts* 6 U22
Berriedale *H'land* 28 F17
Berriew *Powys* 10 S17
Berrow *Som'set* 4 V17
Berwick *E Sussex* 6 W24
Berwick-Upon-Tweed *Northum* 21 L19
Bessbrook *Armagh* 33 P11
Bethersden *Kent* 7 V25
Bethesda *Gwyn* 8 R15
Bettws Bledrws *Ceredig'n* 9 T15
Bettyhill *H'land* 28 E15
Bettystown *Meath* 37 Q11
Betws *Bridg* 9 U16
Betws-y-Coed *Conwy* 8 R16
Beulah *Powys* 9 T16
Beverley *ER Yorks* 17 Q23
Beville *Mayo* 34 P5
Bewcastle *Cumb* 21 M18
Bewdley *Worcs* 10 T19
Bexhill *E Sussex* 7 W24
Bexley *Gtr Lon* 6 V24
Bibury *Glos* 5 U20
Bicester *Oxon* 11 U21
Bickington *Devon* 4 W16

Burton upon Stather *N Lincs* 17 Q22
Burton Upon Trent *Staffs* 11 S20
Burtonport *Donegal* 32 N7
Burwash *E Sussex* 7 W24
Burwell *Cambs* 12 T24
Bury St. Edmunds *Suffolk* 13 T25
Bury *Gtr Man* 15 Q19
Bushey *Herts* 6 U23
Bushmills *Antrim* 33 M10
Butler's Bridge *Cavan* 36 P9
Butlerstown *Cork* 39 U6
Buttermere *Cumb* 20 N17
Buttevant *Cork* 39 T6
Buxted *E Sussex* 6 W24
Buxton *Derby* 15 R20
Bweeng *Cork* 39 T6
Byfield *Northants* 11 T21
Byfleet *Surrey* 6 V23
Bylchau *Conwy* 8 R16

C

Cabinteely *Dublin* 37 R11
Cabrach *Moray* 29 H17
Cabragh *Tyrone* 33 P10
Cadamstown *Offaly* 36 R8
Caenby Corner *Lincs* 17 R22
Caergwrle *Flints* 10 R17
Caerleon *Newp* 4 U18
Caernarfon *Gwyn* 8 R15
Caerphilly *Caerph* 4 U17
Caersws *Powys* 8 S17
Caerwent *Monmouths* 4 U18
Caher *Clare* 35 S6
Caher *Galway* 34 R5
Caher *Tipperary* 39 T8
Caherciveen *Kerry* 38 U3
Caherconlish *Limerick* 39 S7
Caherdaniel *Kerry* 38 U3
Cahermore *Cork* 38 U3
Cahermurphy *Clare* 38 S5
Cairinis *W Isles* 26 G9
Cairndow *Arg/Bute* 23 K14
Cairnryan *Dumf/Gal* 18 N13
Caister-on-Sea *Norfolk* 13 S27
Caistor *Lincs* 17 R23
Calanais *W Isles* 26 F10
Caldbeck *Cumb* 20 N17
Calder Bridge *Cumb* 14 P17
Caldercruix *N Lanarks* 19 L16
Caldicot *Monmouths* 4 U18
Caledon *Tyrone* 33 P10
Calgary *Arg/Bute* 22 J11
Callan *Kilkenny* 40 S9
Callander *Stirl* 24 K15
Callington *Cornw'l* 3 X15
Callow *Galway* 34 R3
Callow *Mayo* 35 Q5
Calne *Wilts* 5 V20
Calshot *Hants* 5 W21
Calstock *Cornw'l* 3 X15
Calta *Galway* 35 R7
Calverton *Notts* 11 R21
Cam *Glos* 5 U19
Camber *E Sussex* 7 W25
Camberley *Surrey* 6 V22
Cambo *Northum* 21 M20
Camborne *Cornw'l* 2 X13
Cambridge *Cambs* 12 T24
Camden *Gtr Lon* 6 U23
Camelford *Cornw'l* 2 W14
Camlough *Armagh* 33 P11
Cammachmore *Aberds* 25 H19
Camolin *Wexford* 40 S11
Camp *Kerry* 38 T4
Campbeltown *Arg/Bute* 18 M12
Campile *Wexford* 40 T10
Camrose *Pembs* 9 U13
Camross *Wexford* 40 T10
Canisbay *H'land* 29 E17
Cannich *H'land* 27 H14
Canningstown *Cavan* 36 Q9
Cannington *Som'set* 4 V17
Cannock *Staffs* 10 S19
Canonbie *Dumf/Gal* 20 M18
Canterbury *Kent* 7 V26
Canvey *Essex* 7 U25
Caol *H'land* 23 J13
Caolas Stocinis *W Isles* 26 G10
Caoles *Arg/Bute* 22 J10
Capel Curig *Conwy* 8 R16
Capel St. Mary *Suffolk* 13 T26
Capel *Surrey* 6 V23
Cappagh *Cork* 39 T7
Cappagh *Galway* 35 R7
Cappagh White *Tipperary* 39 S7
Cappamore *Limerick* 39 S7
Cappeen *Cork* 39 U6
Cappoquin *Waterford* 39 T8
Carbis Bay *Cornw'l* 2 X13
Carbost *H'land* 26 H11
Carbost *H'land* 26 H11
Carbury *Kildare* 37 R10
Cardiff *Card* 4 V17
Cardigan *Ceredig'n* 9 T14
Cardington *Beds* 12 T23
Cardross *Arg/Bute* 19 L14
Cargill *Perth/Kinr* 24 J17
Carhampton *Som'set* 4 V17
Carisbrooke *I/Wight* 5 W21
Cark *Cumb* 15 P18
Carlabhagh *W Isles* 26 F10
Carlanstown *Meath* 37 Q10
Carleton Rode *Norfolk* 13 S26
Carlingford *Louth* 37 P11
Carlisle *Cumb* 20 N18
Carlops *Scot Borders* 20 L17
Carlow *Carlow* 40 S10
Carlton Colville *Suffolk* 13 T27
Carlton Miniott *N Yorks* 16 P21
Carlton *N Yorks* 16 Q21
Carlton *Notts* 11 S21
Carlton-in-Lindrick *Notts* 16 R21
Carluke *S Lanarks* 19 L16
Carmarthen *Carms* 9 U15
Carmyllie *Angus* 25 J18
Carna *Galway* 34 R4
Carnachuin *H'land* 24 H16
Carnaross *Meath* 37 Q10
Carncastle *Antrim* 33 N12
Carndonagh *Donegal* 32 M9
Carnew *Wicklow* 40 S11
Carney *Sligo* 32 P6
Carnforth *Lancs* 15 P18
Carnlough *Antrim* 33 N12
Carno *Powys* 8 S16
Carnoustie *Angus* 25 J18
Carnwath *S Lanarks* 20 L16
Carracastle *Mayo* 35 Q6
Carradale *Arg/Bute* 18 L13
Carragh *Kildare* 37 R10
Carran *Clare* 35 R5
Carraroe *Galway* 34 R4
Carrbridge *H'land* 28 H16
Carrick *Donegal* 32 N6
Carrick *Arg/Bute* 23 K14
Carrickart *Donegal* 32 M8
Carrickbeg *Waterford* 40 T9
Carrickboy *Longford* 36 Q8
Carrickfergus *Antrim* 33 N12
Carrickmacross *Monaghan* 37 Q10
Carrickmore *Tyrone* 33 N9
Carrick-on-Shannon *Roscommon* 36 Q7
Carrick-on-Suir *Tipperary* 40 T9
Carrigaholt *Clare* 38 S4
Carrigahorig *Tipperary* 36 R7
Carrigaline *Cork* 39 U7
Carrigallen *Leitrim* 36 Q8
Carriganimmy *Cork* 38 U5
Carrigfadda *Cork* 38 U5
Carrigkerry *Limerick* 38 T5
Carrignavar *Cork* 39 U7
Carrigtohill *Cork* 39 U7
Carronbridge *Dumf/Gal* 19 M16
Carrowbehy *Roscommon* 35 Q6
Carrowkeel *Donegal* 32 M8
Carrowkeel *Donegal* 32 M9
Carrowkeel *Galway* 35 R7
Carrowkennedy *Mayo* 34 Q4
Carrowreagh *Antrim* 33 M11
Carrowreilly *Sligo* 35 P6
Carrowroe *Longford* 36 Q8
Carryduff *Down* 33 N12
Carsaig *Arg/Bute* 23 K12
Carsphairn *Dumf/Gal* 19 M15
Carstairs *S Lanarks* 20 L16
Carterton *Oxon* 5 U20
Cartmel *Cumb* 15 P18
Cashel *Galway* 35 Q6
Cashel *Tipperary* 39 S8
Castle Acre *Norfolk* 13 S25
Castle Cary *Som'set* 4 V18
Castle Donington *Leics* 11 S21
Castle Douglas *Dumf/Gal* 19 N16
Castlebar *Mayo* 34 Q5
Castlebellingham *Louth* 37 Q11
Castleblakeney *Galway* 35 R7
Castleblaney *Monaghan* 37 P10
Castlebridge *Wexford* 40 T11
Castlecomer *Kilkenny* 40 S9
Castleconnell *Limerick* 39 S7
Castlecor *Cork* 39 T6
Castledawson *Londonderry* 33 N10
Castlederg *Tyrone* 32 N8
Castledermot *Kildare* 40 S10
Castlefinn *Donegal* 32 N8
Castleford *W Yorks* 16 Q21
Castlegregory *Kerry* 38 T3
Castlehill *Mayo* 34 P4
Castleisland *Kerry* 38 T5
Castlelyons *Cork* 39 T7
Castlemaine *Kerry* 38 T4
Castlemartin *Pembs* 9 U13
Castlemartyr *Cork* 39 U7
Castleplunket *Roscommon* 35 Q7
Castlepollard *Westmeath* 36 Q9
Castlerea *Roscommon* 35 Q7
Castlerock *Londonderry* 33 M10
Castleside *Durham* 21 N20
Castleton *Derby* 15 R20
Castleton *N Yorks* 17 P22
Castletown Bearhaven *Cork* 38 U4
Castletown Geoghegan *Westmeath* 36 R9
Castletown *Laois* 36 S9
Castletown *Meath* 37 Q10
Castletown *H'land* 28 E17
Castletown *I/Man* 14 P14
Castletownroche *Cork* 39 T7
Castletownshend *Cork* 38 U5
Castlewellan *Down* 33 P12
Caston *Norfolk* 13 S25
Castor *Peterbro* 12 S23
Catcleugh *Northum* 21 M19
Caterham *Surrey* 6 V23
Caton *Lancs* 15 P18
Catrine *E Ayrs* 19 L15
Catsfield *E Sussex* 7 W24
Catterall *Lancs* 15 Q18
Catterick Camp *N Yorks* 16 P20
Catterick *N Yorks* 16 P20
Catton *Northum* 21 N19
Caulkerbush *Dumf/Gal* 20 N16
Causeway *Kerry* 38 T4
Cavan *Cavan* 36 Q9
Cavangarden *Donegal* 32 N7
Cawdor *H'land* 28 G16
Cawood *N Yorks* 16 Q21
Cawston *Norfolk* 13 S26
Caythorpe *Lincs* 12 R22
Cefn-mawr *Wrex* 10 S17
Celbridge *Kildare* 37 R10
Cemaes *Angl* 8 R15
Cemmaes Road *Powys* 8 S16
Cenarth *Carms* 9 T14
Ceres *Fife* 25 K18
Cerne Abbas *Dorset* 5 W19
Cerrigydrudion *Conwy* 8 R16
Chacewater *Cornw'l* 2 X13
Chaddesley Corbet *Worcs* 10 T19
Chadwell St. Mary *Thurr'k* 7 V24
Chagford *Devon* 3 W16
Chalfont St. Giles *Bucks* 6 U22
Chalford *Glos* 5 U19
Chalgrove *Oxon* 6 U21
Challacombe *Devon* 3 V16
Challock *Kent* 7 V25
Chandler's Ford *Hants* 5 W21
Chanonrock *Louth* 37 Q10
Chapel en le Frith *Derby* 15 R20
Chapel St. Leonards *Lincs* 17 R24
Chapeltown *S Lanarks* 19 L15
Chapeltown *S Yorks* 16 R21
Chard *Som'set* 4 W18
Charing *Kent* 7 V25
Charlbury *Oxon* 11 U21
Charlemont *Armagh* 33 P10
Charlestown *Mayo* 35 Q6
Charlestown of Aberlour *Moray* 29 H17
Charleville *Cork* 39 T6
Charlton Horethorne *Som'set* 5 W19
Charlton Kings *Glos* 10 U19
Charlton *Wilts* 5 U19
Charlwood *Surrey* 6 V23
Charminster *Dorset* 5 W19
Charmouth *Dorset* 4 W18
Chartham *Kent* 7 V26
Chasel *Mayo* 34 Q4
Chatham *Medway* 7 V25
Chathill *Northum* 21 L20
Chatteris *Cambs* 12 T24
Chatton *Northum* 21 L20
Chawleigh *Devon* 3 W16
Cheadle *Gtr Man* 15 R19
Cheadle *Staffs* 11 S20
Chedburgh *Suffolk* 13 T25
Cheddar *Som'set* 4 V18
Cheddleton *Staffs* 10 R19
Chellaston *Derby C* 11 S21
Chelmarsh *Shrops* 10 T19
Chelmsford *Essex* 7 U24
Cheltenham *Glos* 10 U19
Chepstow *Monmouths* 4 U18
Cherhill *Wilts* 5 V20
Cheriton Fitzpaine *Devon* 4 W16
Cheriton *Hants* 5 V21
Chertsey *Surrey* 6 V23
Chesham *Bucks* 6 U22
Cheshunt *Herts* 6 U23
Chester *Ches* 10 R18
Chesterfield *Derby* 16 R21
Chester-le-Street *Durham* 21 N20
Chew Magna *Bath/NE Som'set* 4 V18
Chewton Mendip *Som'set* 4 V18
Chichester *W Sussex* 6 W22
Chiddingfold *Surrey* 6 V22
Chideock *Dorset* 4 W18
Chigwell *Essex* 6 U24
Chilcompton *Som'set* 4 V18
Chilham *Kent* 7 V25
Chillington *Devon* 3 X16
Chilton *Durham* 21 N20
Chingford *Gtr Lon* 6 U24
Chinnor *Oxon* 6 U22
Chippenham *Wilts* 5 V19
Chipping Campden *Glos* 11 T20
Chipping Norton *Oxon* 11 U20
Chipping Ongar *Essex* 7 U24
Chipping Sodbury *S Glos* 5 U19
Chirbury *Shrops* 10 S17
Chirk *Wrex* 10 S17
Chirnside *Scot Borders* 21 L19
Chiseldon *Swindon* 5 U20
Chitterne *Wilts* 5 V19
Chobham *Surrey* 6 V22
Chollerton *Northum* 21 M19
Cholsey *Oxon* 5 U21
Chorley *Lancs* 15 Q18
Chorleywood *Herts* 6 U22
Christchurch *Cambs* 12 S2
Christchurch *Dorset* 5 W2
Christow *Devon* 4 W1
Chudleigh *Devon* 4 W1
Chulmleigh *Devon* 3 W1
Church Hill *Donegal* 32 N
Church Hill *Fermanagh* 32 P
Church Stretton *Shrops* 10 S1
Church Village *Rh Cyn Taff* 9 U1
Churchdown *Glos* 10 U1
Churchill *Oxon* 11 U2
Churchstow *Devon* 3 X1
Churchtown *Cork* 39 U
Churchtown *Wexford* 40 T1
Chwilog *Gwyn* 8 S1
Cilgerran *Pembs* 9 T1
Cille Bhrighde *W Isles* 22 H
Cilycwm *Carms* 9 T1
Cinderford *Glos* 5 U1
Cirencester *Glos* 5 U2
Clabby *Fermanagh* 32 P
Clabhach *Arg/Bute* 22 J1
Clachan na Luib *W Isles* 26 G
Clachan *Arg/Bute* 18 L1
Clachan *H'land* 27 H1
Clackmannan *Clack* 24 K1
Clacton-on-Sea *Essex* 7 U2
Cladich *Arg/Bute* 23 K1
Clady Milltown *Armagh* 33 P1
Clady *Tyrone* 32 N
Claggan *H'land* 23 J1
Claigan *H'land* 26 H1
Clanabogan *Tyrone* 32 N
Clane *Kildare* 37 R1
Clanfield *Hants* 6 W2
Claonaig *Arg/Bute* 18 L1
Clapham *Beds* 12 T2
Clapham *N Yorks* 15 P1
Clara *Offaly* 36 R
Clarahill *Laois* 36 R
Clare *Suffolk* 13 T2
Clarecastle *Clare* 39 S
Clareen *Offaly* 36 R
Claregalway *Galway* 35 R
Claremorris *Mayo* 35 Q
Claretuam *Galway* 35 R
Clarina *Limerick* 39 S
Clarinbridge *Galway* 35 R
Clash *Cork* 39 U
Clashmore *Waterford* 39 T
Clashmore *H'land* 28 G1
Claudy *Londonderry* 32 N
Clavering *Essex* 12 U2
Claverley *Shrops* 10 S1
Clawton *Devon* 3 W1
Clay Cross *Derby* 11 R2
Claydon *Suffolk* 13 T2
Claypole *Lincs* 12 R2
Cleadale *H'land* 22 J1
Cleady *Kerry* 38 U
Cleator Moor *Cumb* 14 N1
Cleethorpes *NE Lincs* 17 Q2
Cleeve Prior *Warwick* 11 T2
Cleggan *Galway* 34 Q
Clehonger *Heref'd* 10 T1
Cleobury Mortimer *Shrops* 10 T1
Clevedon *N Som'set* 4 V1
Cleveleys *Lancs* 15 Q1
Cley *Norfolk* 13 S2
Clifden *Galway* 34 R
Cliffe *Medway* 7 V2
Cliffony *Sligo* 32 P
Clifford *Heref'd* 10 T1
Clipston *Northants* 11 T2
Clitheroe *Lancs* 15 Q1
Clive *Shrops* 10 S1
Clogh *Kilkenny* 40 S
Clogh *Antrim* 33 N1
Cloghan *Donegal* 32 N
Cloghan *Offaly* 36 R
Cloghan *Westmeath* 36 Q
Cloghane *Kerry* 38 T
Cloghaneely *Donegal* 32 M
Cloghboy *Donegal* 32 N
Clogheen *Tipperary* 39 T
Clogher Head *Louth* 37 Q1
Clogher *Roscommon* 36 Q
Clogher *Tyrone* 32 P
Cloghjordan *Tipperary* 36 S
Cloghran *Dublin* 37 R1

D

E

F

G

H

I

K

L

Macroom Cork 39 U6
Madeley Staffs 10 S19
Madley Heref'd 10 T18
Maentwrog Gwyn 8 S16
Maesteg Bridg 9 U16
Maghera Londonderry 33 N10
Magherafelt Londonderry 33 N10
Magheragall Antrim 33 N11
Magheraveely Fermanagh 32 P9
Maghery Donegal 32 N7
Maghery Armagh 33 N10
Maghull Mersey 15 Q18
Magor Monmouths 4 U18
Maguiresbridge Fermanagh 32 P9
Maiden Bradley Wilts 5 V19
Maiden Newton Dorset 4 W18
Maidenhead Windsor 6 U22
Maidstone Kent 7 V25
Malahide Dublin 37 R11
Maldon Essex 7 U25
Malham N Yorks 15 P19
Malin Donegal 32 M9
Malin More Donegal 32 N6
Mallaig H'land 23 H12
Mallaranny Mayo 34 Q4
Mallow Cork 39 T6
Mallwyd Gwyn 8 S16
Malmesbury Wilts 5 U19
Malpas Ches 10 R18
Maltby le Marsh Lincs 17 R24
Maltby S Yorks 16 R21
Malton N Yorks 17 P22
Manafon Powys 8 S17
Manby Lincs 17 R24
Manchester Gtr Man 15 R19
Manea Cambs 12 T24
Manfieldstown Louth 37 Q11
Mangotsfield S Glos 5 V19
Manningtree Essex 13 U26
Manorbier Pembs 9 U14
Manorhamilton Leitrim 32 P7
Manselstown Tipperary 39 S8
Mansfield Notts 11 R21
Mansfield Woodhouse Notts 11 R21
Manton Rutl'd 12 S22
Manulla Mayo 35 Q5
Marazion Cornw'l 2 X13
March Cambs 12 S24
Marden Heref'd 10 T18
Marden Kent 7 V24
Mareham le Fen Lincs 12 R23
Maresfield E Sussex 6 W24
Marfleet Kingston/Hull 17 Q23
Margam Neath P Talb 9 U16
Margate Kent 7 V26
Marham Norfolk 13 S25
Market Bosworth Leics 11 S21
Market Deeping Lincs 12 S23
Market Drayton Shrops 10 S19
Market Harborough Leics 11 T22
Market Lavington Wilts 5 V20
Market Rasen Lincs 17 R23
Market Warsop Notts 11 R21
Market Weighton ER Yorks 17 Q22
Markethill Armagh 33 P10
Markfield Leics 11 S21
Markinch Fife 25 K17
Marks Tey Essex 7 U25
Markyate Herts 6 U23
Marlborough Devon 3 X16
Marlborough Wilts 5 V20
Marlow Bucks 6 U22
Marnhull Dorset 5 W19
Marple Gtr Man 15 R19
Marshchapel Lincs 17 R24
Marshfield S Glos 5 V19
Marske by the Sea Redcar/Clevel'd 16 N21
Marston Magna Som'set 4 W18
Martham Norfolk 13 S27
Martin Hants 5 W20
Martley Worcs 10 T19
Martock Som'set 4 W18
Marton Lincs 17 R22
Marykirk Aberds 25 J18
Marypark Moray 28 H17
Maryport Cumb 20 N17
Marytavy Devon 3 W15
Marywell Aberds 25 H18
Marywell Angus 25 J18
Masham N Yorks 16 P20
Mathry Pembs 9 U13
Matlock Derby 11 R20
Mattishall Norfolk 13 S26
Mauchline E Ayrs 19 L15
Maud Aberds 29 G19
Maughold I/Man 14 P15
Maulyneill Kerry 38 U4
Maum Galway 34 Q4
Mawgan Cornw'l 2 X13
Maxwellheugh Scot Borders 21 L19
Maybole S Ayrs 19 M14
Mayfield E Sussex 7 V24
Mayfield Staffs 11 R20
Maylough Galway 35 R6
Maynooth Kildare 37 R10
Mayo Bridge Down 33 P11
Mayo Mayo 35 Q5
Mealabost W Isles 26 F11
Mealsgate Cumb 20 N17
Measham Leics 11 S20
Medstead Hants 6 V21
Meenaneary Donegal 32 N6
Meidrim Carms 9 U15
Meifod Powys 10 S17
Meigh Armagh 37 P11
Meigle Perth/Kinr 25 J17
Melbourn Cambs 12 T24
Melbourne Derby 11 S21
Melksham Wilts 5 V19
Mell Louth 37 Q11
Mellon Charles H'land 27 G12
Mellor Lancs 15 Q18
Melmerby Cumb 21 N18
Melrose Scot Borders 21 L18
Melsonby N Yorks 16 P20
Meltham W Yorks 15 Q20
Melton Constable Norfolk 13 S26
Melton Mowbray Leics 11 S22
Melton Suffolk 13 T26
Melvaig H'land 27 G12
Melvich H'land 28 E16
Menai Bridge Angl 8 R15
Mendlesham Suffolk 13 T26
Menlough Galway 35 R5
Mennock Dumf/Gal 19 M16
Menston W Yorks 15 Q20
Menstrie Clack 24 K16
Meonstoke Hants 5 W21
Meopham Kent 7 V24
Mere Brow Lancs 15 Q18
Mere Wilts 5 V19
Meriden W Midlands 11 T20
Merriott Som'set 4 W18
Merthyr Tydfil Merth Tyd 9 U17
Merton Gtr Lon 6 V23
Meshaw Devon 3 W16
Messingham N Lincs 17 Q22
Metfield Suffolk 13 T26
Metheringham Lincs 12 R23
Methil Fife 25 K17
Methlick Aberds 29 H19
Methven Perth/Kinr 24 K16
Methwold Norfolk 13 S25
Mevagissey Cornw'l 2 X14
Mexborough S Yorks 16 R21
Mey H'land 29 E17
Micheldever Hants 5 V21
Michelmersh Hants 5 V20
Mickleover Derby C 11 S20
Mickleton Durham 21 N19
Mickleton Glos 11 T20
Mid Lavant W Sussex 6 W22
Middle Barton Oxon 11 U21
Middleham N Yorks 15 P20
Middlemarsh Dorset 5 W19
Middlesbrough Middlesbro 21 N21
Middleton Cheney Northants 11 T21
Middleton in Teesdale Durham 21 N19
Middleton on the Wolds ER Yorks 17 Q22
Middleton Arg/Bute 22 K10
Middleton Gtr Man 15 Q19
Middleton Norfolk 12 S24
Middleton-on-Sea W Sussex 6 W22
Middletown Armagh 33 P10
Middlewich Ches 10 R19
Middlezoy Som'set 4 V18
Midhurst W Sussex 6 W22
Midleton Cork 39 U7
Midsomer Norton Bath/NE Som'set 5 V19
Milborne Port Som'set 5 W19
Mildenhall Suffolk 13 T25
Milestone Tipperary 39 S7
Milford Haven Pembs 9 U13
Milford Cork 39 T6
Milford Donegal 32 M8
Milford on Sea Hants 5 W20
Milford Surrey 6 V22
Millbrook Meath 36 Q9
Millbrook Cornw'l 3 X15
Millford Armagh 33 P10
Millisle Down 33 N12
Millom Cumb 14 P17
Millport N Ayrs 18 L14
Millstreet Cork 38 T5
Millstreet Waterford 39 T8
Milltown Cavan 36 P9
Milltown Galway 35 Q6
Milltown Kerry 38 T3
Milltown Kerry 38 T4
Milltown Monaghan 33 P10
Milltown Malbay Clare 38 S5
Milltown Antrim 33 N12
Milltown Londonderry 33 M10
Milnathort Perth/Kinr 24 K17
Milngavie E Dunb 19 L15
Milnthorpe Cumb 15 P18
Milovaig H'land 26 H10
Milton Abbot Devon 3 W15
Milton Keynes M/Keynes 12 T22
Milton H'land 27 G14
Miltown Kildare 37 R10
Milverton Som'set 4 V17
Minane Bridge Cork 39 U7
Minchinhampton Glos 5 U19
Minehead Som'set 4 V17
Minera Wrex 10 R17
Minety Wilts 5 U20
Mingary H'land 22 J11
Minnigaff Dumf/Gal 19 N15
Minstead Hants 5 W20
Minster Kent 7 V25
Minster Kent 7 V26
Minsterley Shrops 10 S18
Mintlaw Aberds 29 G19
Mirfield W Yorks 16 Q20
Misterton Notts 17 R22
Misterton Som'set 4 W18
Mistley Essex 13 U26
Mitchel Troy Monmouths 4 U18
Mitcheldean Glos 5 U19
Mitchelstown Cork 39 T7
Moate Westmeath 36 R8
Modbury Devon 3 X16
Modreeny Tipperary 36 S7
Moelfre Angl 8 R15
Moffat Dumf/Gal 20 M17
Mohill Leitrim 36 Q8
Moira Down 33 P11
Mold Flints 10 R17
Monaghan Monaghan 33 P10
Monar Lodge H'land 27 H14
Monasterevin Kildare 36 R9
Moneygall Offaly 39 S8
Moneyglass Antrim 33 N11
Moneymore Londonderry 33 N10
Moneyneany Londonderry 33 N10
Moniaive Dumf/Gal 19 M16
Monifieth Angus 25 K18
Monikie Angus 25 J18
Monivea Galway 35 R6
Monkland Heref'd 10 T18
Monkokehampton Devon 3 W15
Monkstown Cork 39 U7
Monkton S Ayrs 19 L14
Monmouth Monmouths 4 U18
Montacute Som'set 4 W18
Montgomery Powys 10 S17
Montrose Angus 25 J19
Monymusk Aberds 25 H18
Mooncoin Kilkenny 40 T9
Moone Kildare 40 S10
Moorfields Antrim 33 N11
Morar H'land 23 J12
Morchard Bishop Devon 4 W16
Mordiford Heref'd 10 T18
Morebattle Scot Borders 21 L19
Morecambe Lancs 15 P18
Moretonhampstead Devon 3 W16
Moreton-in-Marsh Glos 11 U20
Morley W Yorks 16 Q20
Mornington Meath 37 Q11
Morpeth Northum 21 M20
Mortehoe Devon 3 V15
Mortimer's Cross Heref'd 10 T18
Morwenstow Cornw'l 2 W14
Mossley Antrim 33 N12
Mossley Gtr Man 15 Q19
Moss-side Antrim 33 M11
Mostyn Flints 15 R17
Motcombe Dorset 5 V19
Motherwell N Lanarks 19 L16
Mottisfont Hants 5 V20
Moulton Lincs 12 S23
Moulton Northants 11 T22
Moulton Suffolk 13 T25
Mount Bellew Bridge Galway 35 R7
Mount Ida Down 33 P11
Mount Nugent Cavan 36 Q9
Mount Talbot Roscommon 35 Q7
Mountain Ash Rh Cyn Taff 9 U17
Mountcharles Donegal 32 N7
Mountfield Tyrone 32 N9
Mountjoy Tyrone 32 N9
Mountmellick Laois 36 R9
Mountnorris Armagh 33 P11
Mountrath Laois 40 R9
Mountshannon Clare 35 S7
Mountsorrel Leics 11 S21
Mousehole Cornw'l 2 X12
Mouswald Dumf/Gal 20 M17
Moville Donegal 33 M9
Moy H'land 28 H15
Moy Tyrone 33 P10
Moyad Down 37 P11
Moyard Galway 34 Q3
Moyasta Clare 38 S4
Moycullen Galway 35 R5
Moymore Clare 39 S6
Moynalty Meath 37 Q10
Moyne Longford 36 Q8
Moyne Tipperary 39 S8
Moyroughly Westmeath 36 R8
Moyvally Kildare 37 R10
Moyvore Westmeath 36 Q8
Much Dewchurch Heref'd 10 U18
Much Marcle Heref'd 10 U19
Much Wenlock Shrops 10 S18
Muchalls Aberds 25 H19
Muckross Kerry 38 T5
Muff Donegal 32 M9
Muine Bheag Carlow 40 S10
Muineagh Donegal 32 M8
Muir of Ord H'land 28 G15
Muirdrum Angus 25 J18
Muirhead N Lanarks 19 L15
Muirkirk E Ayrs 19 L15
Muker N Yorks 15 P19
Mulben Moray 29 G17
Mullagh Cavan 37 Q10
Mullagh Galway 35 R7
Mullagh Meath 37 R10
Mullaghnaneane Sligo 32 P6
Mullan Fermanagh 32 P8
Mullans Town Tyrone 33 N9
Mullanys Cross Sligo 35 P6
Mullarts Antrim 33 M11
Mulldonagh Londonderry 32 N9
Mullinahone Tipperary 39 S8
Mullinavat Kilkenny 40 T9
Mullingar Westmeath 36 Q9
Mullion Cornw'l 2 X13
Mullughmore Sligo 32 P7
Mundesley Norfolk 13 S26
Mundford Norfolk 13 S25
Mungret Limerick 39 S6
Munlochy H'land 28 G15
Murlaggan H'land 23 J13
Murroogh Clare 34 R5
Murton Durham 21 N21
Musbury Devon 4 W17
Musselburgh E Loth 25 L17
Muthill Perth/Kinr 24 K16
Mybster H'land 28 F17
Myddfai Carms 9 U16
Myddle Shrops 10 S18
Mydroilyn Ceredig'n 9 T15
Mynydd Isa Flints 10 R17
Myshall Carlow 40 S10

N

N. Queensferry Fife 24 K17
Naas Kildare 37 R10
Nad Cork 39 T6
Nafferton ER Yorks 17 P23
Nailsea N Som'set 4 V18
Nailsworth Glos 5 U19
Nairn H'land 28 G16
Nannerch Flints 14 R17
Nantwich Ches 10 R18
Nappa N Yorks 15 Q19
Naran Donegal 32 N7
Narberth Pembs 9 U14
Narborough Leics 11 S21
Naseby Northants 11 T22
Naul Dublin 37 Q11
Navan Meath 37 Q10
Navenby Lincs 12 R22
Neale Mayo 35 Q5
Neath Neath P Talb 9 U16
Necton Norfolk 13 S25
Needham Market Suffolk 13 T26
Needingworth Cambs 12 T23
Nefyn Gwyn 8 S14
Neilston E Renf 19 L15
Nelson Lancs 15 Q19
Nenagh Tipperary 39 S7
Nenthead Cumb 21 N19
Neston Ches 15 R17
Nether Stowey Som'set 4 V17
Netheravon Wilts 5 V20
Netherbury Dorset 4 W18
Netherton Northum 21 M19
Nethy Bridge H'land 28 H16
Netley Hants 5 W21
Nettlebed Oxon 6 U22
Nettleham Lincs 17 R23
Nettleton Lincs 17 R23
Nevern Pembs 9 T14
New Abbey Dumf/Gal 20 N16
New Aberdour Aberds 29 G19
New Alresford Hants 5 V21
New Birmingham Tipperary 39 S8
New Buckenham Norfolk 13 T26
New Buildings Londonderry 32 N9
New Chapel Cross Kerry 38 U3
New Clipstone Notts 11 R21
New Costessey Norfolk 13 S26
New Cumnock E Ayrs 19 M15
New Deer Aberds 29 G19
New Earswick C/York 16 Q21
New Edlington S Yorks 16 R21
New Galloway Dumf/Gal 19 M15
New Holland N Lincs 17 Q23
New Inn Cavan 36 Q9
New Inn Galway 35 R7
New Inn Laois 36 R9
New Luce Dumf/Gal 18 N14
New Mills Derby 15 R20
New Milton Hants 5 W20

O

P

Q

R

S

T

U

V

Valley *Angl* 8 R14
Ventnor *I/Wight* 5 W21
Ventry *Kerry* 38 T3
Verwood *Dorset* 5 W20
Veryan *Cornw'l* 2 X14
Vicarstown *Laois* 40 R9
Vickerstown *Cumb* 14 P17
Virginia *Cavan* 36 Q9
Virginia Water *Surrey* 6 V22

W

Waddesdon *Bucks* 6 U22
Waddingham *Lincs* 17 R22
Waddington *Wexford* 40 T10
Waddington *Lincs* 12 R22
Wadebridge *Cornw'l* 2 W14
Wadhurst *E Sussex* 7 V24
Wainfleet All Saints *Lincs* 12 R24
Wakefield *W Yorks* 16 Q21
Walberswick *Suffolk* 13 T27
Walcott *Lincs* 12 R23
Walderslade *Medway* 7 V25
Waldron *E Sussex* 6 W24
Walford *Heref'd* 10 T18
Walkerburn *Scot Borders* 20 L18
Walkeringham *Notts* 17 R22
Wallasey *Mersey* 15 R17
Wallingford *Oxon* 5 U21
Wallsend *Tyne/Wear* 21 N20
Walmer *Kent* 7 V26
Walpole *Norfolk* 12 S24
Walsall *W Midlands* 11 S20
Walsham le Willows *Suffolk* 13 T25
Walsoken *Cambs* 12 S24
Waltham Abbey *Essex* 6 U24
Waltham Forest *Gtr Lon* 6 U24
Waltham on the Wolds *Leics* 11 S22
Waltham *NE Lincs* 17 Q23
Walton *Cumb* 21 N18
Walton-on-Thames *Surrey* 6 V23
Walton-on-the-Naze *Essex* 7 U26
Wanborough *Swindon* 5 U20
Wandsworth *Gtr Lon* 6 V23
Wangford *Suffolk* 13 T27
Wansford *Peterbro* 12 S23
Wantage *Oxon* 5 U21
Warboys *Cambs* 12 T23
Ward *Dublin* 37 R11
Wardington *Oxon* 11 T21
Wardle *Ches* 10 R18
Ware *Herts* 6 U23
Wareham *Dorset* 5 W19
Wargrave *Wokingham* 6 V22
Waringstown *Down* 33 P11
Wark *Northum* 21 M19
Warkworth *Northum* 21 M20
Warley *W Midlands* 11 T20
Warminster *Wilts* 5 V19
Warrenpoint *Down* 37 P11
Warrington *Warrington* 15 R18
Warton *Lancs* 15 P18
Warwick *Warwick* 11 T20
Washaway *Cornw'l* 2 X14
Washford *Som'set* 4 V17
Washingborough *Lincs* 17 R23
Washington *Tyne/Wear* 21 N20
Washington *W Sussex* 6 W23
Watchet *Som'set* 4 V17
Watchfield *Oxon* 5 U20
Waterbeach *Cambs* 12 T24
Waterford *Waterford* 40 T9
Watergrasshill *Cork* 39 T7
Waterhead *Angus* 25 J18
Waterhouses *Staffs* 11 R20
Wateringbury *Kent* 7 V24
Waterlooville *Hants* 6 W21
Waterside *Londonderry* 32 N9
Waterville *Kerry* 38 U3
Watford *Herts* 6 U23
Wath upon Dearne *S Yorks* 16 R21
Watlington *Norfolk* 12 S24
Watlington *Oxon* 6 U22
Watten *H'land* 28 F17
Watton *Norfolk* 13 S25
Waunfawr *Gwyn* 8 R15
Weachyburn *Aberds* 29 G18
Wearhead *Durham* 21 N19
Weasenham *Norfolk* 13 S25
Weaverham *Ches* 15 R18
Weaverthorpe *N Yorks* 17 P22
Wedmore *Som'set* 4 V18
Wednesbury *W Midlands* 10 S19
Wednesfield *W Midlands* 10 S19
Weedon Bec *Northants* 11 T21
Weeley *Essex* 7 U26
Welbourn *Lincs* 12 R22
Weldon *Northants* 12 T22
Weldon *Northum* 21 M20
Welford *Northants* 11 T21
Welford *W Berks* 5 V21
Wellesbourne *Warwick* 11 T20
Wellingborough *Northants* 12 T22
Wellington *Som'set* 4 W17
Wellington *Telford* 10 S18
Wellingtonbridge *Wexford* 40 T10
Wellow *Bath/NE Som'set* 5 V19
Wells *Som'set* 4 V18
Wells-next-the-Sea *Norfolk* 13 S25
Welney *Norfolk* 12 S24
Welshampton *Shrops* 10 S18
Welshpool *Powys* 10 S17
Welton *Lincs* 17 R23
Welwyn Garden City *Herts* 6 U23
Wem *Shrops* 10 S18
Wembury *Devon* 3 X15
Wemyss Bay *Invercl* 18 L14
Wendover *Bucks* 6 U22
Wensley *N Yorks* 15 P20
Wenvoe *V/Glam* 4 V17
Weobley *Heref'd* 10 T18
Werrington *Cornw'l* 3 W15
West Auckland *Durham* 21 N20
West Bergholt *Essex* 13 U25
West Bridgford *Notts* 11 S21
West Bromwich *W Midlands* 11 S20
West Burton *N Yorks* 15 P20
West Calder *W Loth* 20 L16
West Coker *Som'set* 4 W18
West Dean *Wilts* 5 V20
West End *Hants* 5 W21
West Felton *Shrops* 10 S18
West Grinstead *W Sussex* 6 W23
West Haddon *Northants* 11 T21
West Kilbride *N Ayrs* 18 L14
West Kingsdown *Kent* 7 V24
West Kirby *Mersey* 15 R17
West Linton *Scot Borders* 20 L17
West Looe *Cornw'l* 3 X15
West Lulworth *Dorset* 5 W19
West Malling *Kent* 7 V24
West Meon *Hants* 5 V21
West Mersea *Essex* 7 U25
West Moors *Dorset* 5 W20
West Rasen *Lincs* 17 R23
West Thorney *W Sussex* 6 W22
West Wellow *Hants* 5 W20
West Woodburn *Northum* 21 M19
Westbourne *W Sussex* 6 W22
Westbury *Shrops* 10 S18
Westbury *Wilts* 5 V19
Westbury-on-Severn *Glos* 5 U19
Westbury-sub-Mendip *Som'set* 4 V18
Westcott *Surrey* 6 V23
Westerham *Kent* 6 V24
Westfield *E Sussex* 7 W25
Westhill *Aberds* 25 H19
Westhoughton *Gtr Man* 15 Q18
Westleton *Suffolk* 13 T27
Westminster *Gtr Lon* 6 U23
Weston *Staffs* 10 S19
Weston-Super-Mare *N Som'set* 4 V18
Westonzoyland *Som'set* 4 V18
Westport *Mayo* 34 Q4
Westruther *Scot Borders* 21 L18
Westward Ho! *Devon* 3 V15
Wetheral *Cumb* 20 N18
Wetherby *W Yorks* 16 Q21
Wetwang *ER Yorks* 17 P22
Wexford *Wexford* 40 T11
Weybourne *Norfolk* 13 S26
Weybridge *Surrey* 6 V23
Weyhill *Hants* 5 V20
Weymouth *Dorset* 5 W19
Whaley Bridge *Derby* 15 R20
Whalley *Lancs* 15 Q19
Whalton *Northum* 21 M20
Whaplode *Lincs* 12 S23
Whatton *Notts* 11 S22
Whauphill *Dumf/Gal* 19 N14
Wheathampstead *Herts* 6 U23
Wheathill *Fermanagh* 32 P8
Wheatley Hill *Durham* 21 N21
Wheatley *Notts* 17 R22
Wheatley *Oxon* 5 U21
Wheaton Aston *Staffs* 10 S19
Wheldrake *C/York* 17 Q22
Whicham *Cumb* 14 P17
Whickham *Tyne/Wear* 21 N20
Whimple *Devon* 4 W17
Whipsnade *Beds* 6 U22
Whissendine *Rutl'd* 11 S22
Whitburn *W Loth* 20 L16
Whitby *N Yorks* 17 P22
Whitchurch *Bristol* 4 V18
Whitchurch *Bucks* 6 U22
Whitchurch *Devon* 3 W15
Whitchurch *Hants* 5 V21
Whitchurch *Heref'd* 4 U18
Whitchurch *Shrops* 10 S18
White Bridge *H'land* 24 H14
White Castle *Donegal* 32 M9
Whitecross *Armagh* 33 P11
Whitegate *Clare* 35 S7
Whitegate *Cork* 39 U7
Whitehaven *Cumb* 20 N16
Whitehead *Antrim* 33 N12
Whitehill *Fermanagh* 32 P8
Whitehouse *Arg/Bute* 18 L13
Whitekirk *E Loth* 25 K18
Whiteparish *Wilts* 5 V20
Whitfield *Kent* 7 V26
Whithorn *Dumf/Gal* 19 N15
Whitland *Carms* 9 U14
Whitley Bay *Tyne/Wear* 21 M21
Whitsome *Scot Borders* 21 L19
Whitstable *Kent* 7 V26
Whitstone *Cornw'l* 3 W15
Whittington *Derby* 16 R21
Whittington *Lancs* 15 P18
Whittington *Shrops* 10 S18
Whittington *Staffs* 11 S20
Whittlebury *Northants* 11 T22
Whittlesey *Cambs* 12 S23
Whittlesford *Cambs* 12 T24
Whitwell *Derby* 16 R21
Whitwell *I/Wight* 5 W21
Whitwick *Leics* 11 S21
Whitworth *Lancs* 15 Q19
Whixley *N Yorks* 16 P21
Wick *H'land* 29 F17
Wick *S Glos* 5 V19
Wick *V/Glam* 4 V16
Wick *Wilts* 5 W20
Wicken *Cambs* 12 T24
Wickford *Essex* 7 U25
Wickham Market *Suffolk* 13 T26
Wickham *Hants* 5 W21
Wicklow *Wicklow* 40 S11
Wickwar *S Glos* 5 U19
Widdrington *Northum* 21 M20
Wide Open *Tyne/Wear* 21 M20
Widecombe *Devon* 3 W16
Widemouth *Cornw'l* 2 W14
Widnes *Halton* 15 R18
Wigan *Gtr Man* 15 Q18
Wigmore *Heref'd* 10 T18
Wigmore *Medway* 7 V25
Wigston *Leics* 11 S21
Wigton *Cumb* 20 N17
Wigtown *Dumf/Gal* 19 N15
Willand *Devon* 4 W17
Willaston *Ches* 15 R17
Willenhall *W Midlands* 10 S19
Willersley *Heref'd* 10 T17
Willesborough *Kent* 7 V25
Williamstown *Galway* 35 Q6
Willingdon *E Sussex* 7 W24
Willington *Beds* 12 T23
Willington *Durham* 21 N20
Williton *Som'set* 4 V17
Willoughby *Lincs* 17 R24
Wilmington *Devon* 4 W17
Wilmslow *Ches* 15 R19
Wilnecote *Staffs* 11 S20
Wilton *Wilts* 5 V20
Wimblington *Cambs* 12 S24
Wimborne Minster *Dorset* 5 W20
Wincanton *Som'set* 5 V19
Winchcombe *Glos* 11 U20
Winchelsea *E Sussex* 7 W25
Winchester *Hants* 5 V21
Windermere *Cumb* 15 P18
Windgap *Kilkenny* 40 T9
Windsor *Windsor* 6 V22
Windygates *Fife* 25 K17
Wing *Bucks* 6 U22
Wingate *Durham* 21 N21
Wingham *Kent* 7 V26
Winkleigh *Devon* 3 W16
Winscombe *N Som'set* 4 V18
Winsford *Ches* 10 R18
Winslow *Bucks* 11 U22
Winster *Derby* 11 R20
Winston *Durham* 21 N20
Winterborne Abbas *Dorset* 4 W18
Winterborne Stickland *Dorset* 5 W19
Winterton *N Lincs* 17 Q22
Winterton *Norfolk* 13 S27
Wirksworth *Derby* 11 R20
Wisbech St. Mary *Cambs* 12 S24
Wisbech *Cambs* 12 S24
Wisborough Green *W Sussex* 6 V23
Wishaw *N Lanarks* 19 L16
Witchampton *Dorset* 5 W19
Witchford *Cambs* 12 T24
Witham *Essex* 7 U25
Witheridge *Devon* 4 W16
Withern *Lincs* 17 R24
Withernsea *ER Yorks* 17 Q24
Withington *Glos* 5 U20
Witley *Surrey* 6 V22
Witnesham *Suffolk* 13 T26
Witney *Oxon* 5 U21
Wittersham *Kent* 7 V25
Wiveliscombe *Som'set* 4 V17
Wivelsfield *E Sussex* 6 W23
Wivenhoe *Essex* 7 U25
Wix *Essex* 13 U26
Woburn Sands *M/Keynes* 12 T22
Woburn *Beds* 12 U22
Woking *Surrey* 6 V22
Wokingham *Wokingham* 6 V22
Wolf's Castle *Pembs* 9 U14
Wollaston *Northants* 12 T22
Wolsingham *Durham* 21 N20
Wolverhampton *W Midlands* 10 S19
Wolverton *M/Keynes* 11 T22
Wolviston *Stockton* 21 N21
Wombwell *S Yorks* 16 Q21
Wonersh *Surrey* 6 V22
Wonston *Hants* 5 V21
Woodbridge *Suffolk* 13 T26
Woodbury *Devon* 4 W17
Woodchester *Glos* 5 U19
Woodchurch *Kent* 7 V25
Woodcote *Oxon* 6 U21
Woodenbridge *Wicklow* 40 S1
Woodford *Galway* 35 R
Woodgreen *Hants* 5 W2
Woodhall Spa *Lincs* 12 R2
Woodhouse Eaves *Leics* 11 S2
Woodhouse *S Yorks* 16 R2
Woodlawn *Galway* 35 R
Woodley *Wokingham* 6 V2
Woodstock *Oxon* 5 U2
Woodtown *Meath* 37 Q1
Woofferton *Shrops* 10 T1
Wookey Hole *Som'set* 4 V1
Wookey *Som'set* 4 V1
Wool *Dorset* 5 W1
Woolacombe *Devon* 3 V1
Woolavington *Som'set* 4 V1
Wooler *Northum* 21 L1
Woolwich *Gtr Lon* 6 V2
Wooperton *Northum* 21 M2
Woore *Shrops* 10 S1
Wootton Bassett *Wilts* 5 U2
Wootton Bridge *I/Wight* 5 W2
Wootton Wawen *Warwick* 11 T2
Worcester *Worcs* 10 T1
Worfield *Shrops* 10 S1
Workington *Cumb* 20 N1
Worksop *Notts* 16 R2
Wormit *Fife* 25 K1
Worsbrough *S Yorks* 16 Q2
Wortham *Suffolk* 13 T2
Worthing *W Sussex* 6 W2
Wotton under Edge *Glos* 5 U1
Wragby *Lincs* 17 R2
Wrangle *Lincs* 12 R2
Wrea Green *Lancs* 15 Q1
Wrentham *Suffolk* 13 T2
Wretham *Norfolk* 13 T2
Wrexham *Wrex* 10 R1
Writtle *Essex* 7 U2
Wroughton *Swindon* 5 U2
Wroxham *Norfolk* 13 S2
Wroxton *Oxon* 11 T2
Wyberton *Lincs* 12 S2
Wye *Kent* 7 V2
Wylye *Wilts* 5 V2
Wymondham *Leics* 12 S2
Wymondham *Norfolk* 13 S2

Y Felinheli *Gwyn* 8 R1
Yalding *Kent* 7 V2
Yarcombe *Devon* 4 W1
Yardley Hastings *Northants* 12 T2
Yarm *Stockton* 16 N2
Yarmouth *I/Wight* 5 W2
Yarnton *Oxon* 5 U2
Yarrow *Scot Borders* 20 L1
Yate *S Glos* 5 U1
Yatton *N Som'set* 4 V1
Yaxley *Cambs* 12 S2
Yeadon *W Yorks* 16 Q2
Yealmpton *Devon* 3 X1
Yelverton *Devon* 3 X1
Yeovil *Som'set* 4 W1
Yetminster *Dorset* 4 W1
York *C/York* 16 Q2
Youghal *Cork* 39 U
Youlgreave *Derby* 11 R2
Yoxall *Staffs* 11 S2
Yoxford *Suffolk* 13 T2
Ysbyty Ifan *Conwy* 8 R1
Ysbyty Ystwyth *Ceredig'n* 9 T1
Ystalyfera *Neath P Talb* 9 U1
Ystradgynlais *Powys* 9 U1

Zennor *Cornw'l* 2 X1